Shopper's Checklist

Supershopper alert! How can you become a more savvy collectibles shopper? Take a technique from the shopping maven: Use a shopper's checklist as you prowl the collectibles markets. Photocopy the checklist so you can use a new one as you consider each purchase. Write in complete descriptions on the lines and check off the boxes that apply.

I love this item, but its value depends on its...

Name of item: _____

Color: _____

Finish: _____

Maker: _____

Provenance (history): _____
_____
_____

Place I found it: _____
_____

Date: _____

Condition:
□ mint   □ excellent   □ good   □ fair   □ poor

Construction:
□ mint   □ excellent   □ good   □ fair   □ poor

Design:
□ unique   □ exceptional   □ unusual   □ typical of type

Demand:
□ excellent   □ good   □ fair   □ poor

Rarity:
□ extremely rare   □ very rare   □ rare   □ commonplace

Deposit left:
□ yes   □ no

Research: _____
_____
_____
_____

Notes: _____
_____
_____
_____

alpha books

Collector's Card File

This card provides a convenient and easy way for you to keep track of the items in your collection, their value, and their history. Photocopy the card so you can use a fresh one each time you buy a piece to add to your collection. Carry a stack of blank photocopied cards with you when you shop at antique shows, auctions, flea markets, shops, and so on. You can tally your purchases and fill out the cards at the end of the day or during a natural break in shopping: at lunch or dinner, for example. Don't wait too long after the purchase to complete the card, because then you may forget important details such as the date of the sale.

The cards also provide an accessible record for insurance purposes. I recommend that you staple the sales receipt, any documentation (assessment, letters, newspaper articles, etc.), and a photograph of the item to each card for further ease of record-keeping.

Type of collectible: _____

Date of purchase: _____

Place of purchase: _____

Purchase price: _____

Assessed value: _____

Description of item:

    Size: _____

    Shape: _____

    Material: _____

    Color: _____

    Condition: _____

    _____

    _____

    Label: _____

    Manufacturer: _____

Research: _____

_____

Other notes: _____

_____

_____

_____

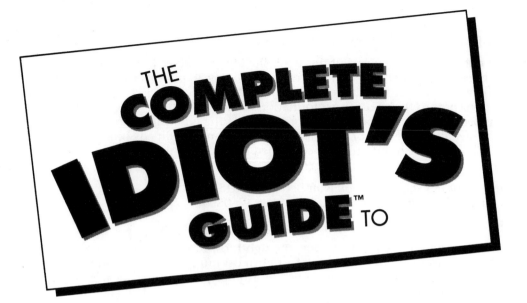

THE **COMPLETE IDIOT'S GUIDE**™ TO

Buying and Selling Collectibles

by Laurie Rozakis, Ph.D.

alpha books

A Division of Macmillan General Reference
A Simon & Schuster Macmillan Company
1633 Broadway, New York, NY 10019

International Standard Book Number: 0-02-861595-6
Library of Congress Catalog Card Number: 96-080407

99 98 97   8 7 6 5 4 3 2 1

Interpretation of the printing code: the rightmost number of the first series of numbers is the year of the book's printing; the rightmost number of the second series of numbers is the number of the book's printing. For example, a printing code of 97-1 shows that the first printing occurred in 1997.

Printed in the United States of America

Publisher
Theresa H. Murtha

Editor
Lisa Bucki

Copy/Production Editors
Lori Cates
Mike McFeely

Cover Designer
Mike Freeland

Illustrator
Judd Winick

Designer
Glenn Larsen

Indexers
Robert Long
Debra Meyers
Greg Pearson
Benjamin Slen

Production Team
Angela Calvert, Tricia Flodder, Malinda Kuhn,
Linda Knose, Pamela Woolf

Contents at a Glance

Part 1: Why Is There a Boom in Collectibles?   **1**

  1 It's Mine... I Saw It First! The Mania to Collect   3
     *Learn the history of modern collecting, find out what
     makes a "thing" become a collectible, and more.*

  2 If Someone Makes It, Someone Else Collects It   15
     *Discover if you're a collector or an investor and get the
     inside skinny on hot collectibles.*

  3 Shop 'Till You Drop   25
     *Find out how to be a smooth shopper and learn the best
     places to find collectibles (including during your vacation).*

  4 Hey, Big Spender... Buying Like an Expert   37
     *Determine the fair price for a collectible that you want
     to buy and find out how to bargain easily and effectively.*

  5 Treasures and Turnips: Selling Your Collectibles   51
     *See how to appraise your collectibles like a pro and get the
     inside skinny on the best markets for collectible sales.*

  6 Guarding the Family Jewels: Your Collection   65
     *Discover how to display, store, clean, and insure your
     collection.*

**Part 2: All in the Family: Ephemera, Stamps, Coins,
and Paper Money**   **87**

  7 Pulp (Non)fiction   89
     *Learn about baseball cards, sports cards, bookplates, playing
     cards, postcards, and other ephemera.*

  8 Truth, Justice, and the American Way: Comic Books   105
     *Find out the history of comic books and find out how to start
     your own comics collection.*

  9 Lick That: Stamps   117
     *Discover the different types of postal stamps and stamp-like
     things you can collect.*

 10 Gilt Trip: Collecting Coins   133
     *Learn the history of coin collecting and discover what you
     need to start your own coin collection.*

 11 ~~Love~~ Money Makes the World Go 'Round   143
     Find out how to start and maintain a paper money collection.

Part 3: Hot Stuff   **155**

 12 Book Learnin'   157
     *Learn the history of books and discover which books
     make the best collectibles.*

13 The China Syndrome   169
    Discover which china is collectible—and which is not.

14 Fun and Games   183
    Find out why kids' toys aren't for kids anymore.

15 Home Sweet Collectible   197
    See what household items, quilts, radios, and tools make
    collectors faint with anticipation.

16 As Clear as Crystal   209
    Discover which types of glass people are collecting now—
    and which ones are likely to be popular in the future.

Part 4: **Master of Arts: Furniture and Art**   **223**

17 Different Strokes for Different Folks: Collecting Paintings 225
    Find out how to buy paintings and drawings with confidence
    and skill.

18 Say Cheese, Please: Photographs   237
    Find out how to build a collection of photographs that suits
    your taste—and pocketbook.

19 Pretty as a Picture: Drawings   247
    Survey different kinds of collectibles drawings, including
    Fractura, silhouettes, paper cutting, and caricatures.

20 Some Day My Prints Will Come: Prints and Lithographs 257
    Learn how prints are made and find out which prints send
    collectors into a frenzy of acquisition.

21 Feathering the Nest: Furniture and Rugs   267
    Find out which types and styles of furniture are most
    collectible.

Part 5: **All that Glitters Isn't Gold—but It's Probably**
         Collectible   **281**

22 Are Diamonds a Collector's Best Friend? Collecting
    Jewelry   283
    Learn about collecting antique jewelry, precious gemstones,
    gold, and Native American jewelry.

23 Heavy Metal   297
    Acquaint yourself with silver, pewter, copper, brass, bronze,
    iron, and steel collectibles.

Appendix A Future Collectibles   309
    Find out what you should be saving now—in hopes of it being
    worth big bucks later!

Appendix B Further Reading   315
    Where to turn for more advice on pricing your finds.

Index   323

Contents

Part 1: Why Is There a Boom in Collectibles? 1

1 It's Mine... I Saw It First! The Mania to Collect 3

You Bought a *What*? 4
The Collectibles Craze 6
Inside a Collector's Mind 6
So Should You Save that Wrapper? 7
The Rewards of Collecting 9
The Least You Need to Know 13

2 If Someone Makes It, Someone Else Collects It 15

If It Walks Like a Duck… 16
Are You a Collector or an Investor? 18
Collectible vs. Antique 19
    Collectibles 20
    Antiques 20
    Collectible Art 20
    The Good, Bad, and Really Bad 21
Voodoo Economics and Collectibles 21
What's Hot—and What's Not 22
What Is a Collection? 24
The Least You Need to Know 24

3 Shop 'Till You Drop 25

The Rules of Acquisition 26
Smart Shoppers 30
Don't Scratch Your Nose! Shopping at Auctions 30
    Read the Auction Catalog 31
    Read the Reference Literature 32
    Get Price Estimates 32
    Mark the Items You Want—and What You'll Pay
      for Each 32
    View the Items 32
    Reserves 32
    Bidding 33
Shopping at Antique Shops 33

Shopping at House Sales/Flea Markets/Swap Meets 33
Shopping by Mail Order 34
Order Me Another Margarita, Dahling... and Then
 Let's Hit the Shops 35
The Least You Need to Know 36

4 Hey Big Spender... Buying Like an Expert   37

How Much Is that Doggie (Statue) in the Window? 38
Damage Control 38
So Can You Knock Off a Few Bucks? 39
Even, Steven: Trading 41
Buying for Big Bucks: Top Five Hints for Hitting the
 Collectibles Jackpot 42
Provenance—A Collectible's Family Tree 43
Buy High, Sell Low 44
All in the Family: Uncle Sam 44
Pitfalls 45
 Damaged Goods 46
 Speculation 46
 "Need, Speed, Greed"—What About Fakes? 47
The Least You Need to Know 49

5 Treasures and Turnips: Selling Your Collectibles   51

This Little Piggy Went to Market 52
Pennies from Heaven: Pricing Collectibles 52
 Tools of the Trade 52
 Appraise Like a Pro 53
 This Little Piggy Sold Roast Beef: Know the Market 55
 The Secret to Selling Success 55
Selling Privately 56
 Let Their Fingers Do the Walking: Advertising 56
 Show and Tell 56
 Money Business 56
Selling at Yard Sales 57
 Neither Rain Nor Shine... 57
 Alert the Media 57
 Tricks and Tips 58
Selling to Dealers 58

It's Show Time! Selling at Antique Shows and
Flea Markets 58
   Hey, Check It Out! 59
Selling at Auctions 60
   Types of Auctions 60
   Pricing 61
   Timing Is Everything 61
   Fees 61
   Talk the Talk and Walk the Walk 62
The Least You Need to Know 63

6 Guarding the Family Jewels: Your Collection   65

Cataloging: Do You Know What You Own? 66
   Do You Know What's in Your Collection? 73
A Place for Everything and Everything in its Place:
Displaying and Storing 75
   Albums and Scrapbooks 75
   Cabinets 75
   Glass 75
   Paper Collectibles (Books, Comic Books, Autographs,
     Prints, Stamps, Paper Money, Baseball Cards,
     and so on) 76
   Pewter 77
   Stuffed Toys 77
   Wood 77
With Collectibles, Is Cleanliness Really Next to
Godliness? 78
   Ceramics (Porcelain, China, Bone China, Stoneware,
     Ironstone) 79
   Copper 80
   Glass and Crystal 80
   Iron 80
   Paper Collectibles (Books, Comic Books, Prints,
     and so on) 81
   Pewter 81
   Silver 81
   Stuffed Toys 82
   Wood 82
Insurance 101: Plain Language About Protecting Your
Collection 83
The Least You Need to Know 85

Part 2: All in the Family: Ephemera, Stamps, Coins, and Paper Money   87

7 Pulp (Non)fiction   89

Ephemera 90
The Paper Chase 91
Baseball Cards 92
    First Base: The History of Baseball Cards 92
    First Base: The Golden Era #1 92
    Second Inning Stretch: A Lull in the Action 93
    Second Base: The Golden Era #2 93
    Seventh Inning Stretch: Another Break for War 93
    Third Base: Modern Baseball Cards 94
    Home Run: Collecting Baseball Cards 94
Hey, Sport: Sports Cards 96
    Be a Sport: Collecting Sports Cards 96
Bookplates 97
It's Your Deal: Playing Cards 98
Postcards 98
Theater Memorabilia 99
    Sign on the Dotted Line 99
    Stage-Struck 99
    Get with the Program 100
Movie Memorabilia 100
    Cels 100
    Poster Girl 100
    Loose Paper 102
A Striking Example of Collectibles: Matchbooks 102
The Least You Need to Know 103

8 Truth, Justice, and the American Way: Comic Books   105

Bam! Pow! Zap! A Short History of Comic Books 106
    It's a Bird, It's a Plane… 106
    The Horror, The Horror 107
    They're Back… 108
    Comics Today 109
Taking the Plunge 109
Don't Step on Superman's Cape 111
Making the Grade 111
A Nip and a Tuck 112

Walk the Walk and Talk the Talk 113
Art for Art's Sake 115
The Least You Need to Know 115

9 Lick That: Stamps **117**

Stamp Collecting 101 118
Getting Your Feet Wet 118
    Getting to Know You, Getting to Know All
        About You 119
    Form and Function 119
    Stop the Presses! How Stamps Are Printed 121
Stamp-o-Rama: Acquiring Stamps 122
    Used, Not Abused 122
    Mixtures and Packets 123
    Dealers 123
    Mail Order 124
    Auctions 124
    Another Opening, Another Show: Stamp Shows 125
    Even-Steven: Trading 126
Tools of the Trade 126
What to Collect? 128
Don't Bet the Ranch: Stamps as Investments 130
A Little Face Time 131
The Least You Need to Know 132

10 Gilt Trip: Collecting Coins **133**

CoinAge: The History of Coins 134
    It's Greek to Me 134
    When In Rome... Get Some Coins 134
    Coin of the Realm: Medieval Coins 134
    Colonial Coins 135
    Bad Spellers of the World Untie: Modern Coins 135
Don't Take Any Wooden Nickels: Starting a Coin
    Collection 136
    Heads or Tails? Learning the Parts of a Coin 136
    Tools of the Trade 137
    Grading Coins 137
A Penny Saved Is a Dollar Earned: Sources for Coins 138
    Pennies from Heaven: Circulation 138

Coin Dealers 138
Other Collectors 139
Taking Care of Your Collection 139
The March of Dimes: Collection vs. Investment 140
Plunking Down Your Spare Change 140
The Least You Need to Know 141

11 ~~Love~~ Money Makes the World Go 'Round   143

If These Bills Could Talk: A Brief History of Paper
  Money 144
  The First Money 144
  We're in the Money: The Development of Money
    in America 144
  The South Will Rise Again—But Its Money Won't 145
Dollars and Sense: Why Collect Paper Money? 146
The Almighty Dollar 146
  Know Your Money 147
Building Your Collection 148
  Top U.S. Notes for Collectors 148
  Hot Foreign Money 149
Money Matches Everything... Or, You Can't Go Wrong
  with Money 150
  Making the Grade 151
  Cash on the Barrelhead 151
Pass the Bucks: Handling and Preserving Money 152
  Wash and Wear Money 152
  Strut Your Stuff... Not 152
  Penny Wise, Pound Foolish 153
The Least You Need to Know 154

Part 3: Hot Stuff   155

12 Book Learnin'   157

Book 'em, Danno 158
It's What's Inside that Counts 159
How Not to Get Rich Quick Collecting Books 159
  Kid 'n' Play 159
  A Good Book—But Not a Good Investment: Bibles 160

Leader of the Pack: First Editions 161
   Identifying a First Edition 162
   Who's Hot… And Who's Not? 163
   Dressed for Success: Collectible Condition 164
   Gilding the Lilly 165
Hot Tip: Old Atlases 165
Building a Book Collection 165
   If These Books Could Talk (and Some Can) 166
   To Each His Own Taste 167
   Serious Shopping 167
The Least You Need to Know 168

13 The China Syndrome   **169**

Shards of History 170
Kissing Cousins: Earthenware, Stoneware, Bone China,
   Ironstone, and Porcelain 170
   Salt of the Earth: Earthenware 170
   Stoneware 172
   Roll 'Dem Bones: Bone China 173
   Always a Bridesmaid, Never a Bride: Ironstone............ 173
   Putting on the Ritz: Porcelain 174
In Your Dreams: Building a Collection 178
   Dating Porcelain 178
   Good, Better, Best: Condition 179
   MacCollectibles: Limited Editions............................... 179
Something's Rotten in China: Reproductions, Forgeries,
   Fakes, and Just Plain Stupidity 180
   Reproductions.. 180
   Forgeries 180
   Fakes.. 180
   Stupidity 181
The Least You Need to Know 181

14 Fun and Games   **183**

Not for Kids Anymore 184
All Dolled Up 184
   Block Heads: Wooden Head Dolls 185
   Bisque Heads 185
   Papier-Mâché Heads 185

Paper Dolls 186
Date with a Doll 186
Barbie: The Plastic Bombshell 187
Character Counts.. 187
Lost in Lilliput: Dolls' Houses and Miniatures 187
The Magic Kingdom of Collectibles: Disneyana 188
Mechanical Toys 189
The Die Is Cast 190
A Penny Saved Is a Penny Earned: Penny Banks 190
Action and Rarity... 191
Getting in on the Action 191
Grin and Bear It: Teddy Bears 193
Losing Your Marbles 194
Modern Toys 195
The Least You Need to Know 195

15 Home Sweet Collectible   **197**

Having Your Hobby and Drinking It, Too: Beer Cans 198
Beer, Here 198
Bottoms Up 199
Bottle Babies 200
Bottoms Up 202
Cleaning Bottles 202
Whatever Winds Your Watch 203
Something to Write Home About: Pens...................... 204
Domestic Goddess Strikes It Rich! 204
Living in an Amish Paradise: Quilts 205
What's the Frequency, Kenneth? (Radios) 207
Let's Twist Again, Like We Did Last Summer: Records 207
Tool Time 208
The Least You Need to Know 208

16 As Clear as Crystal   **209**

The Cadillac of Glass: Crystal 210
Bump and Grind: Cut Crystal 210
A Rose By Any Other Name Wouldn't Smell as Sweet:
Waterford 213
Steuben (Corning) 213
Feeling the S-q-u-e-e-z-e: Pressed Glass 213

Other 20th-Century Glass 215
Art Glass 215
Carnival Glass: Poor Man's Tiffany 217
Crystal on Steroids: Depression Glass 217
Oo La La: Lalique 218
Make Room for Coffeepots: American and European
Glass of the 1940s and 1950s 218
Paperweights 220
Collecting Glass 221
Glass Wannabes 222
The Least You Need to Know 222

Part 4: Master of Arts: Furniture and Art   **223**

**17 Different Strokes for Different Folks: Collecting
Paintings**   **225**

Be Art Smart 226
Art 101 227
Know Thyself 228
Do Squeeze the Charmin! 229
Hit the Books: Research 229
Paying the Piper 231
Value 231
Paintings as Investments 234
Damaged Goods 234
Liar, Liar, Pants on Fire: Fakes and Frauds 235
The Least You Need to Know 236

18 Say Cheese, Please: Photographs   **237**

Look at the Birdie 238
America in Amber: Daguerreotypes 240
Smile! 240
Size Does Matter 241
No Red Eye 241
Market Forecast 242
Better Safe than Sorry 242
So You Want To Put Together a Collection of Photos 242
A Few Grand 243
A Fist Full of Bucks 244

Safekeeping 245
    Be Good 245
    Here's Why 245
The Least You Need to Know 245

19 Pretty as a Picture: Drawings   247

Pain on Paper? 248
Quick Draw McGraw: A Brief Survey of Drawings 249
Culture Vulture 249
The Material Is the Message 249
    Paper Trail 250
    Inky Dinky Bottle of Inky 250
    Get the Point: Pens and Pencils 251
Just Plain Folk 252
    Drawings 252
    Fancy Schmancy Fractura 252
    The Shadow Knows: Silhouettes 253
Cut and Paste 254
The Line Kings 254
    Back in Time 254
    Big Men on Campus 255
    Takin' Care of Business 255
The Least You Need to Know 255

20 Someday My Prints Will Come: Prints and Lithographs   257

Psst! Wanna Come to My Room and See My Etchings? ... 258
    Engraving 258
    Intaglio Printing 258
    Etching 258
    Lino Cutting 259
    Lithography 259
    Relief Printing 260
    Surface Printing 261
    Woodcut Printing 261
    Wood Engraving 262
False Profits 262
Stop the Presses! 263
Go West, Young Collector 264
Go East, Too 265
The Least You Need to Know 265

21 Feathering the Nest: Furniture and Rugs   **267**

Strike a Pose: Identifying Furniture Style Periods 268
  Grim and Guilt-Ridden Pilgrim Furniture 269
  A Well-Turned Leg: Queen Anne 269
  The Best Seat in the House: Chippendale 270
  Hepplewhite 270
  Sheraton 271
  The Empire Strikes Back 271
  Victorian 271
  Mission Impossible? 272
  Art Deco 273
Rock 'Round the Clock: Furniture from the 1940s
  and 1950s 273
Shake and Bake 274
Moving in for the Kill 275
  Follow the Rules 275
  Check and Double-Check 276
Magic Carpet Ride 277
  Flying Carpets: Oriental Rugs 277
  Hooked Rugs 278
The Least You Need to Know 280

**Part 5: All that Glitters Isn't Gold—but It's Probably
Collectible**   **281**

**22 Are Diamonds a Collector's Best Friend? Collecting
Jewelry**   **283**

Oldies but Goodies: Antique Jewelry 284
  Plunging In! 284
  Dating 285
  Material Girl 287
Gemstones: Gravel with an Attitude 287
  Truth or Dare 288
  Amethyst to Zirconium 288
  Truth in Advertising 290
All That Glitters Isn't 14K 291
  Somewhere Over the Rainbow 291
  What's Up, Doc? 292
Native American Jewelry 293

Netsuke 293
Happy Days Are Here Again: Jewelry of the 1940s
    and 1950s 294
The Least You Need to Know 295

23 Heavy Metal   297

The Silver Standard 298
    American Sterling 298
    American Coin Silver 299
    English Sterling Silver 300
    Continental Silver 301
    Sterling Silver from the Former Soviets 301
    Danish Silver 301
    Victorian and Modern Silverplate 302
The Baser Metals: Pewter, Copper, Brass, Bronze, Iron,
    Steel 304
    "The Poor Man's Silver": Pewter 304
    The Alloy Kids: Copper, Bronze, Brass 305
    Man of Steel (and Iron) 306
Collectors' Darlings 307
    Ring Around the Bottle: Bottle Tickets 307
    A Good Night's Sleep: Brass Beds 307
    Lithographed Tins 308
The Least You Need to Know 308

A Future Collectibles   309

Ephemera 310
The Future Is Plastic 311
    Snowglobes 311
    What's Up, Doc? 311
Bits and Bytes 311
The Medium Is the Message 312
Royal Nonsense 312
Get the Scent 312
VidKids 312
Vice 313

B Further Reading   315

General Guides 315
Forgery and Fakes 316

Chapter 7: Pulp (Non)fiction 317
    Advertising Items 317
    Baseball Cards 317
    Movie Memorabilia 317
Chapter 8: Comic Books 317
Chapter 9: Stamps 318
Chapter 10: Coins 318
Chapter 11: Paper Money 318
Chapter 12: Books 319
Chapter 13: China 319
Chapter 14: Toys and Games 320
    Disneyana 320
    Mechanical Banks 320
    Toys and Games 320
Chapter 15: Household Items 320
Chapter 16: Crystal 320
Chapters 17–20: Fine Art 321
Chapter 21: Furniture and Rugs 321
Chapter 22: Jewelry 321
Chapter 23: Precious Metals 322

Index   **323**

Foreword

In the absence of scientific proof, I firmly believe I was genetically programmed to collect from birth.

I started with the Nancy Drew (as well as the Dana Girls and Cherry Ames, Nurse/Detective) series and a foreign doll collection. In my teen years I discovered antique jewelry, which is still my passion (and perhaps addiction). Along the way I have also collected paper advertising fans, old advertisements for Jello and women's cosmetics, Piano Babies, Snowbabies, Depression glass, old books, hat pins, baskets, Limoges china, and old furniture. Today, in addition to collecting antique and period jewelry, I pursue many items of the Arts and Crafts movement including furniture, metalwork, leather hand-tooled purses, hand-painted china, and embroideries.

When I was asked to write this foreword, I thought about who would be reading this book. I decided I would build a profile in my mind by thinking about any friends I had who were collectors.

To my amazement, when I began to think of who I know who might collect one or more items, I discovered that *almost everyone I know collects something!* The collections range from World's Fair spoons, fish-related objects, pop-up books, blue-and-white china, Bakelite radios, old records, and pig and elephant figurines, to old irons, vintage fabrics, enameled boxes, old doorstops, figurative napkin rings, baskets, stamps, coins, watches, and posters.

My son, who is nine, collects magic tricks, comic books, Goosebumps books, and super-hero figures. Even my husband, who would never call himself a collector, collects CDs and has a "mini-collection" of cufflinks. It was actually more difficult for me to identify people I know who do *not* collect something.

I believe that inside most people a budding collector hides, waiting to be set free. But collecting is a tricky business for neophytes and they need to proceed with caution. Until now there has been no manual to help a beginning collector learn how to collect. I wish *The Complete Idiot's Guide to Buying and Selling Collectibles* had been around when I first started collecting! I might have avoided some of the lessons I learned the hard (and sometimes expensive) way.

I once heard Gloria Lieberman, vice president of the Boston auction firm Skinner Inc., say, "If you don't make mistakes you're not doing enough collecting." There is truth to what she said, and it certainly made me feel less foolish about mistakes I have made along the way. However, the information in this book can clearly help someone who is beginning to form a collection avoid many commonly made mistakes. It will provide you with a great deal of useful information to make you an informed collector.

In-depth knowledge of a particular collectible comes only with years of buying, selling, and handling many pieces of that collectible. But knowing how to get started as a collector is invaluable, and *The Complete Idiot's Guide to Buying and Selling Collectibles* will give you that knowledge and a great deal more.

Laurie Rozakis has pulled together a real "bible" for collectors. It's the equivalent of years of experience in one book. Not only does she provide ideas for what you can collect and an overview of the hottest collectibles in today's market, she also gives essential information for collectors of anything—how to bargain, pitfalls to look for (including fakes, damaged goods, and the dangers of speculating), determining a fair price to pay, how to appraise collectibles, and how to care for and insure them. I learned all of these key points only after years of collecting and taking appraisal courses at a university.

Whether you have already started a collection, are thinking about starting one for yourself or your children, or are considering investing in collectibles, this book can be a fabulous resource. Read it through, take it with you when you are out collecting, and refer to it often as you build your collection.

Happy Hunting!

Elyse Zorn Karlin

Elyse Zorn Karlin is a freelance writer who specializes in the areas of antiques, collectibles, and parenting. She is the author of Jewelry and Metalwork in the Arts and Crafts Tradition *(Schiffer Publishing, 1993), and* Children Figurines of Bisque and Chinawares, 1850–1950 *(Schiffer Publishing, 1991). She is the editor of The American Society of Jewelry Historians newsletter. She is a member of both the Executive Board and the Board of Trustees of The American Society of Jewelry Historians.*

Introduction

In 1996, the One True Card—a mint condition 1910 Honus Wagner baseball card—was put up for auction. The card bears the undeniably homely image of a long-dead baseball player who was known to trade baseballs for buckets of beer. The card sold for $640,500. That's right, $640,500. According to the best estimates, fewer than 40 of the Honus Wagner cards exist, and only ten of them are in collectible condition.

At the same auction…

> ➤ Bill Bradley's New York Knicks jersey sold for $15,000; his gym shorts for $2,200.

> ➤ A humidor made from a leather football and signed by football great Knute Rockne fetched $4,500.

> ➤ Babe Ruth's ink handprint went for $14,930.

But that's chump change compared to the $75 million a buyer shelled out for a Vincent van Gogh painting in 1990. How about the nearly $13 million paid for an eleven-sided pear-shaped 101.84-carat diamond now known as *Mouwad Splendor*? A copy of the *Gutenberg Bible* sold for $5,390,000 in 1987.

Does a Shaker chest of drawers catch your eye? One collector anted up $99,000 for this piece of furniture. Even a tiny Shaker box, less than three inches in diameter, passed hands for $12,000. Here are the prices for other recent prizes: $63,000 for a mechanical bank (1993), $55,000 for a Steiff teddy bear (1989), and $100,000 for a duck decoy (1995).

Noel Coward once said that the best souvenirs were memories. Fat lot he knew, we dedicated collectors jeer. It's pretty difficult to frame, catalog, or display a memory. The resale value is pretty weak on memories, too. We like our souvenirs solid, something you can admire, fondle, and display. There's no denying that many collectors feel stirrings of avarice when a lovely collectible comes on the market.

If you've ever tried to find a parking spot at a flea market on a Saturday morning or jostled for space at an auction, you've been one of the millions of Americans in search of a "find." You're looking for things of beauty and value. In a larger sense, however, you are also seeking a piece of the past. Beautiful objects from the past provide evocative memories of the rosy world of family memories and historic events. They connect us to our heritage and our world.

My purpose in writing this book is to help the newcomer discover how to become a savvy collector. You'll learn which collectibles are hot—and which are not. I'll show you what's available in the major collecting fields and give you some brief historical background on the evolution of style and taste. You'll learn how to distinguish between real collectibles and fakes, frauds, and just plain stupidity.

What You'll Learn in This Book

This book is divided into five parts that take you though the process of becoming a confident collector. As you read, you'll see that collecting things involves much more than shopping and buying—that's the easy part! By the end of the book, you'll know how to create a collection of items of beauty and value.

Part 1, Why is There a Boom in Collectibles?, first explores some recent "finds" and their prices. Then you survey the history of modern collecting so you can find out what makes an item "become a collectible and discover the pleasures that collecting can bring. In this part, you'll also discover if you're a collector or an investor, learn how a "collection" is defined, and get the inside skinny on the hot collectibles. Then I'll teach you how to be a smooth shopper. You'll learn how to determine a fair price for a collectible that you want to buy and find out how to bargain easily and effectively. Next, see how to appraise your collectibles like a pro and get the inside skinny on the best markets for collectible sales. Finally, discover how to display, store, clean, and insure your collection.

Part 2, All in the Family: Ephemera, Stamps, Coins, and Paper Money, provides a detailed description of family-oriented collectibles: baseball cards, sports cards, bookplates, playing cards, postcards, comic books, stamps, coins, and paper money. You'll discover the different types of postal stamps and stamp-like things you can collect. Then I'll explain the history of coin collecting so you can find out what you need to start your own coin collection. Find out how to start and maintain a paper money collection, too.

Part 3, Hot Stuff, describes collectible books, china, toys, household items, and glass. This portion of the book starts off with the history of books so you can discover which books make the best collectibles. Next, you'll learn which china is collectible—and which is not. You'll find out why kids' toys aren't for kids anymore and see what household items, quilts, radios, and tools make collectors faint with anticipation. The part winds up with a discussion of collectible glass. The chapter explains which different types of glass people are collecting now—and which ones are likely to be popular in the future.

Part 4, Master of Arts: Furniture and Art, helps you find out how to buy paintings and drawings with confidence and skill. This section also tells you how to build a collection of photographs that suits your taste—and pocketbook. Next, there's a survey of different kinds of collectible drawings, including fractura, silhouettes, paper cutting, and caricatures. Then learn how prints are made and find out which prints send collectors into a frenzy of acquisition. Finally, find out which types and styles of furniture and rugs are most collectible.

Part 5, All That Glitters Isn't Gold—but It's Probably Collectible, helps you learn about collecting antique jewelry, precious gemstones, gold, netsuke, and Native American jewelry. You will also acquaint yourself with silver, pewter, copper, brass, bronze, iron, and steel collectibles.

Lastly, there's **Appendix A**, which forecasts which of today's items are likely to become tomorrow's collectibles. This will help you get the jump on the competition! **Appendix B** is a bibliography, in case you want to do some extra reading on specific collectibles.

More for Your Money!

In addition to all the explanations and teaching, this book has other types of information to make it even easier for you to learn how to be a confident collector. Here's how to recognize these features:

Big Deals

Fascinating facts that clue you into the important antique and collectible sales. You'll learn what the movers and shakers are buying—so you can join their ranks!

Connoisseur

These hints help you become a specialist by teaching you how to judge the best of the best. Here's where I clue you into collectibles you may never have even considered valuable!

Learn the Lingo

Like every other expert field, collecting and antiquing has its own jargon. Here's where I explain these terms so you can talk the talk and walk the walk like a pro.

Tricks of the Trade

Check out these insider tips, designed to make it easier for you to buy, sell, and appraise collectibles and antiques.

Caveat Emptor

These warnings help you become a more knowledgeable collector. They help you avoid the small mistakes—and the costly ones.

Acknowledgments

As always, thanks to my wonderful husband and great kids. Your pride and support make it all possible. Dear hubby, thank you especially for your expert input on Chapter 8 and repeated fact checking. It's useful to have a famous comic book writer and landmark production executive living in the house.

Special Thanks to the Technical Reviewer...

The Complete Idiot's Guide to Buying and Selling Collectibles was reviewed by an antiques and collectibles expert who double-checked the technical accuracy of what you'll learn here, to help us ensure that this book gives you everything you need to know to begin building your collection.

Special thanks are extended to Gary R. Wallace, president and principal auctioneer of Gary R. Wallace Auctioneers, Inc. of Ossipee, NH. The firm conducts over 50 antique and specialty auctions yearly. Gary Wallace started buying, selling, and collecting at the age of 14 and opened his antique and auction business in Newton, MA when he was 17 years old. Now 43 years old, he transacts millions of dollars' worth of sales yearly at his permanent facility in the beautiful White Mountain region of New Hampshire.

Trademarks

All terms mentioned in this book that are known to be or are suspected of being trademarks or service marks have been appropriately capitalized. Alpha Books and Macmillan General Reference cannot attest to the accuracy of this information. Use of a term in this book should not be regarded as affecting the validity of any trademark or service mark. The following trademarks and service marks have been mentioned in this book: Waterford, Lalique, Precious Moments, Disney, Nucut, Near-cut, Deep cut, Press-cut, Swarovski, Steuben, Corning, Favrile, Aurene, Crystal Glass, Dunbar Glass, Heisey Glass, New Martinsville Glass, Pilgrim Glass, Westmoreland Glass, Bacarrat, Clichy, St. Cloud, Cambridge Glass Company, Jeanette Glass Company, L.E. Smith, J.H. Millstein, T.H. Stough, Victory Glass, Avon, Beam, Mont Blanc, Waterman, Stanley, Barbie, Hess, Lehmann, Tootsie, Dinkie, Ives, Van Briggle, Newcomb, Red Wing, Dedham Pottery, Fulper Pottery, Buffalo Pottery, Deldare Ware, Cowan Pottery, Wedgwood, Dansk, Lenox, Coalport, Mason's, Villeroy & Boch, Fiesta Franciscan, Metlox, Russel Wright, Vernon, Homer Laughlin, Pfaltzgraff, Mikasa, Sango, Lusterware, Belleek, Bing & Grondahl, Hummel, Lladro, West Brothers, Stickey, Marvel comics, and DC Comics.

Dedication

This book is for my mother, Queen of the Garage Sales, a collector without peer. Thank you for introducing me to the world of china, silver, crystal, statues, linen, cels, cloisonné, and tchotskes of every stripe. I'll even show you this dedication if we're on speaking terms when the book comes out.

Part 1
Why Is There a Boom in Collectibles?

First collector: "Sonny, when I was just a little whippersnapper, you could pick Shaker chairs from the trash heap and trade a dozen eggs for a handful of old stamps."

Second collector: "And comic books were 10 cents each and Depression glass was given away."

Usually recollections from the past are a bit distorted, but in this case most of the stories you hear about the good old days of antiquing are true. There was a time—and not too long ago, either—when antiques were as abundant as parking tickets. Alas, the past is no more.

Today, the mania to collect has reached such a fever pitch that some objects in antique shops don't have time to get dusty before they're snapped up. Prices for many collectibles are rising higher than Don King's hair and faster than the national debt. Why? What has caused our national obsession with collecting? That's what you'll discover in this part of the book. So strap on your fanny pack and let's get to work finding those bargains.

Chapter 1

It's Mine... I Saw It First! The Mania to Collect

In This Chapter

➤ Explore some recent "finds" and their prices

➤ Learn the history of modern collecting

➤ Find out what makes a "thing" become a collectible

➤ Discover the pleasures that collecting can bring

Do you lust after comic books? Then you might as well go for the gold, the cherry on any comic collector's cupcake: *Action #1,* the 1938 comic book that marks the first appearance of that hunk in red and blue spandex, Superman. A mint copy of *Action #1* just sold for $180,000. Perhaps you prefer more metallic Americana. An original Coca-Cola sign recently sold for $24,000. Want a piece of Camelot? Jackie O's pearls—the fake ones, yet—were auctioned amid much hoopla for $211,500. How about $772,500 for a set of JFK's golf clubs—even though the golf bag was badly tattered?

Everyone collects something. Some people seek out valuable comics; others yearn for rare paintings, striking photographs, first-edition prints, or one-of-a-kind sculpture. Beautiful furniture, textiles, and china are hotly sought-after collectibles; jewelry and gems are always popular. And who doesn't have a stamp or coin collector in the family? There are people who squirrel away gum wrappers; others have fine hubcap collections. If the object exists, someone somewhere collects it... and loves that collection.

In this chapter, you will learn about the human desire to collect objects of beauty and value. You will discover that the urge to collect is as old as time itself—and as powerful. In addition, you will find out how modern collecting got started. This chapter will help you discover that you're not alone in your desire to collect whatever you collect, whether it be fine art or gum wrappers.

Big Deals

In 1874, Illinois farmer Joseph F. Glidden invented the first practical barbed wire for fencing. Greeted with rage, it inspired bitter feuds when land boundaries were disputed. However, a decade later, more than 120 million pounds of barbed wire were being sold a year. In 1957, Jesse S. James of Maywood, California, started a barbed wire collection. James meticulously catalogs and arranges his collection of antique barbed wire on 1 ½-by-3-foot panels, each containing 30 pieces that are 18 inches long. James is not alone in his passion; barbed wire has become a sharp collectible.

You Bought a *What?*

The urge to collect is as ancient as the drive for food, clothing, and shelter. Historically, only the nobility, the highest-ranking members of the church, and the very wealthy had the time and the funds to patronize the arts. Artifacts of the past were high-priced, scarce, and somewhat intimidating. Art auctions were held in Imperial Rome, featuring war booty and elegant fakes. In the 1400s, the great nobles of France and Italy followed Machiavelli's advice to princes to "also show his esteem for talent, actively encourage able men, and pay honor to eminent craftsmen." The great nobles' treasure troves manifested the glory of the state but were highly seasoned by each individual noble's personal taste and training.

Connoisseur
Pioneered especially by Sotheby's auction house in London, pop memorabilia has become big business—particularly if it's associated with such superstars as the Beatles and Elvis. For example, John Lennon's 1965 Rolls-Royce Phantom V touring limo, emblazoned with psychedelic designs, sold at Sotheby's for $2,299,000 in 1985. Elvis's 1942 Martin D-18 guitar used to record his first singles, 1954–56, fetched $180,000 in 1991.

Prehistoric collectors took this biological imperative to the max: They believed they could transport their collections with them from this world to the next. Today, we can determine the social status of the ancients by the items found in their tombs. For example, art was an important status symbol in the past. It has lost none of its value today.

As a more affluent middle class began to emerge, they, too, were eager to acquire art and artifacts—if only to display evidence of their upward mobility! But it was not until the Industrial Revolution that the average Joe or Jane could even begin to think of satisfying the lust for collectibles. For most people in the first half of the 19th century, life was too "nasty, brutish, and short" to allow for the luxury of amassing pretty things. Only members of the upper classes had the money and time to collect fine paintings, ancient coins, rare musical instruments, and the like. During the second half of the 19th century, the development of new types of machinery allowed goods to be mass-produced. This drastically affected the lives of our forebears. Items that were previously created by hand through laborious effort could now be produced easily and quickly—and churned out by the tens of thousands. Factories sprung up in nearly all the large cities, ushering in a plethora of consumer goods. Couldn't get to the shop? Not to worry—Sears and Roebuck had a catalog that was heavy enough to break your foot. Didn't want to read all those pages? The traveling salesman would bring these new marvels right to your door and talk the money right out of your pocket.

> **Connoisseur**
> One of the world's most unusual collections belongs to Fay and Jimmy Rodolfos of Woburn, Massachusetts: They collect Dionne Quintuplet memorabilia. The quints were born on May 28, 1934 to Oliva and Elzire Dionne in rural Ontario, Canada. They were the first identical set of quints that had ever survived. Elzire was 25 years old at the time and already had given birth to six children. She received no prenatal care with the quints until a week before their birth; the first three girls were delivered by midwives before the doctor arrived. The Rodolfos' collection includes "Famous Fives" dolls, postcards, scrapbooks, lamps, newspaper and magazine articles, photos, paper dolls, and much more.

Thanks to the Industrial Revolution, even the poorer classes could become collectors. No doubt they still couldn't ante up enough for an Old Master, diamond pendant, or walnut whatnot, but they *could* now afford to collect such mass-produced paper items as cards, matchbooks, and bookmarks that were given away by the thousands. Marbles, tops, and small toys were almost as easy to procure and barter.

Naturally, this distressed some fastidious collectors whose acquisitions of rare and beautiful objets d'art were announced with pomp and circumstance. It remains a thorn in the side of a few high-minded antique dealers who sneer at the tendency of people to collect anything of lesser magnitude than 14th-century ivory diptychs. But the anguished cries of the antique elite have been shouted down by the squeals of joy from the new members of the sport of millionaires and monarchs.

Throughout the first half of our own century, factories improved both the quality and quantity of these goods. Comic books, inexpensive cameras, baseball cards, Depression glass, records, radios, and toys flooded the market. The enormous quantity of goods led to a change in the mass consciousness. Gone was Grandma's "A stitch in time saves nine" mentality. In its place was the belief in the value of replacement. With goods so inexpensive, why would anyone take the time and trouble to repair an item? Better to throw it out and get a new one.

The Collectibles Craze

You have learned that people are driven to seek food, clothing, shelter… and antiques. Until recently, we were able to hold our last need in check. All that changed about a generation ago when people suddenly went gaga over collectibles.

The collectibles craze kicked in over 30 years ago, in the 1960s. Up until then, people believed that they could buy bigger and better things every year. As long as technology continued to chug along, materials were available, and labor was cheap, we could have what we wanted when we wanted it.

Learn the Lingo
A **collectible** is an item of perceived beauty and value that people seek to own. An **antique**, in contrast, must be at least 100 years old.

But life began to change in the 1960s, and not just because the mini-skirt was invented. The price of many raw materials began to climb; labor followed suit. Producers began to snip a little here and there. The design might have become a little less detailed. Perhaps the fabric was not as thick. As inflation rose, Americans saw their dollar not stretching as far as it had just a few years before. The good old days of steady prices and improving quality slipped away in the wake of the Vietnam War and the increasing spiral of inflation.

Some people cued in to these changes earlier than others. A handful of these far-seeing folks went out and bought old models of such items as radios, appliances, and toys, recognizing their superior quality and design. These items usually cost very little, because most people still wanted new goods.

Inside a Collector's Mind

Goods from the past represent different things to different people. Collectors are motivated by some or all of these feelings:

➤ A desire to forge links to the past

➤ A love of nostalgia

➤ A belief that old items are made better

➤ A connection to childhood and simpler times

➤ A genuine admiration for the item

➤ A lust to make money

So Should You Save that Wrapper?

How does something become a collectible? Although anything can become a collectible, it's undeniable that certain objects become more valued than others. What makes some objects eagerly sought collectibles while others languish on the back shelves? Why, for example, are pulp magazines from the 1920s more sought after than their far rarer counterparts from the turn of the century?

All items pass through the same three steps when they develop from being a functional item into being a collectible:

➤ **Step 1: Item is a thing.** The item is valued for its function. Very few people, if any, collect it. The item has virtually no value as a collectible.

➤ **Step 2: Interest builds.** The item attracts interest and collectors perk up. This creates a supply-demand situation that often drives prices up.

➤ **Step 3: Item is a collectible.** The item becomes a collectible. Many people want to possess it for its appearance, not its function.

In addition to these characteristics, there are several other qualities that make an item into a collectible. Here's my Fab Five list:

1. **Perceived beauty.** There is no doubt that beauty is in the eye of the beholder, especially when applied to collectibles. Nonetheless, a true collectible, like a beautiful person, has an appeal that is recognized by virtually everyone. Even if the item doesn't strike your fancy for some reason, you can still recognize its appeal to others. There's a sexiness about the item that gives a familiar tingle. You can appreciate its craftsmanship, color, or shape; admire its glitter or gleam. Collectors develop a feel for each item's appeal by viewing and handling a variety of the same objects. For example, if you are looking at stamps, see how you feel about the color, shape, size, and design of each stamp.

Connoisseur
A well-bred foal can appreciate by its second birthday to become one of the most expensive animals on earth. Beginning in the 1970s (fueled in part by Arab oil money), the price of racehorses skyrocketed. In 1985, 24 fine yearlings sold for $1 million each, eight others went for over $2 million, and one especially sweet horsey fetched $13.1 million at the Keeneland Select Sales auction in Lexington, Kentucky. Prices softened a bit the following year, but even so, the Maktoum family of oil-soaked Dubai plunked down $40.2 million for 57 one-year-old racehorses.

Caveat Emptor
The speed with which an item becomes a collectible determines how stable its value will be. In most cases, the more slowly an item becomes a collectible, the stronger the market for the item will continue to be.

The artist's reputation is also a factor here. For example, some people sign up on waiting lists for Bev Doolittle prints before they're released, based on the artist's reputation and the beauty of her previous work.

Caveat Emptor

"Instant collectibles" were created to cash in on the collecting craze. They are aimed at the everyday person who believes he or she is investing in a legitimate collectible. Instant collectibles come in many forms; the most common are the "limited edition" plates, statues, figurines, ingots, and medals. Buy instant collectibles solely if you like them as home decorations; they are unwise investments.

2. **Quantity.** Some collectibles become hot because there are enough of them to fire up a market. But if there are too many of them, the item will likely never become a collectible because everyone would have it. The market would be flooded by the item. My husband, Bob Rozakis, is a recognized authority on comic books and comic art. He has been in the comic book business for nearly a quarter of a century. Every year, starry-eyed people come up to him at conventions and parties and say, "Gee, I'd have a copy of *Action #1* if my mother hadn't thrown it out when I (went into the Army, left for college, got married, had a sex change operation, etc.)." My husband always responds, "If everyone had a copy of the comic, it would be too common to be a collectible. What makes that comic—and others like it—a hot collectible is that very few people have a copy of it."

As a result, people who hoard today's objects because they think they will become tomorrow's collectibles would be much better off spending their time cleaning out their closets. By their combined efforts, these people are working against each other. For an object to become a collectible, there must be enough of them to spark interest—but not enough to make them commonplace.

3. **Price.** How much an item costs is very important to whether or not it becomes a collectible. Nearly all collectibles start off being affordable to most people, thus creating a broad base of support. Within nearly all collectibles, there are fewer items that are more expensive, and finally the fewest examples that are most costly.

   For instance, many stamp collectors are kids who start their collections by steaming canceled stamps off envelopes. As they grow up, they buy the stamps they can afford, such as limited issues and first-day covers. If they become sufficiently affluent, the collectors can buy more and more expensive stamps to add to their collections. But if an item becomes too expensive, only the most wealthy collectors can afford to stay in the game.

4. **Links to the present.** Collectibles that have the greatest appeal usually have parallel items in the present. For example, there are antique toys and new toys; old portraits and new portraits. Collectors like to collect items that are still being created in some form. This gives the present-day collection a vitality lacking in items that have merely historical interest.

5. **Historical links.** Most collectibles stir powerful feelings about the past, a time we imagine was kinder and gentler. For example, Beatles memorabilia brings back memories of the exciting 1960s; movie posters from the 1920s carry echoes of the silent films. The more a group of popular culture items captures the mood of the past, the more likely the items are to become collectibles—if they are not already valued.

The Rewards of Collecting

Why collect? You've learned that collecting is an innate drive. It prompted Og and Grog to stash pretty bones in the back of their cave; it moved King Tut to load his tomb with enough gold to sink an ocean liner. Throughout the ages, people have been moved to collect things that strike their fancy—so you're in good company! Take a closer look at your feelings about collecting by filling out the Collecting Inventory Worksheet in this section.

Collecting gives spiritual, educational, emotional, and cultural satisfaction. Because there's no limit to the items people can collect, there's something for everyone. Following are some of the primary advantages you can gain from collecting. Use these advantages as ammunition the next time your partner complains, "You're buying *more* ink stands? Don't we have enough by now to supply the whole danged U.S. Congress?" Your answer? You probably collect to…

1. **Express yourself.** Today, we're often labeled by our jobs. I'm a professor and a writer; you may be a doctor, accountant, postal carrier, or bus driver. At parties, people say to me, "Oh, you're a teacher." Sometimes I'm labeled by my children's accomplishments or even by my husband's career. Like you, I'm rarely appreciated for myself. Collecting something special, something that you have selected, allows you to express yourself. Your collection shows the world that you are special.

2. **Meet people.** Whether you're a new parent isolated by the demands of babykins, a recent divorcee or widow(er), or just an average Joe or Jane burdened by the demands of family and work—it's difficult to meet people. Sure, we grab some "face time" with our coworkers at the water cooler and schmooze over our egg salad at lunch, but it's really hard to connect with the people who share our interests. How often do you find yourself talking about work when you'd really rather be talking about the antique table you got at auction last Saturday or the perfume bottles you picked up at the little antique store in Saratoga? A collectibles show or convention is a great way to bring together people with common interests.

   It's not surprising that many collectors have best friends who are also collectors. Some have even met their spouses over a convention table or at a flea market. And people who collect together tend to stay together—unless your partner gets to the item that you want first!

3. **Relieve stress.** No time to eat. No time to think. No time to breathe! Find yourself s-q-u-e-e-z-e-d in this box? You're not alone. Whether you're a corporate lawyer or a librarian, a homemaker or a hatmaker, you're pulled in a dozen different directions every day. We live in a very stressful age, pressured to achieve and accomplish with nary a chance for winding down.

   Collecting allows you the opportunity to relax and refresh your soul. I've seen highly placed business people, their faces lined with tension and their shoulders slumped with exhaustion, barking orders to equally harried subordinates as the job never seems to get done. But on the weekend, these same people, their faces alight with pleasure, are jovial and relaxed as they catalog their stamps, sort their coins, or hunt out an ivory statue to add to their collection. Less fattening than chocolate, less expensive than a Caribbean vacation, less sadistic than a Stairmaster, collecting allows you to unwind and enjoy life.

Tricks of the Trade
Sometimes dealers will buy a **lot** of merchandise, accepting items they don't want for those they collect and trade. A stamp dealer, for example, might take some old books as part of a lot. A doll collector of my acquaintance snared some great finds from an antique furniture dealer this way.

4. **Expand your knowledge.** Collectors learn fascinating facts about history, economics, math, social science, and art—to name just a few fields. Depending on your collecting interest, you might find out more about modern art, printing, or metalwork, for example.

   If you're like the rest of us, it's likely you never got drafted to play major league football or tapped to sing on Broadway. Your still life of cereal-and-strawberries isn't displayed in the Museum of Modern Art; you probably hung up your toe shoes a few years ago. But many successful collectors have attained a level of personal excellence in an area they—and others—find compelling. They are sought after for their knowledge and respected by others for what they know. Collecting gives you the opportunity to gain knowledge that you find interesting. It lets you be the head weenie at the roast.

5. **Have fun.** Most of us spend all day chained to a desk and all night sprawled in front of the TV. In between, we do endless loads of laundry, bankrupt ourselves at the supermarket, and make only marginally successful attempts to get fit. Collectibles get you up and out to spend time with people who have similar interests.

6. **Make money.** Finally, many collectors have learned that they can make a tidy piece of change through their collection. An experienced collector, for instance, can often find bargains from dealers. If you're willing to develop a keen eye, study hard, and do your homework, there's gold in them thar collectibles. See Chapters 4 and 5 for detailed ways to make money buying and selling your collectibles.

Collecting Inventory Worksheet

To see where you stand, complete this worksheet. Use your (collectible) Mount Blanc pen. If necessary, add some blank paper to provide more room for your answers.

1. List your current collections or the items you would like to collect.

   ❏ _____

   ❏ _____

   ❏ _____

   ❏ _____

   ❏ _____

2. What are the best pieces you have in your collections? What makes them so special?

   ❏ _____

   ❏ _____

   ❏ _____

   ❏ _____

   ❏ _____

3. What are your strengths as a collector?

   ❏ _____

   ❏ _____

   ❏ _____

   ❏ _____

   ❏ _____

continues

11

Collecting Inventory Worksheet, continued

4. What are your weaknesses as a collector?

❏ _____

❏ _____

❏ _____

❏ _____

❏ _____

5. List the things you would collect if you had the time, money, or expertise.

❏ _____

❏ _____

❏ _____

❏ _____

❏ _____

6. List five reasons why you enjoy collecting or think you would enjoy collecting.

❏ _____

❏ _____

❏ _____

❏ _____

❏ _____

The Least You Need to Know

➤ No matter what people admit in public, everyone collects something. And they feel very passionate about their collections.

➤ The Industrial Revolution enabled everyday people to satisfy their urges to collect pretty things.

➤ Collecting is a great way to express yourself, meet people, relieve stress, expand your knowledge, have fun, and maybe even finance that sports car you've wanted since you were 18.

Chapter 2

If Someone Makes It, Someone Else Collects It

In This Chapter

➤ Discover if you're a *collector* or an *investor*... or a pack rat with an attitude

➤ A detailed look at the difference between a *collectible* and an *antique*

➤ Learn how a "collection" is defined

➤ Get the inside skinny on the hot collectibles; find out which ones are sizzling *now*

The Guggenheims, Vanderbilts, and Astors collected art and homes. Queen Elizabeth of England has her horses; ex-Princess Di goes for baubles with hefty price tags. Baseball great Reggie Jackson collects cars. Comedian Morey Amsterdam collected figurines of cellists. Robert Goulet collects frog tschotchkes; Red Skelton collects clown statues. What conclusions can we draw from this? If someone makes it, someone else will collect it. But there's more to collecting than the lust for acquisitions, as you will learn in this chapter.

Collecting beautiful and valuable objects has it all: a satisfying aesthetic experience, the possibility of economic gain, and pride of ownership. In addition, your collection makes an important statement about you and what you represent. Whether you are aware of it or not, your collection projects an image of how you perceive yourself and how you want others to perceive you.

This chapter focuses on *you* and collecting. First, you'll take a short, painless quiz to determine whether you have the heart and soul of a true collector. Then I'll show you how to figure out whether you prefer to collect or invest. As you will discover, this distinction makes a big difference in your approach to the topic.

Then I'll give you a clear-cut definition of *collectible* and *antique* so that you can tell how objects are classified by the pros. Then it's a quick class in Economics 101 so that you understand how the antique and collectible markets operate. Finally, you find out which collectibles are *in*—and which ones are *out*.

Altogether, the information in this chapter will help empower you to stop amassing "stuff" and start collecting items of value and pleasure. I'll give you the tools you need to realize that you *can* be a successful collector—that you can enjoy collecting as a pastime, hobby, or career.

Big Deals

➤ According to the *1996 Guinness Book of World Records,* the largest collection of beer cans belongs to (the envelope, please)... William B. Christiensen of Madison, Wisconsin. Bill has more than 75,000 different beer cans from around the world.

➤ So far, a Rosalie Pilsner is the most expensive beer can ever sold; it fetched $6,000 in the U.S. in 1981.

➤ And beer labels? Jan Solberg of Oslo, Norway had collected 424,868 different beer labels as of June 1995.

➤ "Don't kick the can" is the motto of the Beer Can Collectors of America. After all, the can might be a collector's item.

If It Walks Like a Duck...

You can tell a zebra by its stripes, a duck by its quack. Psychologists claim to be able to tell a collector just as easily by similarly clear-cut signs. No less august figures than Sigmund Freud and Charles Darwin believed that collecting was instinctive. Other psychologists, in contrast, have argued that collecting is a culturally stimulated experience like the urge to crunch your abs or eat something squishy we can't pronounce. But, hey, we don't remember who *those* psychologists were. At any rate, take the Collector Quiz in this chapter to see if you've got the mentality of a collector.

Collector Quiz

Sharpen your (1939 World's Fair) pencil. Then take this quiz to see whether you have the authentic collector mentality.

Yes   No

❏   ❏   As a child, you hoarded treasures in your special treasure box. This was usually an old cigar box or candy container, but a shoe box with a lid would do in a pinch.

❏   ❏   As you grew up, you replaced all those cat's-eye marbles and baseball cards with more expensive and meaningful memorabilia.

❏   ❏   You would still have your baseball cards if your mother (sister, aunt, father, etc.) had not thrown them out when they cleaned out the attic (garage, closet, basement, etc.). You remind your mother (etc.) of this transgression at least once a year—normally at a major family gathering.

❏   ❏   Certain objects give you great pleasure because of their beauty and value.

❏   ❏   If you had more money, you would collect more expensive and beautiful objects.

❏   ❏   You feel that possessing something beautiful is an exhilarating experience, a real rush.

❏   ❏   You believe that your collection or collections say something about you, your values, and beliefs.

❏   ❏   You agree that a person's collection reveals his or her cultural, social, and economic status.

❏   ❏   You have lusted after someone else's collection or any part thereof.

❏   ❏   You get so excited when you see toys you played with as a child for sale at garage sales that you buy them.

Bonus Questions:

❏   ❏   At least once in your life, you have spent too much for an object because you believed that it would appreciate in value. Or just because you really liked it. A lot.

❏   ❏   You lose track of time when you stare at your treasures. Hours can pass this way.

continues

Collector Quiz, continued

❏ ❏   You have been known to fondle the objects you collect.

❏ ❏   Your heart goes pitter-patter when you are near one of your beloved possessions.

❏ ❏   You dream about finding the rarest item associated with your hobby— *Action #1* comic, for example.

❏ ❏   You would never consider selling your collection unless your family was starving and the rent was six months overdue—and then you'd still stop and think...

Score:

1–2 yes answers	You have been known to drive by a flea market without kicking yourself in the morning.
3–4 yes answers	You can pass up the pot holder shaped like a turkey but not the bargain-priced Renoir.
5–6 yes answers	No antique store is safe when you're loose.
7–8 yes answers	You've been bitten by the "collecting bug;" hide your charge card.
9–10 yes answers	You're the real thing, bunky: Collector Americanus.
Yes to all the bonus questions	Either you can write this book or add it to your book collection.

Are You a Collector or an Investor?

Each of us hopes that our family heirlooms and flea market finds will turn out to be worth a fortune. But a collector isn't in it solely for the bucks. Study the following lists to see whether you can tell the difference between a collector and an investor. Which descriptions cling to you like a wet (collectible) T-shirt?

Collectors...

➤ Save a collectible because they like the item.

➤ Consider items in the collection as children to be cherished.

➤ Are interested in buying, selling, trading—and possessing.

➤ Are passionately in love with the items they collect.

➤ Get pleasure from their collection that cannot be reckoned in terms of money.

Investors…

➤ Buy the item only because they want to resell it at a profit.

➤ Consider items in the collection to be merchandise.

➤ Are interested in buying, selling, and trading.

➤ Are excited over the thought of making a profit from the item, not possessing it.

➤ Are business people, first and foremost.

This is no time to sit on the fence, kiddo. You can't be a wuss with *me* because collectors and investors often work at cross-purposes. After all, a collector wants to own the finest pieces… but these are the very pieces that a dealer needs to turn a profit. Therefore, you have to stand your ground now. What will it be? Collector or investor? Not deciding before you start buying will make it impossible for you to collect with a pure heart or invest with a sharp mind.

Put down your (antique jade) worry beads and dry your tears. I'll let you off the hook a little. Today, it is very hard to be a pure collector. The finest pieces in just about any collection usually cost some serious money. As a result, you are going to have to learn to wheel and deal to build a respectable collection. That's why you bought this book, after all.

Consider becoming a collector, but adopt and use the best traits of a dealer. Learn to use a dealer's methods to get what you want for your collection. Buy what you can, keep the best for yourself, and resell the rest. That way, you can have your cake—and display it, too.

Collectible vs. Antique

I wish people would ask: "Can I give you a vacation home in Aspen?" or "How *did* you get to be so gorgeous?" but instead they always ask me these three questions:

1. What is a *collectible*?

2. What is an *antique*?

3. When does a collectible become an antique?

Collectibles

The word *collectible* has been defined as often as the terms *Liberal* and *Conservative*—and just as erroneously. Here's a definition you can use: "A *collectible* is an item that was originally made to serve a utilitarian purpose but has since transcended its original function through intense collector interest."

Occasionally, a collectible may not have any true quality, or its quality may be completely beside the point. The point of these collectibles is association, rather than intrinsic merit. The powder brush that Anne Boleyn used on the morning of her execution and the string of pearls that Marie Antoinette wore before her head was parted from her body both have a value of their own as ivory and pearl, but their value is nowhere near as important as their association. The same is true of the black leather jacket that John Lennon wore in 1962 (sold for a staggering $47,900 at a recent auction) or Jimi Hendrix's black felt hat (which went for a respectable $24,000).

Antiques

An *antique* is also an object that people collect because it is beautiful, rare, unique, or any combination of these attributes. But an antique is different from a collectible in one

Connoisseur
"You have to be an antique to appreciate them."—Fay Madigan Lange

major way: An antique must be at least 100 years old. We have the U.S. Customs service to thank for this distinction; leave it to the government to set us straight. But according to this definition, no consideration is given to quality, style, craftsmanship, or any other aspect. According to law, a collectible becomes an antique simply when Willard Scott can celebrate its 100th birthday on the *Today* show. But most dealers and collectors consider 50 to 100 years an acceptable range to rank a "collectible" as an "antique."

The best efforts of the government to the contrary, *antique* is not a precise term. In the beginning of the 19th century, the English painter Thomas Rowlandson is rumored to have made this point while a chamber pot was being auctioned off: "What am I to bid for tomorrow's antique?"

Collectible Art

Collectible art is an all-purpose term that includes the visual, decorative, and functional arts. A true collectible encompasses the creations of old masters and rare antiques to almost anything that required skill and talent to create. For example, a toaster is a functional object whose purpose is to turn mushy bread a crispy brown. A painting, in contrast, serves only to embellish a home or office. Neither the toaster nor the painting becomes a collectible, however, unless enough people decide to regard it as one.

The Good, Bad, and Really Bad

To some people, antique = quality = value. As a result, they lust after not only true objects of value, but also seek out anything "old" or "collectible." The primary requirement is age, and not even a whole lot of that. As a result, the market became clogged with good, bad, and really bad. The only characteristic all this stuff had in common was age—it was all produced in the past. The equation? Antique = old.

Going by this yardstick, everything would become an antique if we wait long enough: a magnificent painting, a rusty flyswatter, and even aged Aunt Alice. Following this reasoning to its logical conclusion, the number of "antiques" is virtually unlimited, but the amount of "collectible" art is quite limited. Sometimes it is easy to tell the difference, but more often it is not, especially to newcomers to the field of collecting. By the end of this book, you will learn that age does not equal value. In many years, a fine work of art will become a rare treasure; in an equal number of years, a piece of trash becomes an old piece of trash—whether we call it an antique or not.

Big Deals

Sid Sackson has the largest and most extensive private collection of board games in the world. His collection totals about 50,000 games and complete reproductions of equipment and rules. His collection fills several rooms in his home. Sackson also has a library of more than 1,000 game books in 13 languages and over 2,000 magazines on games.

Voodoo Economics and Collectibles

Age is one of the sieves that separates the wheat from the chaff, or in our case, the true collectibles from the merely old stuff. The value of an object is determined in large part according to the law of *supply and demand.*

A diminished supply of anything—gasoline, houses, or diamonds—raises its demand and price. The increased price, however, will often decrease the demand, resulting in an astonished, "You expect me to pay *what* for this old picture?" Once again, this lowers the price.

Despite what our economists would have us believe, these checks and balances work well with guns and butter, but not with collectibles. With collectibles, the rise in price alone can spark enough interest to increase demand and further spike the price. The spiral can continue forever, as long as the supply remains finite. In terms of collectibles, here's how supply and demand work:

➤ **Demand.** The demand for any collectible is first created by its beauty and later by its performance on the market.

Caveat Emptor
A thing of beauty is a joy forever—or until it breaks, chips, scratches, peels, or flakes.

➤ **Supply.** The supply is determined by the creator and should balance with the anticipated demand.

➤ **Supply/Demand Ratio.** This is the most crucial factor in the collector market. The demand for a collectible must exceed its supply to tickle our collector bone. Therefore, the desirability of any collectible is linked to its supply/demand ratio. Without that challenge and excitement, there's no thrill of the hunt. And so there's no hunter.

What's Hot—and What's Not

To become a major collectible, an item must cause enough people to look at it with admiration. Like sneakers, restaurants, movie stars, and ice-cream flavors, some collectibles are more in demand than others. What objects become collectibles? We all know that beautiful furniture, carpets, rugs, coins, stamps, and fine art are sought after. So are fine books, porcelain, exquisite jewelry, textiles, and prints.

But what about the collectibles that aren't so well-known to the newcomer to Collection World? Here's the inside scoop, a list of the hottest collectibles on the market today. These items are *smokin'* but only if they're vintage, one-of-a-kind, out of print, or rare...

➤ Advertising items

➤ Antique clothing

➤ Autographs

➤ Barbed wire

➤ Baseball cards

➤ Beer cans

➤ Bottle caps

➤ Boy Scout memorabilia

➤ Cameras (old and well-made)

➤ Clocks

➤ Coin-operated machines

➤ Animation art

➤ Ashtrays

➤ Banks (antique metal toys)

➤ Barbershop things

➤ Beatles memorabilia

➤ Bicycles

➤ Bottles

➤ Buttons (antique)

➤ Christmas items

➤ Coca-Cola memorabilia

➤ Comic art

- ➤ Comics
- ➤ Dinnerware
- ➤ Elvis Presley memorabilia
- ➤ Folk art
- ➤ Glassware
- ➤ Hollywood memorabilia
- ➤ Jazz memorabilia
- ➤ Kitchen implements
- ➤ Locks (antique)
- ➤ Matchbooks
- ➤ Military items
- ➤ Movie memorabilia
- ➤ Musical instruments
- ➤ Newspapers (old)
- ➤ Norman Rockwell items
- ➤ Paper money
- ➤ Perfume bottles
- ➤ Plates
- ➤ Political items
- ➤ Posters
- ➤ Pottery (art pottery)
- ➤ Quilts (old, handmade)
- ➤ Rock and roll memorabilia
- ➤ Rubber stamps (old)
- ➤ Sheet music
- ➤ Silver items
- ➤ Sports memorabilia
- ➤ Country store items
- ➤ Dolls
- ➤ Fishing lures
- ➤ Gemstones
- ➤ Hat pins
- ➤ Items associated with magic
- ➤ Keys (old)
- ➤ Lightbulbs (early)
- ➤ Marbles (old)
- ➤ Menus
- ➤ Minerals
- ➤ Music boxes
- ➤ Native American art
- ➤ Non-sports cards
- ➤ Olympic pins and other memorabilia
- ➤ Paperweights
- ➤ Pin-ups
- ➤ Playing cards
- ➤ Postcards
- ➤ Postmarks
- ➤ Pulp magazines
- ➤ Railroad memorabilia/trains
- ➤ Royal Doulton china items
- ➤ Schoolhouse items
- ➤ Shells (unique)
- ➤ Soda cans (vintage)
- ➤ Stock certificates

continues

continued

➤ Stoneware

➤ Temperance memorabilia

➤ Thimbles

➤ Tools

➤ Trading cards

➤ Wine

➤ Teddy bears

➤ Theatre items

➤ Tobacco items

➤ Toys

➤ Walt Disney items

What Is a Collection?

Everything and anything had a place in the great "collections" of the 17th century: porcelain, clocks, mermaids, Aztec headdresses, silk, cameos, jewels, scientific instruments, busts, statues, shells, medals, pistols, enamels, suits of armor, weapons, and strange furniture. But a collection is more than a random accumulation of objects. That's the mess the Collier Brothers created with their piles of newspapers and trash. A collection, in contrast, is a methodical arrangement of objects of beauty and value. A collection has a plan, a governing principle.

The Least You Need to Know

➤ Be a collector, but use the best traits of a dealer.

➤ Buy what you can, keep the best for yourself, and resell the rest.

➤ A *collectible* is an item that was originally made to serve a utilitarian purpose but has since transcended its original function through intense collector interest.

➤ An *antique* is a collectible that is at least 50 to 100 years old.

➤ The law of supply and demand applies to collectibles only so far. With collectibles, the rise in price alone can spark enough interest to increase demand and further spike the price.

➤ A *collection* is an assortment of valued objects arranged according to a plan.

Chapter 3

Shop 'Till You Drop

In This Chapter

➤ Find out how to be a smooth shopper

➤ Learn the best places to find collectibles—and why

➤ Discover ways to combine a great vacation with shopping for collectibles

The California gold mines are kaput, pirate loot lies buried under the briny depths, and the stock market is in a swoon. Nonetheless, more treasure hunting goes on today than ever before.

Today, fortune hunters search under porches of old houses, in dust-clogged attics, and at antique stores. They haunt flea markets and swap meets, charity bazaars and house-wreckers' lots. They are the first at auctions, whether they are held in the country or city. Some even have an antique dealer on retainer. The current collecting boom has made superstars out of everyday stuff and some not-so-everyday stuff: jail padlocks, railroad spikes, first-edition books, and stamps.

In this chapter you will get the lowdown on "antiquing." You will learn the ins and outs of buying the objects you desire for your collection. We will start at the very beginning, with the Rules of Acquisition. It's a jungle out there, kiddo. I wouldn't send you out without arming you with sufficient knowledge.

Next, I'll take you on a tour through Collectible Country. We will visit great places to buy antiques and collectibles. On our tour, you will learn the advantages and disadvantages of shopping in each venue. Along the way, you will get great tips that will help you shop like a pro. So put on your walking shoes and let's get started.

Big Deals

R.S. "Dick" Kemp of New Hampshire collects trucks. Big trucks. He has over 100 old trucks (mostly Mack) that date back as far as 1916. Kemp began his collection in 1952 with a 1930 Bulldog Mack that he bought for $50. Only 63 Mack trucks were built in 1947, and Kemp owns two of them. Kemp learned to drive a truck when he was 14 years old and was driving a big rig for a living by the time he was 16. If trucks tickle your fancy, Kemp displays his collection in Kemp's Mack Truck Museum.

The Rules of Acquisition

Buying is easy. Today, spending money is as simple as whipping out the credit card (with a flourish) and chanting the familiar mantra, "Charge it, fella." But buying wisely is hard. Remember: Shoppers are made, not born. In this section, you will discover ways to create a collection of beauty and value—without mortgaging the ranch or selling your firstborn. (Unless your firstborn is an adolescent; then be my guest.)

How good a shopper are you? That is, what is your Shopper's Quotient (SQ)? There's a way you can find out without having to make any costly collector mistakes. Complete the simple true/false Test Your SQ quiz on the next page.

Whether you have the SQ of a novice or an expert, you can benefit from studying my Top Ten Rules of Acquisition.

1. **Buy only what you can appreciate, enjoy, and live with.** This is the #1 rule of collecting. Consider embroidering this rule into a sampler or tattooing it around your navel. If you don't like the object (and I mean really like it), don't buy it. Remember: You could end up with a cast-iron gargoyle leering at you from the mantle or an insufferably cute shepherdess statue turning your stomach. And no one will take it off your hands.

2. **To start, play it safe.** When you're first starting out, it's not the time to take a walk on the wild side. Plunge in slowly; the water can be really cold. To start, look for "blue-chip" items—collectibles that have recognized value. As you gain knowledge and confidence, you will become less conservative.

3. **Buy things in good (or great) condition.** Not all beautiful things are created equal; some may come with defects. Most concealed defects will have very little effect on the collectible's aesthetic value—but they can have a tremendous effect on its market prospects. A $10 difference in the cost of a collectible can result in a $1,000 difference in its value and sale price.

Test Your SQ (Shopper's Quotient)

Test your SQ—Shopper's Quotient—with this easy quiz. Write T if you think the statement is true or F if you think the statement is false.

_____ It's better to buy first and think later. Otherwise, the bargain might get away and you could miss a once-in-a-lifetime deal.

_____ Even if you detest an item, it's a good idea to buy it to round out your collection or hold for later resale.

_____ Start by buying big; this is no time to be a wuss.

_____ It's a waste of time to make friends with the owner of your local antiques shop; they usually don't know enough to help with specialty items.

_____ The condition of an item should *not* be a crucial factor in your decision to buy it.

_____ The best buys are usually found in unexpected places: barns, flea markets, and swap meets.

_____ People rarely get good deals in antique shops.

_____ Collectibles have fixed values.

_____ Don't rely on yourself; you must seek out experts to verify your feelings.

_____ Try not to ask questions. It will just make you look foolish and lessen your chance of getting a good deal.

Answers

Every statement is false. However, if you answered...

All false	I'd trust you with my AmEx any day.
6–9 false	You've been mallcrawling, haven't you?
5–3 false	Warning: Untrained shopper. Shop only at your own risk.
1–2 false	Don't buy a thing until you read the Top Ten Rules of Acquisition.

4. **Develop a critical attitude.** You have smart brains; after all, you wouldn't be a collector if you didn't. Now is the time to think for yourself. It doesn't hurt to be a little cynical. Be suspicious of excessive claims made about an object. Comments like "one of a kind," "worth a fortune," and "you'll never get a bargain like this again" should set off alarms. If something seems too good to be true, it very likely is.

5. **Remember that a collectible is worth only what someone will pay for it.** "You'll make a bundle on this item!" "A real treasure—certain to zoom in value," "You can't lose money on this baby." Ever hear these phrases? If you're lucky, the speaker was easy to recognize by his greasy handlebar mustache and sinister laugh. More likely, however, the speaker was a sweet little old lady with apple cheeks, the owner of an adorable antique store tucked into a country inn. It's all the same—you were targeted. Remember: No matter what someone tells you, no matter what value may be listed in a book, a collectible is worth only what someone will pay for it. See rule #1.

6. **Buy the best you can afford.** Remember the advice your mama gave you (or should have): It's just as easy to fall in love with a rich mate as a poor mate. Mama was on to something here. Listen up, collectors: It's just as easy to swoon over a collectible with good prospects as it is to fall for one with lousy prospects. No argument here; just a question: "How can I tell which collectible will soar in value—and which will sink faster than a gangster with cement overshoes?" That's covered in Chapter 4, "Hey, Big Spender… Buying Like an Expert."

7. **Cozy up to a dealer.** The probability of finding an antique shop in your neighborhood that has exactly what you want all the time is about as likely as the check being in the mail. However, it's always a good idea to investigate all local resources thoroughly and completely. You may not find what you want every time, but a reputable dealer can help you locate items that you want or need to round out your collection. Knowledgeable dealers make excellent resources, too, especially regarding appraisals and authentication.

Connoisseur
Serious collectors very often have their dealers set aside special pieces for them. The dealers give their special customers "first crack" at the item. This is another advantage to establishing a professional relationship with a dealer.

8. **Ask questions.** You can tell that the gewgaw on the shelf is pretty; you think it must be valuable because it's carrying a hefty price tag. But what makes it so valuable? Don't be afraid to ask. Ask the salesperson what makes it worth collecting and why. Keep asking until you get an answer that makes sense to you. An inquiring mind makes you seem more intelligent, not less.

9. **Location, location, location.** Those are the three rules of real estate and they also apply to collecting. Americans cherish the myth that gold can be found in dross; the messier and more rundown the store, we think, the more likely we are to find the bargain of the century.

Specialty stores have cottoned to this mind-set years ago; some shop owners intentionally display items in disarray. They throw heaps of sweaters or shoes on a table, knowing that most customers will assume that heaps of messy items translate to a great deal. Never assume. Don't think that a very elegant store has nothing to offer or that a poorly-lit barn will offer untold treasures. Often, just the opposite is true: Solid deals can be made in an elegant antique store but the barn is packed with dreck. Ma and Pa Kettle wised up years ago; it's likely that by the time *you* get to the barn, they sold all the good stuff to the fancy antique store down the road a piece.

> **Caveat Emptor**
> Never buy any collectible that you don't fully understand. If you can't "see" what makes something so special, back off. If you don't understand why it's so expensive, run, don't walk. Wait until you do understand. Then you can buy. This holds true for stinky French cheese, co-op apartments, and exercise machines as well.

10. **Do your homework.** You'll find plenty of information in this book, and there's reams and reams more available. Study the major publications such as *Antiques* and *Maloney's Antiques and Collectibles Resource Directory*. You can get these in many libraries. Also look for local magazines such as *Arts Weekly* (CT), *Maine Antiques Digest* (ME), and *Antiques Trader* (St. Louis, MO). Publications such as these are often free at shows and auctions.

    Don't forget to browse the Web for info. At different Web sites, you'll find listings for auctions and private sales. The Web is also a great way to stay current on prices.

    Use the following checklist when evaluating sources such as pricing guides. Remember that prices are regional and thus vary from area to area.

Your source is valid if…

➤ It is recent and timely—values and prices can change very quickly in the antiques and collectibles market. Check prices every six months to keep up to snuff.

➤ Its contents can be verified in at least two other published sources.

➤ The publication has been around long enough to be considered reliable.

➤ It is respected by others in the field.

➤ It is published by a reputable publisher.

➤ The author has no obvious ax to grind.

➤ It makes sense. If the author's claims seem outlandish, they probably are. Trust your gut.

Smart Shoppers

A reporter once asked the legendary bank robber Willy Sutton why he kept breaking into banks. "That's where the money is," Sutton is reported to have answered. Why do collectors frequent flea markets, antique stores, and swap meets? Let me count the ways:

➤ Antique bottles often hide under old porches. They are a wily lot, those old bottles.

➤ A sheaf of official records that Ben Franklin kept while he was Postmaster General was found in the binding of an old book. The binder had put the official records there to stiffen the binding.

➤ In 1968, the last printed copy of the *Declaration of Independence* in private hands was found in the basement of a Philadelphia bookshop—hidden for over half a century. Take a deep breath at this one: It was sold for nearly half a million dollars.

➤ One of the world's rarest stamps, a Hawaiian "missionary," was found under a chunk of peeling wallpaper.

I know you're drooling enough, so I'll stop now…. But here's the truth. The find of a lifetime is just that—a one-shot deal. It's a myth we cherish, like "I'll lose ten pounds in time for my reunion." The truth? Most fine collectibles are purchased at reputable establishments by dealers and collectors who have done their homework. So don't pass up a chance to snoop under the porch or peel the wallpaper from the walls of a crumbling mansion, but spend most of your time shopping at the sources outlined below.

Don't Scratch Your Nose! Shopping at Auctions

You can find a lot of um, neat stuff at auctions, as the following list shows. Which one of these five unusual "steals" appeals to you?

1. **George Washington's laundry bill.** A laundry bill dated 1787 and signed by George Washington and two of his colonels sold for $1,100 at an auction. According to the document, Mary Firth got the job of washing the General's unmentionables as long as she bought her own soap.

2. **Swedenborg's skull.** The skull of Swedish philosopher Emanuel Swedenborg sold at Sotheby Parke Bernet, London, March 6, 1977, for $2,850. The buyer wanted to reunite the skull with its skeleton in Uppsala, Sweden.

3. **Smile!** The earliest known photograph of a photographer taking a picture was auctioned at Christie's, London, in 1977. It sold for $9,860.

4. **Outhouse.** In 1974, a one-seater, 19th-century oak outhouse sold at a New England auction. The going price for the best seat around the house? $140. The lucky buyer wanted to dismantle it and use the pieces to make picture frames.

5. **Baby blues.** At a private auction in Beverly Hills, Judy Garland's false eyelashes sold for $125 in 1979.

Source: Wallace, Irving. The Book of Lists. New York: William Morrow, 1980.

Hey, we're grownup-type people, sophisticated and debonair, certainly able to go into an auction and bid on what we want. Then why do so many people rank major root canal as less terrifying than shopping at auction? Maybe because we say "buying at auction" rather than "buying at *an* auction"? Do these two letters make such a difference? Put 'em back in and banish your fears! Follow the easy techniques described next to overcome Fear of Auction. (Unfortunately, I have no advice to help you deal with root canals.)

Read the Auction Catalog

These usually come out a few weeks before the auction. Here's how to read these unique documents effectively:

➤ First skim the pages. Then go back and focus on those items that you want.

➤ Be sure to read the small print, especially the sections called "Condition of Sale" or "Standard Notices."

➤ There may also be a glossary and a key to abbreviations and terms. Read them all. Important buzzwords include AF ("as found") and "Not subject to return."

➤ Boldface or capitalized entries indicate important pieces.

➤ Think carefully about the wording of each description.

If the auction house does not publish a catalog, be sure to get a copy of the terms—especially if they are not posted. Ask the auctioneer before the sale begins.

Pay careful attention to how an item is described in an auction catalog. Break the auction house code with this model:

Term	Meaning
The picture is ascribed to Van Gogh	The picture is a real Vincent thing, as far as the auction house is concerned
The picture is labeled "Van Gogh"	The picture is probably a copy
The picture is "in the style of Van Gogh"	The picture could be a fake

Read the Reference Literature

Remember: It is highly unlikely that you are going to get a bargain without doing some heavy homework.

Get Price Estimates

Sales rooms usually print a list of price estimates, a range of prices they expect each lot to bring. If there are no written estimates, get a verbal one. But since a significant length of time can elapse between the writing and printing dates, prices may be wildly out of date. Counter this by checking several different sources, including dealers and friends bitten by the collecting bug.

Mark the Items You Want—and What You'll Pay for Each

Next to each item you want, write down how much you are willing to spend for it. The best lots are often left to the end. As a result, you can often get good deals as people run out of money.

Auctions are dramatic and exciting. It is easy to get carried away and spend more than you intended. Marking your top price—and sticking to it—can help you prevent overspending. Save your catalogs. Since they are marked with the estimates, the prices achieved, your estimates, and your purchase prices, they become valuable documents.

View the Items

Never buy anything you have not viewed. Never. Then, take it one step further and be sure to inspect the lots that interest you. I recommend that you check out everything else as well; you never know what will turn up. I could tell you tales that would make your mouth water and your knees shake—but I'm too nice to torture you with "auction envy."

Don't be intimidated: Try to handle all the items you want so that you can see whether there are cracks, repairs, and other problems. For example, it is often easier to find a repair to a porcelain bowl with your finger than with your eye. Ask for what you want to see. Keep asking until you get it. After all, you're shopping for *your* collection.

Reserves

A *reserve* is the price below which the vendor will not sell an item. You want to know the reserve so that you know the lowest possible bid. Some auction houses disclose the reserve price. It will be printed or posted.

Bidding

I know this belongs in Chapter 4, "Hey, Big Spender… Buying Like an Expert," but I got carried away with auction fever. I swear I just went to the auction to look, but I couldn't help it… I started to *buy*. Don't be ashamed; it happens to all of us at least once.

Giving good bid is not the sole privilege of the experienced and well-dressed. Anyone can bid well with a little practice. There are affordable prices at even the most prestigious auctions. In spite of the legend that the man with the itchy nose ended up with the Ming vase, only the auctions depicted in the movies favor subtle Cary Grant eyebrow-arching bids. In real auctions, the normal practice is to make it absolutely clear to the auctioneer that you are bidding. You don't need semaphore: Raising your hand, holding up your catalog, or nodding will work just fine. Besides, although you are legally liable to pay for a lot that is knocked down to you, you will rarely be asked to ante up if you made a genuine error.

> **Caveat Emptor**
> A perfectly proportioned, humble, plain, handmade wooden bench sits on the sidewalk on a construction site on 7th Avenue between 42nd and 43rd Streets in New York City. A sign hangs on the seat's back: "Authentic handcrafted Amish love seat—not for sale." It's not for sale, but it's not Amish either. The bench was made by a 21-year-old laborer; the sign was hung by the project manager.

Shopping at Antique Shops

Antique shops are probably the best place to seriously study the varying qualities of collectibles and antiques. Unless you were voted Class Klutz, shop owners allow you to wander freely and examine the pieces that interest you. You don't even have to put on your Gucci loafers to browse. But even more important, antique shops are learning grounds where you can ask questions. Don't be afraid to ask the key question, "Can you tell me more about this piece?"

Shopping at House Sales/Flea Markets/Swap Meets

It's Saturday morning in the Poconos. The digital clock on the car dashboard reads 6:00. There's nary a creature stirring… except smart shoppers headed to the yard sales, house sales, and flea market/swap meets. They've been up for a while now and they're armed. They wear fanny packs crammed with dollar bills. Some shoppers have as much as $1,000 in cash. They carry self-stick labels with their names on them. They have water bottles, fruit, and sun hats. Days before, they have scoured the ads and mapped out their routes. They shop by area to cover the most places in the least amount of time. As the seconds click by, they are eager to get moving. Better get out of their way. They are fierce.

Tricks of the Trade

Don't count on bad weather keeping the crowds at bay. Some of the largest auction crowds turn up in the middle of blizzards.

If the early bird catches the worm, the early house/yard-sale shopper catches the best collectibles. Every yard sale/flea market maven has a story about the Tiffany studio lamp they bought for 50 cents and resold for $500. The ads say the sales start at 10:00, but these shoppers feign ignorance and beat the crowds by hours. Don't believe me? Hold a yard sale for 9:00—but be ready to get outside by 6:00. When you let down the ropes, the shoppers will dive into your goods like teenagers into a pile of hamburgers. Dashing from treasure to treasure, they put stickers on the items they want.

Follow these steps to get the best deals at these sources for antiques and collectibles:

➤ Shop in the best areas. Unscrupulous sellers have been known to truck in merchandise from other areas, but logic decrees that you are most likely to get the best collectibles in the best locations.

➤ Plan your route the night before. Map it out—and make sure you know how to get to each place.

➤ Get up early. Obscenely early. Then get going. If the sale looks really good, people even sleep overnight outside, waiting for the sale to open. Some people even show up a day or two early. Would I lie to you?

➤ Eat breakfast, even if you hate breakfast. You will need the energy for the fray. Fistfights have erupted over much-desired objects.

Caveat Emptor

Consumer Affairs and The Better Business Bureau handle complaints against a wide variety of businesses. The BBB recently issued a study of complaints against mail-order companies. Their findings? Most complaints were registered against mail-order companies that provide only a post-office box number, fewer against firms that gave a street address, and fewest still against those companies that added a phone number.

Shopping by Mail Order

It is difficult to assess a mail-order firm because you cannot, obviously, visit the premises. You can't meet the staff and check out the shop. However, there are many instances when you must shop by mail order because the items are not available any other way or you have no access to the shops.

Use the Mail Order Buying Checklist before you order a collectible by mail to help determine whether the catalog dealer is reputable.

> ### Mail Order Buying Checklist
>
> ❏ Has the mail-order company been in business for several years?
>
> ❏ Does the store have a solid reputation in the trade?
>
> ❏ Do your friends and fellow collectors have good things to say about the company?
>
> ❏ Does the company make reasonable claims rather than outrageous ones?
>
> ❏ Are prices within accepted limits—neither too low nor too high?
>
> ❏ Does the company project a professional image?
>
> ❏ Have any complaints been lodged against the business by consumers? If so, how have they been resolved?
>
> ❏ Does the mail-order company offer guarantees against problems and damages and a return policy?
>
> ❏ Can you reach a real person with real authority on the telephone—or are you left suspended in digital hell or relegated to a clerk with no authority to resolve a problem?

Order Me Another Margarita, Dahling... and Then Let's Hit the Shops

My friend Tom is a part-time antiques dealer in Hawaii, specializing in legal antique ivory. He times his vacations to New York to coincide with the big city antique shows in the autumn.

Rita buys and sells antique jewelry. She melds business with pleasure by shopping at every store, yard sale, and auction she runs across during her vacations.

What both Rita and Tom—and scores of other collectors—have discovered is the pleasure of planning a vacation around shopping for a collection. I highly recommend this approach because it offers numerous advantages:

➤ The chance of snagging a really remarkable addition to your collection

➤ The delights of a vacation

➤ Possible tax breaks

The Least You Need to Know

➤ Buy only what you can appreciate, enjoy, and live with.

➤ Ask questions to learn what you need to know.

➤ Buy things in the best condition you can afford.

➤ Develop a critical attitude about each item.

➤ Remember that a collectible is worth only what someone will pay for it—no matter what anyone promises.

Chapter 4

Hey Big Spender...
Buying Like an Expert

In This Chapter

➤ Learn how to determine a fair price for a collectible you want to buy

➤ Discover how damages affect a collectible's price

➤ Find out how to bargain easily and effectively

➤ See how to "buy" by trading

➤ Find out how to buy intelligently

Have you ever bought an antique or collectible and come away thinking, "I know I paid too much for this. I should have done better"? Or, have you wanted to buy a decorated jug at a yard sale but didn't know how much to offer? Do fancy antique shops intimidate you? Relax. The answers to all your buying concerns are in this chapter.

In the previous chapter, you learned about places to shop for antiques and collectibles. In this chapter, you will learn specific techniques for becoming a powerful buyer. There's a lot more to it than just spending money! First, I'll teach you all about how to tell whether the offering price is fair. Then you'll learn how damages affect the prices of antiques and collectibles. Next, I'll show you how to bargain like a pro. This is followed by trading, one of the best ways to "buy" antiques and collectibles. Finally, you'll discover some of the most important problems with buying antiques and collectibles—especially how to avoid getting stuck with a fake.

How Much Is that Doggie (Statue) in the Window?

Although the legal definition of an *antique* still requires that the object be 100 years old or older, more and more people are considering collectibles as "young" as 30 or 40 years old as antiques. This expanded definition has come about partly because of the great increase in the prices of "real" antiques. As a result of this rise in prices, certain kinds of antiques are out of reach for the average collector. For instance, silver, pewter, and 18th-century furniture are largely closed to newcomers—even those with relatively deep pockets. Almost no good examples exist outside museums and large private collections, and when a piece is offered for sale, its price is in the stratosphere. This is why intelligent people, people like you, have turned their interest to new, younger collectibles. But this presents its own problems, especially with regard to pricing.

It's unlikely that you will be able to afford a genuine 18th-century highboy—but at least you will know what it costs. The inverse is true of the newer antiques and collectibles. If you have been diligent about saving your pennies, you probably *will* be able to buy many of these hot collectibles—but it's unlikely that you will be able to determine their price that easily. The prices asked for newer collectibles are likely to vary not only from state to state and from city to city, but often from shop to shop within the same community.

Much of the worry about the prices of antiques and collectibles exists because people are not aware that this is a unique business. And it is a business, although some collectors view it more as a divine quest. Antiques dealers, flea market vendors, and auctioneers are business people. They buy and sell, just like other business people. But their work is different from other retail establishments in one crucial area: When they sell an item, they cannot reorder another one. They may not be able to get another comparable piece for weeks, months, years—if ever. And the price is not fixed: The dealer may have to pay more or less for the same object over the years. As a matter of fact, there are no fixed prices at all. The dealer is free to ask what the market will bear.

Damage Control

In addition, many pieces come damaged. Repairs can greatly affect the price of the item. The specific reduction will vary greatly, though, depending not only on the extent of the damage but on how the buyer perceives the damage. Here are some examples:

➤ **Glass.** Damage can destroy the value of a piece. Many dealers will not even handle cracked or chipped glass.

➤ **Paper goods (stamps, money, baseball cards, postcards, playing cards, and so on).** Even slight damage can often be almost impossible to repair and will therefore sharply affect the cost (and value) of the piece.

➤ **Pottery.** Damaged stoneware and other pottery, in contrast to glass, is usually easier to repair and thus the price is not greatly affected.

➤ **Furniture.** The price and value of antique furniture are not greatly affected by slight damage that has been properly repaired. The key words here are "slight" and "properly." In general, you're better off seeking out items that have their original finish.

As a general rule of thumb, you can often count on getting a piece for about 50 percent less than the asking price if there's noticeable damage.

But what a collector is willing to pay for a damaged piece depends on how badly the collector wants the particular piece. Damaged one-of-a-kind or very rare pieces usually fly off the shelf because buyers know they are never likely to get an undamaged one. On the other hand, damaged mass-market items will languish in dusty corners, because collectors know that a better piece is likely to come onto the market soon. What does all this mean? To start, it means that in some instances, you can bargain to get a better deal.

Connoisseur
Cracks and chips in an antique stoneware jug (one more than 100 years old) are considered serious if they pierce the designs. Nonetheless, any damage will affect the value.

Caveat Emptor
Do not accept any prices cited in a guide book as gospel; use them as a guide. They represent prices recently asked in shops and the collectible periodicals and therefore provide only guidelines. Remember that the prices cited in guides are regional as well. All things being equal, an item can fetch more in New York City than in the 'burbs.

So Can You Knock Off a Few Bucks?

Some people are delighted at the opportunity to shave a little off the top; others recoil in horror at the concept of asking for a better price. Here's the number one rule of bargaining: No matter how good a deal you feel you might get by bargaining, it's not worth it if you or the seller feels uncomfortable. Go with your personal style. Bargain if you feel comfortable with it. Don't bargain if it makes you queasy. Otherwise, the item might feel tainted, no matter how much you saved. Then the pleasure is gone.

That said, let's talk about the right way to bargain. First off, avoid the lame, "I spent all my money on donuts so could you charge me less for this vase?" or the déclassé,

"My husband will kill me if I spend more than $5 on this." Nix, "What a piece of trash. I'll give you a buck to take it off your hands." Deep-six, "You have to give me a better price." No one likes to be ordered around.

The key to bargaining is to make the seller feel like he or she has the upper hand. Never insult, demean, or hector as you bargain. Here are my Top Three Best Bargaining Lines:

1. "What's the best you can do on this?"

2. "Can you do a little better on this item?"

3. "Would you take (name a price) for this?"

These questions show the seller that there may be some difficulty involved, given the state of the economy, the mortgage on your house, the price of your teenager's sneakers, and so on. The seller is then in the position of doing you a favor. The seller appreciates your effort. The "you" personalizes the deal; the item falls into second place.

Now, how can you bargain comfortably and easily?

➤ **Know your prices.** Before you can bargain, you have to know what something is worth. It is not unusual for items to be overpriced. I once saw a clock tagged $50 at a flea market. I knew it was worth $30. Knowing its accepted value made it reasonable for me to offer $20 to $25. In this case, bargaining was expected. Other times, collectibles may be priced accurately. I recently saw a newspaper ad for comics priced at $25—a fair price. In that case, $20 is a respectable counteroffer.

➤ **Be reasonable.** As you saw in the previous examples, be reasonable in your offers. If the item is in mint or excellent condition, you can bargain within a range of 5 to 25 percent. If the item is in poor condition, you can offer much less—as much as 75 to 90 percent less. How can you determine how much to try to knock off the price? Read on.

➤ **Be sensible.** If you want the item badly, buy the item. Don't play games if you don't want to sour the deal. When you bargain, you always run the risk of alienating the seller. Remember: A price tag is not a contract. A seller never has an obligation to sell you anything. But if you don't want the item enough to pay more than a specific price, stick to your guns. Don't insult the seller by offering too little, but don't pay too much for something you really don't want.

➤ **Time your purchases.** At flea markets, house sales, swap meets, and the like, you will be able to bargain much more easily at the end of the day than at the beginning. Everyone starts a sale optimistically, but by the end of a hot, buggy afternoon, even the most professional seller is muttering, "You mean I have to pack all this stuff back up and carry it into the truck?" Rather than having to cart everything back into the house/truck/store, most dealers will bargain freely as they are getting ready to leave. This means that you are getting last crack at the merchandise, however, so if you want an item badly, buy it when you see it first thing in the morning.

➤ **Buy more than one item.** Sellers want to sell. The more you buy, the more money they make. This is a key leverage point to bargaining. Here's how you can make this fact work for you: Say you see three perfume bottles you want. Start with the one you want most. Ask the seller, "What's the best you can do on this?" Suppose he sticks to his price of $25. Suggest that you might be interested in Perfume Bottle #2, if the price is right. It is marked $15. Offer $35 for the two bottles. Now indicate that you want Bottle #3 as well. It is marked $12.50. What can he do on that? He might say that you can have all three bottles for $45. Pull out two $20 bills and offer them.

The seller expected to sell one item and receive $25. Now he can sell three items and get $40. If he agrees, you will have gotten the first bottle for its full price, $25, the second bottle for $5 less than its marked price, and the third bottle for $7.50 less. If he doesn't agree, you have the option of still purchasing only the first bottle—or as many as you want—for the stated price.

➤ **Use cash.** Almost all casual purchases of antiques and collectibles are done with cash, even in shops and antique stores. Many (if not most) well-established shops take credit cards, but be aware that the seller is charged five percent by the credit card company for this customer service. In many cases, it's a piece of cake to get a five percent discount simply by paying with cash rather than plastic. When paying with cash, be sure to get a receipt for insurance and tax purposes.

Cash dealing is an art in itself. First, carry enough cash. Today, most of us carry very little cash, relying instead on plastic and checks, so getting into the cash mind-set may take some time. Second, sort and separate your bills into denominations and place the bucks in a safe place on your person. Remember where you put them—I've known flustered buyers to forget where they stashed their money!

➤ **Don't bargain over pennies.** It never fails: Every garage sale/yard sale/flea market, I see a shopper pick up an item with a 50 cent sticker and say, "Will you take a quarter?" Get a life. The seller feels demeaned; the buyer needs a smack to the side of the head with a polo mallet. Bargain when it counts, not for nickels and dimes.

Even, Steven: Trading

One of the best ways to "buy" antiques and collectibles is to trade for them. Say that you have a pair of brass and iron fireplace tongs made in the early 1800s. They are valued at about $200. You don't need them because you have a similar pair in better condition.

One day you are in a local antique shop and you see a fine quality brass merchant's scale, made in the mid-1800s. It would be perfect for your collection, and it's valued at $200. Voilà! A fair trade is born.

Keep trading in mind the next time you're a little cash-poor but inventory-rich.

Buying for Big Bucks: Top Five Hints for Hitting the Collectibles Jackpot

For those of you who are interested in buying antiques and collectibles for profit, I make the following suggestions:

1. **Inflation is good for collectibles.** During an inflationary cycle, people are more apt to buy collectibles at the current price level because they are afraid that the items will cost much more in the future. Conversely, deflation is bad for collectibles. During a deflationary period, people like to keep their money on hand to take advantage of bargains. Historically, collectibles do not sell well during these times.

2. **Always buy the best items in the best condition.** Good cooks know the secret: Start with the freshest, finest ingredients and it's almost impossible to mess up. How bad could the brownies be if you use imported Dutch chocolate and rich creamery butter? Conversely, even the most talented cook can't salvage a dish made with rancid oil or spoiled fish.

   Remember: With collectibles, the law of supply and demand sets the price. The best pieces in the best shape will always be the ones collectors lust after most fiercely. In addition, since wealthy collectors usually go after the best pieces, the best stuff is likely to hold its value better should the economy suffer a downturn. When everyone else has resorted to eating pork and beans and selling their collection, wealthy collectors can afford to grill filet mignon and to hold on to their collectibles until the market rises. Average and poor-quality merchandise is hard to unload during the best of times; it can become an albatross hanging around your neck during a recession.

3. **Go for collectibles that are linked to the present.** Items that are still produced in some form, such as coins, stamps, and furniture, have more appeal than items that are obsolete. There is certainly a market for armor, straight razors, and 45 RPM records, but the market for books, paintings, and glass is bigger and better. A living collection continues to bring collectors to the fold; a dead collection attracts far fewer people.

> **Tricks of the Trade**
> We all tart up a little for company. Almost all dealers use some kind of showcase or stands to display their goods. Consider buying the display as much as the goods. It's a great way to get some fine-looking display cabinets, stands, and the like.

4. **Shun instant collectibles.** Buy these plates, thimbles, cookie jars and whatnots if you like them as household decorations; don't buy them as investments. They hold their value about as well as a snowball holds its shape in August.

5. **Buy with your head, not your heart.** If you love it, buy it for pleasure—but not for investment. The item that appeals to you might be the least valuable item in the genre. That's OK, unless you're interested in resale. If you want to make money from your collection, learn as much as you can before you buy, and buy that which will hold its value or increase.

Provenance—A Collectible's Family Tree

"Well," the seller declared with utter conviction, "my cuckoo clock is undoubtedly priceless because Prince Albert once wound its stem." I moved away *fast*. I didn't want to be the one to break the news that even if the artist-formerly-known-as-Prince wound her cuckoo clock, it likely wasn't worth a bundle.

Many times I have been told that an item is valuable because it is associated with someone famous. This is called *provenance*. I call this the "George Washington slept here" syndrome. First of all, unless the Father of Our Country had sleeping sickness, he couldn't have slept everywhere he was spotted dozing. Second, who cares? The ultimate determinant of value is quality, not prior ownership.

Provenance does not always mean profit. Every collectible has a provenance. It may begin with you, or it may go back several generations in your family. The only time you can cash in on provenance is when these two conditions are met:

➤ The prior owner was very important.

➤ There is clear-cut documentation to back up the claim of provenance.

But even when the provenance is established, the value of the piece must ultimately rest on its own merit—in other words, how good the piece is. Many people have overbid at celebrity auctions, only to wake up the next day with the equivalent of a collector's hangover when they gaze sorrowfully at a load of junk. "I got carried away," is a frequent refrain. For instance, a week after the frantic Sotheby's auction of Jackie Onassis's possessions, the newspapers quietly published stories of buyers who tried to return the baubles they had screamed over. They realized that the items would not hold their value longer than a soap bubble holds its shape.

> **Learn the Lingo**
> **Provenance** is the source or origin of a collectible. A piece's provenance tells who owned the piece at one time. Provenance is also established when a piece is displayed in a museum or sold at an auction.

Buy High, Sell Low

When asked his advice for making a killing on Wall Street, the wealthy financier hooked his fingers in his vest-pocket and drawled, "Buy low, sell high." Simple, no? Then why have so many investors found themselves in the reverse position of buying high, selling low, and losing their shirts?

Caveat Emptor

In 1982, a famous movie producer paid more than $50,000 at auction for the balsa wood sled named "Rosebud" that was used as a prop in Orson Wells' movie *Citizen Kane*. Even though the buyer is likely not worrying about making his next car payment, there's no guarantee that the item will hold its value or increase. Want to avoid collectors' heartache? Buy for pleasure, not profit.

Unlike death and taxes, trying to turn a profit in the collectibles market is not a sure thing. Making money in collectibles is first cousin to making money in the stock market. You can win big… but you can lose big.

Most people who begin collecting like to believe they can get their money back should they need to sell their collection. For those who buy collectibles intelligently, there is a good chance they will come out ahead. I know a comic collector who sold his childhood comic collection at a tidy profit. He used the money to purchase the film rights to the comic character Batman. Rest assured that he is not counting his pennies these days.

But not everyone is so savvy. That's why you bought this book.

All in the Family: Uncle Sam

Assume that tomorrow you buy a stamp that you've been drooling over for years. This makes you a collector. You finance it by selling an autographed letter. This makes you a dealer. In passing, you gaze lovingly at your other investment-grade stamps. You know they will pay for your child's college education. So you're an investor. Collector, dealer, investor: You will very likely wear all three hats. No one cares which hat you wear when.

Actually, you and I don't care, but our uncle does. Our dear Uncle Sam—and his lieutenants at the Internal Revenue Service—have their eyes on you.

As far as the government is concerned, all collectors fit into one of two groups: You either intend to make money from your collection or you don't. If you make money, the government wants its cut. Trades don't exempt you from paying capital gains tax if you make money on the deal. If you don't make money, the government wishes you well. But Uncle Sam is not without mercy. If you intend to make money but actually suffer a loss, the government will share in that loss to some degree. This is true only if you are selling collectibles as a business. Consult your accountant for specific guidelines that apply to your tax situation.

Big Deals

When Frank Horwath of Illinois was just a kid, he began collecting... nails. His father was a carpenter, and young Frank was often called upon to sort the nails. Today, Frank has more than 15,000 varieties of nails, including hand-forged, cast, and machine-made samples. All the nails are documented and mounted on display boards. It is likely the most complete nail collection in the world. Among his treasures is a nail from the Dome of the Rock, the oldest existing Islamic shrine; a nail from the home of William Ellery, one of the signers of the Declaration of Independence; and a collection of nails from most of the state capitol buildings.

But for many collectors, the picture is not so rosy. It is often the people who buy things they do not especially like, just as investments, who get slapped upside their heads when prices plummet. Sometimes they cannot even recoup their initial investments. People who do not learn the ropes often find themselves *on* the ropes. Avoid heartache by following these guidelines for buying collectibles:

➤ **Start small.** Stick with inexpensive collectibles that give you pleasure. This way you are not spending a lot, so you don't have to worry about losing a lot.

➤ **Learn, learn, learn.** Pay attention to what everyone says. Then sift through the information and see what makes the most sense. Double-check it in several sources.

➤ **Keep careful records.** That way, if you do have to sell, you can square things with Uncle Sam easily. I recommend that you use a separate checking account or charge card to purchase antiques and collectibles. Record cash purchases in a ledger.

Caveat Emptor
In 1979, a resourceful promoter placed an ad in *Barron's* magazine called "Collecting as an Investment." Although the article was identified as a paid advertisement, it was widely distributed in mail-order solicitations to the "limited edition" collectors as "an article that appeared in *Barron's*. It worked. The plates zoomed out of the warehouse, but resale value was zilch. Caveat emptor: Faux editorials are still planted in several collectibles and antique publications.

Pitfalls

Like true love and super-premium ice cream, every passion has its downside. With love, it's the morning after; with ice cream, it's those darned calories. When you buy antiques and collectibles, you face equally upsetting dangers: damaged goods, speculation, and fakes. Let's take a look at each of these risks.

Damaged Goods

Take a moment to skim the collectible ads in any newspaper or magazine. I'll bet my collection of antique pins that you'll find one that says, "We buy broken Hummels and other porcelain." Look a little further down the page. Can you find the ad that declares, "We sell repaired Hummels and other porcelain"? Substitute any repairable collectible for "Hummel" and "porcelain" and you'll find this ad all over the world.

What do you do if you discover something "odd" on a collectible? How can you tell if it's a defect or merely an imperfection with no real consequence? If it is your lucky day, maybe the imperfection is even something that adds to the value of the collectible. The problem with damaged goods is that you really can't tell whether the damage is significant—not without help. Here are some solutions:

➤ **Talk to the dealer.** Most dealers can be trusted; after all, their reputations are at stake. That's why many serious collectors use the same dealers over and over. They develop trusting relationships.

➤ **Research the item.** If you have any doubts at all about the item, you have to research it in greater detail. Check pictures in reference texts and price guides; talk to other collectors.

➤ **Get a professional appraisal.** If the collectible is especially valuable, call in an expert to do an appraisal.

The final decision can only be yours. If you are unhappy with what you have discovered, do not buy the object.

Speculation

One time or the other, most collectors get swept away by exceptional market prospects. Like gamblers on a roll, we wager just a little bit more than we plan. A dash of speculation adds a zest to collecting, but heavy speculation is a very different kettle of (collectible) fish.

The logic seems unshakable: "If one of the item is good, ten must be better." Nope. And if dealers seem unwilling to sell, the speculator becomes even more determined. Heavy speculation is risky business. Producers and dealers survive. The big losers are always the speculators themselves.

"Need, Speed, Greed"—What About Fakes?

What are your chances of coming across a fake antique or collectible? Higher than you think... much higher. For example, in the decade and a half that Thomas Hoving was with the Metropolitan Museum of Art, he examined 50,000 works of art in all fields. He claims that *fully 40 percent* were either phonies or so badly restored or so misattributed that they were just the same as forgeries. Since then Hoving is sure that the percentage has risen. What few professionals are willing to admit is that the art and antique world is permeated with fakery.

One reason there are so many fakes around today is due to our own greed. Everyone wants to get rich quick. When the collectibles and antique market exploded in the 1970s and 1980s, fakes flourished. Young instant millionaires and billionaires bought art and antiques for investment or as a sign of prestige and social superiority. Originals were not plentiful enough and fakes filled the gaps. And despite the general crash of the art market, fakes continue to flourish.

Connoisseur
There are three kinds of fakes: the copy, the pastiche, and the attempt to create something new. A fake will often look richer and more appealing than the original. It may look slightly older, too.

For example, about 25 years ago, an unscrupulous art dealer working for John and Yoko Ono Lennon "invented" an Egyptian tomb hidden under tarps in the desert. He used the "tomb" to unload piles of second-rate Egyptian antiques to rich and gullible people. The Lennons were not as stupid as most; they insisted on traveling to Egypt to see "their" tomb. In a panic, the dealer had the Lennons' tarot card reader call them in Cairo and warn them that a dangerous man in Egypt would harm them and they should return to New York at once, which they did. Of course, the tarot card reader was in on the scam. The Lennons avoided buying the fake antiques.

One of the best ways to detect fakes is to handle as many of the objects you want to collect as possible. This will give you the "feel" of the real thing. It is also important to read as much as you can about the collectibles you want. It is not as difficult as you may think and I hope this will become more apparent to you as you read on in this book.

Connoisseur
If enough fakes were made by a particular forger and if enough time passed before they were revealed, they would be used for models of other fakes. Once that happens, it is almost impossible to detect them.

Use the Is it Real? Checklist as you examine each article.

Is it Real? Checklist

❏ Look at the article closely and jot down your first impression. First impressions are almost always right.

❏ Examine the object in as much detail as possible. Take your time and scrutinize every inch of the object. Use a magnifying glass.

❏ Describe the condition of the piece, noting every bump and scrape.

❏ If possible, ask what the thing was used for. As you learned in Chapter 1, until recently, most objects that we now collect served a purpose.

❏ Determine if the condition of the piece supports the way it was used. If not, what appears incongruous?

❏ Describe the style of the work. Is there one single style or many different ones?

❏ Figure out if the date given for the work and its style match.

❏ Gather as much documentation as you can. Remember that such documents are very easy to fake.

❏ See if the item has provenance and if it can be proven.

❏ If the work is extremely valuable, you may want to submit it to sophisticated professional analysis. Some of the tests available include carbon 14, thermoluminescence, ultraviolet, x-ray, and autoradiography (which evaluates particular pigments).

❏ Check rumors in the marketplaces about what the object really is and where it really comes from.

After you have completed the checklist, list all your doubts and track down every one. If you cannot explain each one to your satisfaction, keep looking before you buy.

Ironically, if nothing at all is known about the fake antique or collectible, it is often taken more seriously, since people believe that great works of art will be found in the most unlikely spots.

The Least You Need to Know

➤ The prices asked for newer collectibles are likely to vary widely.

➤ Damages affect the value of collectibles to different extents, depending on the type of damage and the collectible itself.

➤ Be reasonable, sensible, and considerate when you bargain.

➤ Always try to buy the best item in the best condition.

➤ Keep careful records.

➤ Beware of fakes; there are more of them for sale than you think.

Treasures and Turnips: Selling Your Collectibles

In This Chapter

➤ Learn when it's time to start selling some of your collection

➤ Discover how to assess the collectibles market

➤ Learn how to appraise your collectibles like a pro

➤ Get the inside skinny on the best markets for collectible sales

If your luck as a collector has held so far, you may already be experiencing a problem common to most of your collector compatriots: Your purchases are threatening to over-run your home. The garage is full, the attic floor is sagging, the trunk of the car is bulging, and you suspect that a few extra children may be hiding under the boxes in the living room. And there's a great art auction today, a promising garage sale on Saturday, and who could miss the annual swap meet on Tuesday? You're in over your head.

It's time to sell a few things, bunky. Take a deep breath, stop kicking the floor, and get ready to part with some of your purchases.

In this chapter, you will first learn how to price your collectibles. I'll give you step-by-step instructions for figuring out how to appraise your objets d'art. To make it even easier, I've provided helpful worksheets and displays. Then, I'll list the best markets in which to sell your collectibles. I promise to share your pain at parting with some of your collection.

This Little Piggy Went to Market

Cocky seller at an auction: "This vase is priceless."

Eternal optimist at stamp show: "I know I'll get a bundle for my stamps."

Beautiful dreamer at a rare book show: "I'll be able to retire on the money I get for my first edition of *Green Eggs and Ham.*"

Some of these hopeful souls may hit the collectible jackpot, but most will be disappointed. In Chapter 3, you learned the cardinal rule of selling collectibles: *A collectible is worth only what someone will pay for it.* No matter what the guidebook says, what the auctioneer promises, what the shop owner claims—the market is a fickle thing. Yes, 12 ashtrays with Mrs. Onassis' initials from before her marriage to Aristotle Onassis (J.B.K.) sold for $37,000 at Sotheby's April, 1996 sale of Jackie O's effects, but a year earlier, the "Jack Kirby" comic book/art market collapsed when the rarest and earliest comic book featuring the character Thor passed (did not sell) at $15,000. The book would have flown off the podium in 1993 or 1994. How can you sell your collectibles with confidence? Read on to find out.

Pennies from Heaven: Pricing Collectibles

Price an item by learning the five W's:

➤ What is it?

➤ When was it made?

➤ Where was it made?

➤ Who made it?

➤ Why is it worth its value?

Here's how to make this method work for you.

Tools of the Trade

First of all, you can't sell anything until you know what it is worth. You must begin by getting an *appraisal*—a knowledgeable estimate of an object's value. You can do this yourself or hire an appraiser. If your items are very valuable, you will of course want to seek out professional appraisers. But if hiring a professional appraiser will cost you more than the value of the object, it's time to learn how to do it yourself. And if your objects are extremely valuable, you'll want to have an idea of their worth even before you hire an appraiser.

Appraisers would like you to think they use specialized equipment to appraise different objects. They actually use inexpensive, everyday tools—nothing you can't get at your local hardware store. Here are some of the most useful tools to have on hand when you judge the value of a collectible:

> **A black light.** Professionals use a black light to find damage and identify fakes. It's especially useful to analyze glass, find damage in porcelain, discern repairs to furniture and sculpture, and reveal overpainting of pictures. The black light works best in a completely darkened room. A closet works well, but throw the junk and mothballs out first. The black light (which is actually violet or purple) "sees" through the surface to reveal cracks, changes in texture, glue, blotches of paint, and other irregularities. This takes practice; you must know what you're looking for before you use a black light.

> **Price guide.** There are standard, authoritative price guides for every type of collectible, from baseball cards to Barbies, comics to coins, silver to sculpture. These are clearly labeled: The one for comics, for example, is called *Overstreet's Comic Book Price Guide.* You can often get the guide you need from the library. It's important to get the most recent guide, however, to keep up with selling and pricing trends in your field. This will tell you what's hot—and what's not.

Learn the Lingo
An **appraisal** is a written or oral estimate of the value of a collectible in a geographical area at a certain period of time.

Caveat Emptor
Black lights are pricey and you may not want to invest the money in one. You can make your own black light by buying a black light bulb from a hardware store or novelty shop and screwing it temporarily into a lamp. But read the directions carefully before you start, because a black light can be dangerous to your eyes.

Appraise Like a Pro

When you appraise an item, you name it, describe it, and assign it a monetary value. Professional appraisers present their judgments on their stationery to give weight and authenticity to their words. You can appraise an item by preparing a chart like the example appraisal charts in this chapter.

Appraisal Chart—Comic Books

Article	Description	Appraised Value
Captain America #1	VF condition	$36,000
Human Torch #2	GD condition	$ 2,000
Slam Bang #1	VF condition	$ 1,000
More Fun #53	F condition	$30,000
All Flash #1	VF condition	$11,000

Description code
MT	*Mint condition*	*Near perfect in every way*
NM	*Near mint condition*	*Minor imperfections*
VF	*Very fine condition*	*Small creases in spine*
F	*Fine condition*	*Above-average copy*
VG	*Very good condition*	*Average used comic book*
GD	*Good condition*	*Small pieces may be missing*
FR	*Fair condition*	*Centerfold may be missing*

Appraisal Chart—Celebrity Collectibles

Article	Description	Appraised Value
Michael Jackson's glove	White, rhinestone-covered	$27,900
Prince outfit	*Purple Rain* stage costume	$18,600
Teddy bear	Rod-jointed Steiff apricot plush c. 1904	$11,770
Teddy bear	Red plush Steiff once owned by Princess Xenia of Russia; c. 1906-1909	$12,100

When you appraise collectibles for sale, first separate the items into two piles: the items you know about and the items you don't know about. Appraise the items you know about first. Then tackle the unfamiliar ones. They will need some research and time.

Don't be discouraged. You *can* learn to judge quality. Once you begin to examine pieces closely and make comparisons, you will find that you will develop a sixth sense for distinguishing the wheat from the chaff, the Staffordshire from the Precious Moments. You will probably begin looking without clearly knowing what you are looking *for*, but once you see the difference between quality and trash for the first time, you will remember it always. It's like the difference between savoring a real baked potato and choking down potato flakes. (Please don't call me from the potato flake union. I have enough trouble with the potted meat people.)

This Little Piggy Sold Roast Beef: Know the Market

A collectible is usually sold in very much the same place and manner in which it was purchased. For example, if a rare vase bought at an exclusive antiques shop is offered for sale, it will likely be placed at a similar gallery. An old plate bought at a flea market usually ends up being sold at a flea market. Collectibles such as stamps and coins that were purchased at retail establishments will usually be resold at stores when their owners want to trade up or raise cash. Of course there are delicious exceptions, but they are too rare to bet the ranch on. Therefore, by considering the source of your collectible you will have a better idea where and how you can resell it.

Neophyte collectors usually buy from whatever source strikes their fancy—a display in a store window, a flea market, a thrift shop. It really makes very little difference as long as you are pleased with your purchase and intend to enjoy it. It does make a big difference, however, if you are looking to sell your collectible or antique.

There are also regional differences in taste that affect pricing. Victorian furniture, for example, is much more in demand in California than it is in Florida. Regional tastes and preferences have a strong influence on the demand for specific collectibles.

The Secret to Selling Success

Here it is: Buy low, sell high—and sell fast. While prices in the antiques and collectibles market seldom jump as wildly as the Dow Jones, unlike stocks, antiques and collectibles are not easy to store. A thousand shares of Coca-Cola stock can fit in your pocket; an antique console or cabinet might crowd a small room. And while you can usually liquidate 1,000 shares of stock with a telephone call, the same cannot be said of a piece of furniture, a pile of comics, or a series of prints. So sell your unwanted antiques and collectibles fast to keep your cash available for the next deal that comes along.

There are many places to buy antiques and collectibles. Fortunately, there are just as many places to sell them. Each place has its strengths and weaknesses, and successful sellers use nearly all these avenues, depending on what they are selling and when. So let's take a look at some of the best places to sell your prized possessions.

Tricks of the Trade
To restore or not to restore—that is the question. Here is the answer: If it is clean, if it works, and if it looks good, don't restore it. Keep the price down, sell it, and sell it fast.

Selling Privately

Since you have relatively few items for sale, opening a shop or hitting the show circuit is premature. Put an inexpensive classified ad in the newspaper to attract private customers. You can keep the names, addresses, and telephone numbers of especially fine customers to use as you build a client list. This way, the next time you have some items for sale, you can contact these people first—if they haven't already called you 17 times to see if you've gotten anything new.

Let Their Fingers Do the Walking: Advertising

Start by finding out which newspapers are most widely read in your area. Study their ads carefully, compare rates, and make your choice. When you write your ad, use boldface to emphasize the item being sold, stress the positive aspects of the piece, and include the price. This serves to screen out all but the most serious buyers. Here's an ad you can use as a model:

> **ANTIQUE SETTEE.** Circa 1860. Hand-carved walnut. Original finish and upholstery. $500. Call 555-1234 after 5:00 PM.

Show and Tell

As a courtesy to your family, let them know when someone is going to come and see the items you have for sale. Then Grandma can get off the treadmill and Sal won't walk in the room in his skivvies. I recommend that you place the items you have for sale in a separate room, such as a garage. It is uncomfortable for everyone to transact business amid the breakfast dishes.

> **Tricks of the Trade**
> Make sure that any furniture you have for sale is clean and empty. No one wants to open a drawer and find the toddler's old cheese sandwich, Junior's jock strap, or the dog's bone. If this does happen, under no circumstances should you squeal, "Oh! *That's* where it went!"

Money Business

You have stated your price, now let the buyer make an offer. Why? The offer may be more than you intended to settle for. Perhaps you are ready to take as little as $350 for the settee you advertised at $500. The buyer may offer $450. Look momentarily upset and then snap it up and reel it in.

But if the buyer's offer is too low, explain with your Sunday manners that you have too much invested in the piece to let it go for that little. You may also want to groan a little for effect, scratch your head, and look pained. A soft chuckle may also work. Then continue the discussion until a mutually agreeable price can be established. If not, move on to the next buyer.

When you finalize the sale, give a receipt. Indicate the amount, the date, and an exact description of the piece. Mark it "all sales final" and shake hands. If possible, have the buyer sign it and keep a copy. I favor cash over checks and always ask for payment in full.

You may want to accept a deposit to hold the item for a specific length of time. I like a significant deposit—a third to half of the price—to assure prompt pick-up. Always write up a receipt. It's your call whether the deposit is refundable.

Selling at Yard Sales

GIGANTIC FAMILY YARD SALE! Yard and garage sales are other good ways to weed items from your collection. Organizing a multi-family sale is not much more difficult than setting up your own event, but it's worth the effort because it can attract hundreds of additional people and thousands of additional dollars.

Neither Rain Nor Shine...

Sitting over a cup a' java with the neighbors, pick a time for the sale. Don't limit an event of this magnitude to just one day; try to run it over Saturday and Sunday. Avoid scheduling the sale the same time as big local attractions such as country fairs, the high school commencement, traditional travel holidays, and gory trials. Also be on the lookout for major street repairs, which could make it hard for even the most determined customers to reach the sale. Pick the location; it should be the house that is easiest to reach and owned by the most good-natured neighbor.

Alert the Media

Place ads in the newspaper; tack signs and flyers to anything that doesn't move. Here's an effective ad that you can use as a model:

> GIGANTIC FAMILY YARD SALE!
> 62 Sunset Avenue
> OVER 25 HOUSEHOLDS!
> Saturday and Sunday
> June 1 and 2
> 9 a.m.–4 p.m.

Make big, bold signs. I have found that fluorescent orange and yellow paper with black lettering works great. A few days before the sale, mark the route clearly so Wrong-Way Corrigans don't get lost.

Tricks and Tips

I offer these hints as a veteran of many garage and yard sales:

➤ Make sure that the price of every item is clearly marked.

➤ Put away any items that are not for sale. People will attempt to buy *anything*.

➤ Arrange items by types. For example, put all the tools in one area, all the clothing in another, and all the books in a third spot.

➤ Be ready for the early birds. As you have already learned in Chapter 3, the SuperShoppers will be ringing your doorbell at 6:00. Make a lot of coffee.

➤ Have plenty of people to help. Watch for items that "walk away" and people who look less than honest.

➤ Have plenty of change on hand and keep a close eye on the change box.

➤ I've been stung too many times, so I won't accept personal checks. Strictly cash 'n' carry.

➤ Have fun. Let the kids have their own mini-sale of toys and lemonade; have plenty of junk food on hand to add a festive, naughty mood to the day.

Selling to Dealers

Dealers who have a shop or participate in many road shows are often short on inventory. As you gain a reputation as a knowledgeable collector, dealers will become interested in your collection. You can save yourself and the dealer miles, hours, and dollars by taking pictures of pieces that you have for sale. If you are mailing photographs and information to dealers and want your materials returned, indicate so on your cover letter and enclose a stamped, self-addressed envelope.

Consider taking this one step further and looking for specific items that you know certain dealers want. When you make a great find, wash, sort, and label each piece before you present it to the dealer. Make the items as attractive and easy to view as possible—just as a dealer would do.

Do your homework so that you can be straightforward about the price that you want.

It's Show Time! Selling at Antique Shows and Flea Markets

If you have enough merchandise and time, you may want to dip a toe into the antique show/flea market waters. Flea markets are far more casual than antique shows; however, they also tend to attract fewer Daddy Warbucks types. Save your quality items—furniture, glassware, fragile books, and the like—for a major indoor antique show. This will prevent the great unwashed from pawing over your valuables. Either event, however, will give you a greater opportunity to sell a wide range of items.

How can you tell if it's show time?

1. Do you have the physical stamina? We're talking some serious heavy lifting.

2. Do you have the inventory? You can't sell it if you don't have it.

Study the shows before deciding where to exhibit. Match your goods to the spirit of the show and to the cost of the booth. Booths can cost as little as $25 but often range into the hundreds of dollars. Avoid the temptation to bring everything you have. Instead, select those pieces that will draw attention to your booth, that will complement each other, and that will transform a browser into a buyer.

Hey, Check It Out!

Use these suggestions to attract buyers to your booth:

➤ **Avoid clutter.** Give each piece enough space so it can be noticed. Let people see three sides of the bookcase, not just the front.

➤ **Make it easy to shop.** Wide, open paths make it easy for people to reach your booth, especially the physically challenged shopper. Place the larger pieces along the back of the booth, middle-sized pieces in the middle, and low pieces as an island in the middle. As shoppers approach the booth, they are naturally drawn in one end of the booth and out the other.

➤ **Highlight one special piece.** This is your draw, the piece that makes 'em come and look. You may not sell the vase with the $25,000 price tag, but if nearly everyone comes to admire it, you *will* get a chance to sell them something else.

➤ **Provide a lot of light.** Dark booths are unappealing and vaguely sinister. They make it appear as though you are hiding flaws and damages in the merchandise. Light makes everything seem more valuable.

➤ **Price and describe each item.** Make it easy for browsers to know what they are handling. The price tag tells them how much it costs, but the description tells them why it's worth the price.

> **Tricks of the Trade**
> Never assume that everything a dealer has to display has been put out. There may be something more interesting that a dealer is withholding. Use this same approach yourself to get the most return for your money. Hold back some especially interesting items until the end of the sale.

➤ **Dress for success.** Don't look like a schlump. Dress neatly and well. Look alert and happy. This is not the time to schmooze with friends. You're working, so work. If you want to be treated like a professional, you have to look and act the part.

➤ **Keep your booth clean.** No food or drink. This greatly lessens the chance of accidents and damage.

Selling at Auctions

"One forty-seven going once. Do I hear one forty-eight? One forty-eight? Won't someone give me one forty-eight? I've got one forty-eight. Now one forty-nine. Do I hear one forty-nine? Come on, folks, we know this chest is worth two hundred if it's worth a nickel. One forty-nine is a steal. Do I hear one forty-nine? One forty-eight going once. You're going to kick yourself in the morning. One forty-eight going twice. SOLD!"

That simple word "sold" leaves one person elated, several people frustrated, a bunch of people uncertain, and the rest of the audience anxious for the auctioneer to move on to the next item. Nothing in the collectibles business is as unpredictable as an auction, and few places offer such odd deals. Dealers pull out what's left of their hair trying to figure out why a table identical to one priced at $300 in a shop will sell at an auction for $500, but when they decide to auction their identical table the following week, it brings only $200.

So what makes the difference? *You.* Auctions bring together a wildly diverse group of collectors, buyers, investors, and sellers. This lends auctions their excitement and unpredictability. While you will likely not have enough merchandise to hold your own auction, you can take even a few pieces to a local auctioneer for sale.

Types of Auctions

Any collectible and antique can appear on the auction block. Here are a few of the most common types of auctions:

➤ Household auctions (sometimes referred to as an "estate auction"), perhaps the most common type.

➤ Farm auctions (dominated by machinery and tools, but may also include old furniture and household items).

➤ Antiques auctions (held indoors in often lush surroundings).

➤ Consignment auctions (held on a regular basis, such as the second and fourth Sunday of every month). The auctioneer assembles a collection of antiques and household goods to be auctioned off to the highest bidder.

Pricing

Most auctioneers will give you a brief verbal valuation of an object without fee. If you appear to be a serious vendor with some important antiques and collectibles, a valuer will often travel short distances, free, to appraise your collection. In nearly all cases, you will be charged for out-of-town visits. Some valuers ask to see photographs of the items you will be offering for sale before they will comment on the items you are selling.

Timing Is Everything

How quickly can a lot be offered for auction? This is a key point. Since furniture auctions are held frequently, furniture is easily placed for general sale. But special items, such as comics or dolls, may be retained for a collector's sale. This allows the auction house enough time to gather a large enough selection of these items and to contact collectors worldwide. What does this mean to you as the seller? You could wait months until the items you want to sell come under the hammer—but it could be worth it in the end if you receive more money than you could on your own.

Fees

Check the fees beforehand so that there are no unpleasant surprises. I recommend that you visit the auction house in person and get everything in writing. Here are some of the fees you might be charged:

➤ Minimum charges per lot.

➤ Fees if a lot fails to reach its reserve. The auctioneer who received your items for sale will want to agree on a reserve quickly. Do not allow yourself to be pressured. It may be possible to wait to see what interest your goods spark. This will enable you to set a more realistic reserve than if you make a quick decision. The following fees are common in the larger houses, but there are many galleries throughout the country that just charge sales commissions.

➤ Cataloging fees.

➤ Fees for illustrations.

➤ Insurance charges.

➤ Sales commission.

Learn the Lingo
A **reserve** is the price below which the vendor will not sell an item. An auctioneer can tell you the reserve.

Talk the Talk and Walk the Walk

You can't walk the walk if you don't talk the talk. Here are some terms you should know to be a real auction maven:

➤ **Buyer's pool (or buyer's ring).** This is an illegal practice used by a group of buyers, generally big-time dealers, to hold the bidding down on key items in order to increase the profits. Here's how it works: A group of dealers who would normally be bidding against each other agree before the auction which one will "buy" each item and what the top limit will be. When that item comes up, the other dealers in the group do not bid to clear the path for the designated buyer. Afterward, they divvy up the spoils. This can hurt you as a seller because it can drive prices down on items that you have on the block.

➤ **Call-ups.** A person can request that a particular piece be put up for sale as soon as possible. The auctioneer pauses every so often in the bidding and asks for *call-ups*. This allows buyers to get what they want, pack up their tents, and move on to other auctions—or go home to gloat over their purchases. As a seller, call-ups tell you what's hot... and what's not.

➤ **Choice.** This means that the final bidder has the choice of all the items up for sale. It also means that the bidder will have the choice of taking any number of them, from none to all. Thus, if the six glasses were sold *choice*, the buyer could take none, some, or all. Obviously this is not as good for the seller—and that's you in this chapter.

➤ **Consignments.** To help spice up what would otherwise be a dull sale, auctioneers will often take pieces on *consignment*. These great pieces usually come from well-known collectors who are disposing of parts of their collection or from dealers who had items left over from other sales. As a seller, you can offer any item you want on consignment as well.

➤ **Jumping bids.** This is a psychological move used by bidders to discourage other bidders from staying in the game. Let's say the bids are progressing at $5 jumps and the price is currently $200. A bidder wants to knock out the opposition and so *jumps the bid* to $225. This is nice for the seller; it lets you know you have an eager-beaver buyer.

➤ **So much apiece, winner take all.** This is most commonly used with sets of antiques where you will bid on just one of them, but your final purchase price will be the last bid times the number of items. For example, if a set of four glasses is up for bid and the auctioneer announces at the beginning that they will be sold "so much apiece, winner take all," and someone bids for one glass at $10, the final price will be $10 × 4 = $40. This is great for you as a seller, because you will be able to sell more sets of merchandise.

The Least You Need to Know

➤ Start selling items from your collection when the dog disappears under the boxes (and you have a Great Dane).

➤ With some simple household tools and reference materials, you can appraise most collectibles yourself.

➤ If possible, know where the article came from before you try to sell it.

➤ The secret to selling success is buy low, sell high—and sell fast. This frees your cash for other purchases.

Chapter 6

Guarding the Family Jewels: Your Collection

In This Chapter

➤ Figure out what's really in your collection

➤ Discover how to display, store, and clean it all

➤ Learn why you need insurance for your collection

➤ How to figure out what insurance policies are best for you

The average collection represents a considerable emotional and financial investment. You've put a lot of *yourself*—as well as time and money—into gathering your treasured items. A growing collection tends to establish a presence of its own, like a beloved family pet. While all collectors are concerned about taking the best possible care of their collections, relatively few know what to do. As a result, they do not take full advantage of what is easily available to them.

In this chapter, you will learn how to catalog, clean, and protect your collection. You will learn how to find out what you really have in your collection—and why it's vitally important to know. Next, you will find out ways to display your collection and how an effective display can enhance your appreciation many times over. Finally, you'll take my Instant Insurance course so that you can decide what coverage is right for your collection.

Cataloging: Do You Know What You Own?

Quick—how many radios do you have? What is the serial number on your television set? Where did you put cousin Ethel's pearls and Uncle Eric's coin collection? How wide is the antique Chippendale highboy in the foyer? How many Paul buttons do you have in your Beatles memorabilia collection?

Most people put things away carelessly, often cramming things in closets just before the in-laws arrive. Maybe you reassure yourself with a brave, "I'll sort the closet/drawer/attic/ under the bed in a few weeks," but weeks stretch into months and years. By then, you might be too frightened to reach under the bed. Lord knows what's living there.

Bite the bullet, plunge in, and take the chest test. Complete the following Household Inventory Worksheet to start sorting all your possessions. Describe each object in as much detail as possible. Here are some details to include:

➤ Size: height, weight, depth, length

➤ Color

➤ Condition

➤ Number of items (for example, 12 sterling silver soup spoons)

➤ Brand name (for example, International Sterling Silver)

➤ Pattern (for example, Wild Rose)

➤ Age

➤ Serial numbers and other identification marks

➤ Cost

➤ Source

Household Inventory Worksheet

Take a complete inventory of your possessions by completing this worksheet. If you need more space, add additional sheets of paper.

Kitchen

Collectible furniture _____

_____

_____

Collectible ceramics _____

_____

_____

Collectible glass _____

_____

_____

Collectible metalware _____

_____

_____

Collectible household tools _____

_____

_____

Collectible wine _____

_____

_____

continues

67

Household Inventory Worksheet, continued

Other collectibles _____

_____

_____

Dining Room

Silver _____

_____

_____

Crystal _____

_____

_____

China _____

_____

_____

Linen _____

_____

Candlesticks _____

_____

Art _____

_____

Collectible furniture _____

_____

_____

Ceramics _____

_____

_____

Other collectibles _____

_____

_____

Family Room/Living Room

Televisions (make and model) _____

_____

VCR (make and model) _____

_____

Computers (make and model) _____

_____

Stereo (make and model) _____

_____

Cameras (make and model) _____

_____

Art _____

_____

Statues _____

_____

Collectible textiles, such as oriental rugs _____

_____

continues

Household Inventory Worksheet, continued

Prints _____

_____

_____

Collectible furniture _____

_____

_____

Collectible books _____

_____

_____

Collectible dolls, games, toys _____

_____

_____

Collectible clocks _____

_____

Collectible lamps _____

_____

_____

Collectible tools _____

_____

_____

Other collectibles _____

_____

_____

Bedroom #1

Jewelry _____

_____

_____

Quilts _____

_____

_____

Collectible furniture _____

_____

_____

Art _____

_____

_____

Other collectibles _____

_____

_____

Bedroom #2

Collectible furniture _____

_____

_____

Other collectibles _____

_____

_____

continues

Household Inventory Worksheet, continued

Bedroom #3

Collectible furniture _____

_____

_____

Other collectibles _____

_____

_____

Banks and Other Storage Areas

Comics _____

_____

_____

Baseball cards _____

_____

_____

Stamps and coins _____

_____

_____

Collectible books _____

_____

_____

Other collectibles _____

_____

_____

Do You Know What's in Your Collection?

Could you accurately describe every item in your collection if something happened to them? Quickly now, how many of the pens in your collection have black barrels? How many of your prints have wooden frames? How many have metal frames? How many of your candlesticks have fluted bottoms—and how many don't?

So now you've spent a weekend figuring out what you own. Now it's time to take a look at your collection itself using the Collection Inventory Worksheet. In this exercise, you are going to separate the collector from the pack-rat, the connoisseur from the Collier brother.

Collection Inventory Worksheet

Catalog your collection by filling out this chart. If necessary, make additional copies or use additional sheets of paper.

Name of collection_____

Title of piece/ description	Source	Date of purchase	Cost	Current value
1. _____	_____	_____	_____	_____
2. _____	_____	_____	_____	_____
3. _____	_____	_____	_____	_____
4. _____	_____	_____	_____	_____
5. _____	_____	_____	_____	_____
6. _____	_____	_____	_____	_____
7. _____	_____	_____	_____	_____
8. _____	_____	_____	_____	_____
9. _____	_____	_____	_____	_____

continues

Collection Inventory Worksheet, continued

Title of piece/ description	Source	Date of purchase	Cost	Current value
10. _____	_____	_____	_____	_____
11. _____	_____	_____	_____	_____
12. _____	_____	_____	_____	_____
13. _____	_____	_____	_____	_____
14. _____	_____	_____	_____	_____
15. _____	_____	_____	_____	_____
16. _____	_____	_____	_____	_____
17. _____	_____	_____	_____	_____
18. _____	_____	_____	_____	_____
19. _____	_____	_____	_____	_____
20. _____	_____	_____	_____	_____
21. _____	_____	_____	_____	_____
22. _____	_____	_____	_____	_____
23. _____	_____	_____	_____	_____
24. _____	_____	_____	_____	_____
25. _____	_____	_____	_____	_____

Now that you know exactly what is in your collection, where you have stored it, and what it is worth, you can begin learning the best way to take care of it all.

A Place for Everything and Everything in its Place: Displaying and Storing

Why own something beautiful if you can't display it—or at least some of it? But in order to preserve and safeguard your collectibles, it is important to restrict their exposure to harmful elements. Harmful or inadequate displaying and storage methods can speed up the deterioration of your collectibles or result in damage. This is not to say that you can't enjoy your collection, but some pieces are best chuckled over in the dark. First, let's look at two popular storage methods: albums and cabinets. Then we look at specific ways to display and store the most popular types of collectibles.

Albums and Scrapbooks

Ephemera such as playing cards, bookmarks, and stamps should never be stuck into a scrapbook. Even the small, translucent stamp hinges sold in hobby shops are unsuitable. One of the neatest methods to display such items is to cut a diagonal nick in the paper of the album leaf and insert the object in place, like photographs are held in albums with corners.

You can also buy stick-on corners or make them yourself by cutting obliquely across the corners of envelopes.

Cabinets

Nothing sets off your small collectibles like a fine cabinet—and it also serves to protect your collection. Match the type of cabinet to the type of collectible.

➤ Use cabinets with simple rectangular bars for books.

➤ Use cabinets with ornate back paneling for china, crystal, and the like.

➤ Use cabinets with glazed side panels to display objects.

> **Caveat Emptor**
> Beware of cabinet lighting. A too-bright light or one that is left on too long can crack certain types of porcelain, especially pieces that are already damaged. Glass shelving is a good idea because it helps you keep the wattage to a minimum but still get light into all corners of the cabinet.

Glass

The line you are in will move the slowest, anything that tastes good is bad for you, and glass breaks. The general rule of thumb in my house: The more I treasure a piece of glass, the more likely I am to break it. As a result, I strongly recommend that you store glass collectibles in a locked cabinet, under a dome, in a Lucite box, and don't invite me over to handle your glass. Here are some other suggestions:

➤ Handle only one glass collectible at a time.

➤ Glass expands when heated and shrinks when cooled. For this reason, do not store glass near sources of very cold or very hot air, such as air conditioners or heating vents.

➤ Some types of glass can be damaged by sunlight. Discoloration can occur, so keep glass away from the direct rays of the sun.

Paper Collectibles (Books, Comic Books, Autographs, Prints, Stamps, Paper Money, Baseball Cards, and so on)

Even the finest paper is fragile—that's why it's paper and not pre-stressed concrete. Paper can be easily damaged by soiled hands—or even moisture on someone's clean hands. Corners snap off, sheets tear, edges break. To prevent this kind of damage, frame prints immediately, or store them in special sleeves or drawers designed for that purpose. Also:

➤ **Keep light levels low.** Some people cannot so much as look at a pastry without gaining weight. Paper has the same problem with light: Everytime a paper product is exposed to light, damage occurs. Ideally, paper collectibles should be stored in the dark, exposed to light only when needed. If you must use lights, avoid fluorescence. Ultraviolet light is the baddest of the bad light boys because it is a catalyst for many chemical reactions. This includes the formation of acid compounds that can make paper brittle and weak.

➤ **Keep temperature low and constant.** Keep the room temperature between 68° and 72°F, with as little variation as possible. For every 10° drop in temperature, the life of your paper is doubled. High temperatures also support the growth of mold and fungus.

➤ **Keep humidity low and constant.** Relative humidity levels should be no more than 50 percent, no matter what the season. Paper is *hygroscopic*, which means that it gives off and absorbs humidity from its surroundings. Bouncing between high and low levels of humidity accelerates this process. In addition, high humidity allows mold and bacteria to grow, which can lead to a paper breakdown called "foxing."

➤ **Keep items off floors and walls.** It is tempting to display that rare print or bold comic on the wall. Resist the temptation; your heirs will be glad that you did. Elevate stored paper collectibles 6–10 inches off the floor to protect against floods. Never place printed material directly against a wall, especially an outside wall. Condensation can form. Toss in poor air circulation. The result? Mold and mildew.

➤ **Use proper storage containers.** Store books and comics carefully. For comics, use Mylar type "D" or lignin-free boards and boxes. Polypropylene and polyethylene bags are fine for short-term storage of comics and books. Over time, however, the bags will break down. Place your printed material on enameled metal or sealed wooden shelves. In the presence of moisture, woods send off vapors. This forms an acidic compound that can eat away at paper.

➤ **Handle with care.** All printed materials should be handled carefully. Wash your hands before you begin, to prevent potentially corrosive oils from being deposited on the paper. Then lay the book or comic on a flat surface. Turn the pages slowly to prevent damage to the spine, staples, or stitches.

➤ **Frame paper collectibles properly.** Frame shops can provide acid-free mats and special UV-filtering glass, both of which can help prevent damage.

Pewter

The term "pewter" refers to metal that is created by combining different amounts of white alloys, tin, lead, and antimony. The tin content determines the grade of the pewter. According to standards established by the British and American Pewter Guilds, "fine pewter" must contain at least 92 percent tin. Since tin is expensive and lead is not, low-grade pewter can contain as much as 50 percent lead; "pewter-like" collectibles may contain as much as 75 percent lead. As a result, there are many different grades of pewter available to collectors.

Since pewter is a relatively soft metal, keep it away from extreme sources of heat, such as radiators. It's not a great idea to bake it in the sun, either.

Stuffed Toys

Keep stuffed toys away from direct sunlight; they will fade. In this context, "stuffed toys" is an oxymoron, because these "toys" are collectibles that are meant to be displayed, not handled. Consider displaying them on shelves high enough to discourage handling.

Wood

Since wood is from living material, it will change with increases and decreases in moisture. When the air is very humid, wood will swell; when it is very dry, wood can crack. Normal changes in temperature and humidity will not affect properly dried and seasoned wood—but quick and drastic changes will. Follow these suggestions to correctly store wooden collectibles such as furniture and statues:

➤ Do not place valuable wooden collectibles such as antique furniture near air conditioners, air ducts, or radiators.

➤ Do not expose collectible wood to direct sunlight. The light will bleach the wood and lighten its color.

Big Deals

As of May 31, 1993, George E. Terren of Southboro, Massachusetts has the world's largest collection of miniature liquor bottles—31,804.

With Collectibles, Is Cleanliness Really Next to Godliness?

It's spring and the urge to clean has stolen upon you, like your four-year-old at 5:00 a.m. on the only day all week that you can sleep late. The house smells damp and musty; the closets are sour and stale. A perfect excuse to clean your collectibles, you think. But time is short. Why not toss the lot into a dishwasher? The washing machine?

Connoisseur
The first rule of cleaning a collectible is *conservation:* Do nothing that cannot be undone. When in doubt, keep your hands to yourself and consult an expert in cleaning fine collectibles.

Stop. Take a deep breath. When the urge to clean collectibles comes upon you, arrange the band-aids in size order or alphabetize your canned goods. When you have calmed down, turn back to your collection. Then start with these general guidelines. Follow the steps for each specific type of collectible.

Some collectibles are exceptionally durable. For example, museums are filled with porcelain vases that have survived foreign wars, domestic battles, and maniacal cleaning fits. It's pretty hard to destroy a coin, and nails are as hard as, well, nails.

But other collectibles are very fragile. Paper, such as books, stamps, prints, postcards, playing cards, baseball cards, paper money, and comics, can deteriorate very quickly in adverse conditions. Antique textiles can be very fragile, too. Depending on their material and construction, some collectibles require considerably more care than others. Furthermore, what's good for one collectible could be devastating to another. Too much care can be as damaging as too little—and sometimes more so. Certain cleaning processes could make an antique lamp shade as white as rice—or leave it in tatters.

Ceramics (Porcelain, China, Bone China, Stoneware, Ironstone)

Because porcelain is the hardest of all the ceramics, it requires the least care. Since it is completely impervious to water, it is easiest to clean. Do not take this as carte blanche to put your Ming vase in the dishwasher, however. Many porcelain items are extremely fragile. The greatest threat to these items is breakage. Follow these steps when cleaning ceramic products:

➤ You can easily clean slightly dusty items by brushing gently with a small, soft brush.

➤ Do not use feather dusters and cleaning cloths on porcelain figurines and statues. A piece of the statue can catch on the cloth and break off.

➤ There is nothing wrong with simply blowing off a light coating of dust. Don't go for the first-place ribbon in the hog-calling contest, though. Computer stores offer compressed air in a can, used for removing dust from delicate computer parts. This product might be useful for cleaning your collectibles, too. With more soiled porcelain, it's bath time. You will need two sinks or basins. Follow these steps:

1. Line each basin with a thick layer of soft towels.

2. Fill the first basin with a dash of gentle detergent and warm water.

3. Fill the second basin with $1/4$–$1/2$ cup of white vinegar and warm water.

4. Immerse the collectible in the first basin and then rinse in the second.

5. Let the piece air-dry.

6. Never wash more than one piece at a time.

Connoisseur
Use baby shampoo to clean your china. It's gentle and doesn't leave a thick film. In a pinch, it's also a great cleaning agent for hard and gas-permeable contact lenses.

Tricks of the Trade
Here are two neat cleaning suggestions:

1. To make a crack seem to disappear, first soak the object for a few hours in distilled water. Then mix one part hydrogen peroxide to three parts water. Add a drop of ammonia. Give it a nice soak again.

2. To get rid of food stains on china, try a foaming denture cleaner. Test a small, unobtrusive part first. Fruit and ink stains respond well to a paste of household salt. Rust remover works on... you guessed it, rust!

Copper

Unlike silver, copper likes it a little tougher. You can remove small scratches with jeweler's rouge, but something grossly discolored with verdigris needs a harder approach. Start with copper cleaner. If that doesn't work, you can try bleach in boiling water. In extreme cases, a powder cleaner such as Comet will remove stubborn stains.

Glass and Crystal

The cleaner your glass is, the more it will sparkle. Sparkle is what glass does best. Therefore, you should dust your glass collectible daily with a light brush. You should also floss twice a day and get at least 60 minutes of moderate exercise three times a week. So for those of you, like me, who are too busy flossing and jogging to clean your glass collectibles every day, try these cleaning hints:

➤ Experts are divided on recommended methods for cleaning fine crystal. One crystal cleaning camp suggests this method: Soak large pieces in a basin of warm water to which $1/2$ cup of clear ammonia has been added. Rinse in another basin that contains warm water and a dash of clear vinegar.

➤ Another school of thought inveighs against ammonia and water. They recommend washing crystal in isopropyl alcohol because it evaporates completely, leaving no film. I favor this method, but the smell always knocks me for a loop.

➤ Do not soak crystal figurines.

➤ Wear white cotton gloves when you clean your crystal, to prevent smudges and fingerprints.

"Sick glass" has a permanently frosted look. You can have the piece professionally polished to remove outside marks, but inside the bottle is much harder to clean. Gloss over the problem by attaching a piece of cotton to the end of a stick. Soak the cotton in mineral oil and rub it over the marks until they disappear. Be sure to cork the bottle of mineral oil after use to prevent it from evaporating.

Iron

Cast iron is brittle and so must be handled carefully. Unfortunately, it is also a magnet for rust. I prefer to leave the rust because it marks the item as authentic, but if you tend to be compulsive, you can use fine steel wool and oil to work off the rust. Be careful: The item will cease to look antique if you get carried away.

Paper Collectibles (Books, Comic Books, Prints, and so on)

Dust framed prints quickly and lightly with a lint-free cloth or feather duster. If the print is very dirty, remove it from the wall to clean. If you leave it hanging, it could fall and the glass could shatter. More serious for a collector, the dust could work its way behind the glass and damage the print.

➤ Hold the print on an angle so the dust falls away.

➤ Never spray any glass cleaner directly on the surface. The liquid could seep into the frame and damage the print. Instead, gently clean the frame with a cloth that has been lightly dampened with a mild glass-cleaning solution.

➤ Water damages wood. Clean the frame with a dry cloth.

> **Caveat Emptor**
> The Professional Picture Framers Association warns that framed art is not protected forever—regardless of the method used to frame the art. Check the print or picture often for signs of discoloration or insects. You may need to take the print to a framer for evaluation and if necessary, repair.

Pewter

Like most metal collectibles, pewter is easy to clean. But the quality of the pewter dictates how much cleaning it can take. In the past, pewter was kept gleaming by scrubbing it with oil or sand and rushes. Today, tastes have changed.

➤ Remove surface dirt from pewter with a soft brush. Work downward and blow away the dust.

➤ If necessary, pewter can be washed. Soak the object in water. Keep it relatively cool; pewter melts easily.

➤ Use a mild soap and rinse completely.

➤ If this does not restore your pewter to its original tone, you need the services of a professional pewter cleaner.

Silver

Clean large silver items with the highest quality plate powder. Be sure that it is soft enough not to scratch but strong enough to tackle tarnish and discoloration. Remember that silver is a soft metal, so be especially gentle on embossed (raised) surfaces. Be sure to wear plastic gloves; this stuff is nasty to hands. You can attack recalcitrant stains with a mixture of jeweler's rouge and water.

Stuffed Toys

Some older stuffed toys, especially bears, are filled with materials that may attract unwelcome visitors of the insect variety. If you suspect that your stuffed collectibles have unwanted houseguests, you can strip down the doll or bear and give it a chemical bath. First, remove any of the bear's leather or plastic detailing. If these accessories do not come off, stop. Take the collectible to a professional for debugging.

But if you *can* get the bear bare, place it in a container that you have lined with unbleached muslin. Fill two muslin bags with moth crystals and place them next to the bear. Seal the container. Wait about a month. Decant and air out.

Many modern collectible bears and cloth dolls are touted as "washable." Don't believe it. You can wash these collectibles, but you're gambling big time. Washed bears can become stiff, limp, or even disintegrate. Dyes can bleed or mottle. Trims can become damaged; eyes and internal metal parts can rust. Feel free to chuck the kids' toys in the washer to remove the caked oatmeal and applesauce. Vacuum your collectible stuffed toys instead. Follow these easy steps:

➤ Place fiberglass over the bear first to protect eyes and other delicate parts that might be worked loose by too much suction.

➤ Clean the bear's eyes with dry cotton swabs.

➤ Use cornmeal to remove stains. Sprinkle a teaspoon directly on the stain. Allow it 24 hours to set. Then vacuum.

➤ Be very, very careful about using chemical stain removers. I do not recommend them because they can discolor fur. If you feel utterly compelled to use a chemical stain remover on a stuffed bear, be sure to first test it on a hidden part of the body.

Wood

Under no circumstances should wood be washed. In general, clean your wooden treasures with a soft, untreated cloth. I do not recommend any wax or cleaning compound because it could damage the surface.

Big Deals

Let's twist again, like we did last summer…. Starting in 1950, Helge Friholm of Soborg, Denmark, amassed 73,832 different bottle caps from 179 countries. Her collection made the Guinness Book of World Records. Don't get any ideas from this, Gentle Reader.

Insurance 101: Plain Language About Protecting Your Collection

Some collectors are not aware of the true value of their collections because they cannot believe that prices have risen as fast as they have. Even some insurance experts and museum curators may not be sure what a collectible is worth. Rest assured that there is one class of people who know exactly what specific collectibles go for—thieves. That's why insurance was invented. And that's why you should have as much of it as you need or want.

No matter what Ed MacMahon assures you when you're staring bleary-eyed at the television at 3:00 a.m., you are the only person who can decide what kind of insurance you want and how much you are willing to buy. Insuring collectibles is complex because agents deal most often with life insurance, homeowner's insurance, and car insurance—not collectible insurance. Even so-called "insurance experts" may not be sufficiently versed in policies for collectibles. So I've cut through the sales spiel to give you a crash course in Insurance 101. Start here:

➤ Standard homeowner's policies or tenant's policies insure the contents of your home, apartment, or place of residence.

➤ Standard homeowner's policies have limits on the amount of loss you can claim for specific items. For example, even if your coin collection is worth $10,000, you are limited to a clearly specified amount under a standard homeowner's policy. Here are some examples:

$200 limit on coins and gold

$1,000 limit on jewelry

$2,000 limit on firearms

$2,500 limit on silver flatware

➤ Depending on your policy, you will be paid for complete replacement of the item or for the replacement cost minus wear-and-tear (called *depreciation*).

➤ Your insurance claim cannot exceed the amount of your coverage under your basic homeowner's policy. If you have $100,000 insurance coverage, you cannot claim a $150,000 loss. (Actually, you can *claim* anything you want, but you'll get zip.)

➤ Most standard homeowner's policies cover only those hazards listed in the policy, such as fire, lightning, windstorm, riots, vandalism, and theft. Check your policy: You are probably covered for a car running into your house or a blimp landing on your roof—but not for a flood. Your collection might survive blimp pressure, but not water damage.

➤ Many easily available homeowner's insurance policies will not insure especially valuable or irreplaceable collectibles. For this reason, collectors often buy special insurance policies in addition to their regular homeowner's policies.

➤ The easier the collectible is to lose, the more it will cost to insure it. A grand piano sitting in your living room will cost less to insure than the antique pin on your lapel, even if both are worth $50,000. Why? The likelihood of a quick-fingered thief stealing the pin is greater than a refugee from the World Wrestling Federation carrying off your piano.

➤ The cost of the insurance policy for a valuable collection can exceed the cost of the entire collection. If this happens to you, consider insuring only the most valuable pieces in your collection.

➤ Most insurance companies offer special collectible policies for the following items: fine arts, jewelry, cameras, china, crystal, silver, musical instruments, stamps, and coins.

So how can you make sure you get the insurance you need for your collection? Follow these five steps:

Learn the Lingo
Replacement cost means the cost, at the time of the loss, of a new article identical to the one damaged, destroyed, or stolen.

1. Take the time to find a broker who knows the ropes about collectible insurance.

2. Shop around for the best insurance rates.

3. Talk to other collectors in your geographic area.

4. Don't sign anything you don't understand. See the table "The Inside Scoop on the Insurance Biz" for more about policy terminology.

5. Review your policy every year.

The following chart shows some of the most often used insurance policies available for collectibles.

The Inside Scoop on the Insurance Biz

What It's Called...	What You Get...
1. Actual cash value	1. Replacement cost of the item or an item of like kind—minus depreciation.
2. Replacement cost guarantee	2. The lost article replaced with something of the same value by today's standards. The item is not depreciated.
3. Scheduled endorsement	3. An add-on to your policy. In case of loss, you get the appraised value for your collectibles. The collection must be appraised beforehand.
4. Valuable items policy	4. The amount that you and the company agree upon. Since this negotiation may degenerate into the Hundred Year's War, the amount may have to be established by an expert who serves as a mediator. The collection must be appraised beforehand.

The Least You Need to Know

➤ You should catalog all your possessions, especially the items in your collection.

➤ Each type of collectible must be cleaned in a specific way to avoid damage.

➤ Insuring collectibles is complex. Make sure that you get the coverage that you need to protect your specific collection.

Part 2
All in the Family: Ephemera, Stamps, Coins, and Paper Money

The postcard read like any one of millions of notes that college students send to their kinfolk back home: "My tests are over and I'm just starting the second term," scribbled the 19-year-old Georgetown University freshman to his grandmother.

But two things made this postcard special enough that the auctioneer thought it would fetch more than a few dollars. First, there was a photograph on the front, identifying the small town of Hope, Arkansas, as the home of the world's largest watermelon. Second, there was the identity of the card's author, who signed his message "Bill." Above his home address, he had scribbled "Wm. J. Clinton."

What was the top bid for this postcard? More than $4,000. As the fate of this postcard shows, certain ephemeral objects can have tremendous value. In this part, you'll learn how to sift the wheat from the chaff. There are bargains waiting for the plucking. On your mark, get set, go!

YOU KNOW WHAT THEY CALL EARLY AMERICAN POTTERY IN FRANCE?

Chapter 7

Pulp (Non)fiction

In This Chapter

➤ Hit a home run with your baseball card or sports card collection

➤ Get the inside skinny on bookplates, playing cards, postcards, and other ephemera

➤ Discover why theater and movie memorabilia is a sure-fire show-stopper

➤ Strike it big with matchbooks

Before the turn of the century, baseball cards came in packets of tobacco and cigarettes, mere giveaways intended to stiffen the spines of wimpy cigarette packages and entice unwary consumers to sell their souls to Mr. Butts. Today these old baseball cards are worth their weight in gold—almost as much as some of the players. The boom in trading cards has reached the point where they are the main focus of baseball memorabilia shows held throughout the nation. The glossy, four-color cards featuring players from major league teams have developed into sizzlin' collectibles.

In this chapter, you will discover the most desirable collections of ephemera—and what ephemera itself is. You'll learn what you need to know about paper to help you buy the best items in the best condition. Then I'll take you through baseball card batting practice. You will delve into the history of b.b. cards, discover the types of collections, and find out which cards are important—and why.

Next, you'll learn all about bookplates and playing cards. I'll even take you backstage to get the insider's info about theater and movie memorabilia. Finally, we'll strike up an acquaintance with matchbook covers.

Ephemera

What is *ephemera*? Is it a dance craze, a floor cleaner, or an artificial fat? Sorry; it's none of the above. *Ephemera* is printed or handwritten, two-dimensional, and made to be discarded. (No, that does not define your ex.) A devoted ephemerist conveniently ignores the fact that many examples of ephemera—such as modern baseball cards—were created to be collected, not discarded.

As this definition suggests, ephemera is usually paper, although handkerchiefs and badges are also considered fair play by ephemera collectors. Here's a list of the most commonly collected ephemera:

➤ Baseball cards	➤ Lottery tickets
➤ Betting slips	➤ Maps
➤ Birth certificates	➤ Menus
➤ Bookmarks	➤ Mourning cards
➤ Bookplates	➤ Music covers
➤ Calling cards	➤ Posters
➤ Death warrants	➤ Ration cards
➤ Draft cards	➤ Stock certificates
➤ Greeting cards	➤ Theater programs
➤ Grocery stamps	➤ Tickets
➤ Legal documents	➤ Timetables
➤ Letterheads	➤ Valentines
➤ Letters	➤ Wanted posters

Ephemera can be divided into three categories: *fleeting* (lottery tickets), *semi-durable* (postcards), and *everlasting* (commemoratives).

The Paper Chase

"Better living through chemistry" was the mantra for scores of 60s love children and those of us who groove on that tangy diet cola afterburn. Chemicals have brought us such great inventions as plastic storage containers that burp and tomatoes that bounce. But chemicals have been a nasty thing for paper. Before chemicals were introduced into the paper-making process, paper could exist for hundreds of years without turning brown and crumbly. Brown and crumbly is wonderful on a pie crust, but it signals the beginning of the end for paper. You can find books from the 1600s with snowy-white pages, while many books from the 1940s are as brittle as a jilted lover.

One of the most important criteria for assessing paper collectibles is the condition of preservation. Avoid brittle paper like any other 20th-century scourges: cellulite, gas-guzzlers, and buying retail. Once paper has become brittle, nothing can be done to save it. Eventually, it will become dust. Light browning, however, is not a death sentence for paper products. There is effective first-aid available for lightly toasted paper.

Paper conservation has become as much an art as California freeway driving. It's amazing what these paper wizards can do. Using everyday chemicals like benzene, they can take a book apart and bathe each page until the decomposing chemicals have vanished like ring around the tub. Tape marks can be vanquished; stains blown away. Of course, this type of restoration carries a significant price tag. Be sure the collectible is worth it before you commission a professional restorer.

And kiddies, don't try this at home. Paper restoration is a skill that requires special training. No matter what someone says about spraying mildewed books with Lysol, recoloring faded pages with felt-tipped markers, or slapping some flour-and-water paste over rips, resist the urge. Similarly, don't soak anything but yourself in warm water to remove stains. It's a no-go on playing with water-damaged books and book presses, irons, or other painful-looking tools. If you feel the urge to play with paper, go to the diner and color the placemat.

There are some ephemera collectors who do not mind owning a repaired paper item. There are even collectors who seek out damaged paper ephemera for the pleasure of restoring and repairing them. I wish these people well, but I tell you that damaged or repaired paper items should be sold as such.

Normally, the cost of the item drops by half when damaged. Your best defense is a good offense. Examine each prospective buy inch by inch. Do this carefully and thoroughly. Then you can judge the item's condition for yourself.

> **Caveat Emptor**
> Beyond browning, check paper collectibles for rips, tears, creases, stray marks, and soiling. All of these damages drive the price and value south faster than those poor overworked college kids heading to Fort Lauderdale for spring break.

Baseball Cards

Collectors are a passionate lot. They defend their choices with great brio—whether their treasures are budget Elvis-on-velvet or rare cabinets inlaid with mother-of-pearl. Some people love Elvis-on-velvet, others hate it, but no one doesn't like baseball cards. These sweet little cards are as quintessentially American as belly-bomb burgers and spandex pants.

Kids collect baseball cards because they're affordable and fun. In the good old days, you even got a slab of solid pink bubble gum slapped up against the cards. What happens if you don't like the player you get in a pack? You can always put his cards in the spokes of your bicycle. It makes a great noise. Adults love baseball cards because they provide a psychic link to the past. They are easy to store, catalog, and trade… and they can be a super investment.

First Base: The History of Baseball Cards

The first baseball cards were issued around 1886 by the New York-based Goodwin and Company, a tobacco corporation, as incentives for buying their products during an era of intense competition. Mounted on heavy cardboard, these cards were about a third the size of today's b.b. cards. One side featured a black-and-white photo of a player; the other side had a list of other available cards. The promotion worked well, so other cigarette companies quickly stepped into the field.

By the end of the 1890s, the American Tobacco Company so dominated the industry that the lack of competition made offering these cards unnecessary.

As a result, very few cards were produced during the next 15 years. Fortunately for collectors, this sorry state of affairs didn't last forever. In 1909, the "golden age" of baseball cards started.

Connoisseur
Double folder baseball cards come folded over. When opened, they amputate the legs of the first player and reveal a second player standing on his friend's legs. **Triple folders** show an action scene flanked by head shots of two players.

First Base: The Golden Era #1

The "golden age" of baseball cards saw the issuing of the most distinctive, innovative, and valuable cards to date. The cards of this era were characterized by fine artwork, brilliant color, and creative formats such as double and triple folders. In 1915, the tobacco companies stopped including cards with cigarette boxes. The candymakers, however, continued producing and distributing the cards until the 1920s. The "golden age," therefore, lasted from 1909 to the late 1920s. World War I put the kibosh on this shining period. It also marked the permanent departure of the tobacco industry from the baseball card business.

Second Inning Stretch: A Lull in the Action

The 1920s was a relatively quiet period for baseball cards, characterized by cards of questionable quality. The tobacco companies had gotten out of the baseball card business and the gum companies did not exist. What were left were some caramel candy companies and some anonymous manufacturers of low-quality "strip cards." These are small baseball cards with poor art and color.

Second Base: The Golden Era #2

The 1930s marked the "Second Golden Era." It saw the establishment of the baseball bubble gum card, cards most like the ones we know today. In 1933, the Goudy Gum Company of Boston issued the first major set of b.b. cards. It consisted of 240 players, 40 of whom are now members of the Hall of Fame. Six years later, Gum Inc., which later became Bowman Gum, issued their first set entitled "Play Ball—America."

WAGNER, PITTSBURG

MICKEY MANTLE

Would you trade these cards for a utility outfielder, a player to be named later, and an undisclosed amount of cash?

Seventh Inning Stretch: Another Break for War

Baseball card production ended with the beginning of America's involvement in World War II. The need for scrap paper during the war resulted in a scarcity of cards from this era. From 1942 to 1947, almost no cards were produced.

Third Base: Modern Baseball Cards

The embargo ended in 1948, when the Bowman Company produced a 48-card set. The Topps Company entered the market in 1951, remaining virtually the sole manufacturer of baseball cards until the Fleer and Donruss companies entered the business in the 1980s.

By the mid-1970s, baseball cards had become extremely popular. The first price guide came out in 1979. The baseball card phenomenon entered a new phase in the late 1980s. The skyrocketing values of older cards prompted an escalation in competition for a share of the marketplace among card companies. By the mid-1990s, there were at least six major companies, each producing at least two or three different major cards.

Home Run: Collecting Baseball Cards

Baseball card collectors are especially at risk for the collector's lament: "So much to buy… so little time." You need a plan… or another house for your cards. I recommend four ways to organize your collection: *year set, player, team,* and *Hall of Fame standing.* Let's look at each one in detail.

➤ "Collect by year" means to try to complete an entire set of a particular type of card for one year.

➤ "Collect by player(s)" means to obtain every card ever made of a certain player or players. If this plan appeals to you, I recommend that you focus on a player who has entered the major leagues recently. Otherwise, amassing the collection could easily become your life's work.

➤ "Collect by team" means getting all the cards of the players on a specific team. The collection can include only a specific year or span the team's entire history. Most of these types of collectors focus on their home team.

➤ "Collect by Hall of Fame standing" means collecting only those cards of the players who have been inducted into the Hall of Fame. The logic? Cards of superstars will soar in value faster than the cards of average or forgettable players. This has proven to be the case. If you want to jump on this bandwagon, guess which players will make the Hall of Fame, buy and hoard those cards, and kiss that rabbit's foot a few extra times.

Remember location, location, location? With baseball cards it's condition, condition, condition. A card in good condition is worth several times the same card in shoddy condition. How can you tell if a card is *ex-mint* (the fancy-schmancy name for best possible shape)?

➤ The card is clean.

➤ The card has its original gloss.

➤ The card has four sharp corners.

➤ There are no tears, creases, or smudges on the surface.

Big Deals

The Honus Wagner card is the rarest of all baseball cards. Produced by the Sweet Caporal Tobacco Company in 1909–11, the card was recalled when Wagner, who did not smoke, objected to the use of his picture in connection with the tobacco product. This is the prestige card among collectors. In case you intend to rummage through bins at flea markets looking for ol' Honus, start with size. The card is much smaller than today's b.b. cards. The background is orange and Wagner is wearing a Pittsburgh suit. When you find it, remember that I sent you. You can take me out to the ballgame.

You can cozy up to the corner deli owner and get first dibs on his shipment of cards and luncheon meat, but your time is better spent washing the cat. Here are the best ways to shop for b.b. cards:

➤ **Conventions.** Baseball card collecting is very popular throughout the country. As a result, there are scores of b.b. card shows and conventions every weekend. Conventions allow you to buy just the cards you want. That way, you don't get stuck with stacks of useless cards. Look through the newspaper or local "What's Happening" publications to find the conventions in your area.

Caveat Emptor
Beware of cards that have been cut down to make them look new. These cards are considered damaged and have little value to collectors. The easiest way to spot a cut-down card is to carry a test card. Place the suspect card on top of the test card. If the suspect card is smaller than the test card, run.

➤ **Mail order.** Many serious collectors get new cards wholesale through the mail. This is an especially valuable source if you live in a remote area.

Caveat Emptor
Phony fat, phony baloney, phony phones—what's next? You guessed it—counterfeit baseball cards. Once a card is valued at about $100, the chances are someone will make a knock-off. If you're thinking of buying a big bucks card, get the current buzz from the b.b. mags and check carefully with reputable dealers before putting down any cash.

➤ **Friends.** Serious collectors often trade as well as buy cards from fellow aficionados. How can you meet people who are willing to help you build your collection? Set up a network of like-minded fans. Use e-mail, snail-mail, or face-time at conventions.

➤ **Dealers.** Get to know the reputable dealers. Tell them what cards you need so they can help you locate them.

➤ **Family.** Every now and again, Cousin Ralph cleans his attic and comes up with a box of Great Uncle Louie's baseball cards. Let the family know you're interested in b.b. cards. That way, if any turn up, you might get first crack at them.

Hey, Sport: Sports Cards

Baseball cards have become a big-time collectible. As a result, some collectors have turned their attention to other types of sports cards: boxing, football, hockey, basketball, and wrestling, to name just a few. Overall, these cards are much more affordable than baseball cards. Even vintage sports cards in good condition are still available for under $10.

Like baseball cards, sports cards were first produced in the 1880s to protect fragile cigarette boxes and attract buyers to the thrill of emphysema and black lung. During World War I, boxing cards held center ring; by the 1930s, attention had shifted to football heroes. In 1958, the Topps Bubble Gum Company issued a series of basketball cards—a resounding flop. In the 1950s and 1960s, hockey's tremendous popularity in Canada sparked a series of these cards, but they, too, failed. But sports cards might just wind your watch, so read on to find out how to become a savvy collector.

Be a Sport: Collecting Sports Cards

I sent you to conventions and dealers for baseball cards. Sports cards are a horse of a different color, however. With this collectible, start at your local candy or stationery store. There are so many different types of sports cards produced that I recommend you first scope out the field. Look at the display. Buy a few packs to find out what's what.

There are five basic ways to collect sports cards: by *era, type, team, player*, and *sport*. Select a category that is large enough to be fun but not large enough to be an impossible task. Remember, this is a hobby, not an obsession. For example, trying to collect all the football cards ever produced would seriously cut into your leisure time… forever.

If you want to collect for investment, however, the rules change.

1. Consider going for the superstars in a specific sport. These cards appreciate much more quickly and steadily than the cards of average or forgettable players.

2. Avoid cards that have been glued into albums. Cards that are missing part of their backing are worth very little to investors.

3. Only buy cards in the best possible condition—mint or near-mint. In the last few years, prices for baseball cards and other sports cards have fallen dramatically. Recently printed cards are very poor investments. The older, rarer cards are much better bets.

Big Deals

Craig Shergold of Carshalton, England, reported to the *1996 Guinness Book of World Records* that he collected a record 33 million get-well greeting cards by May 1991. The collection stopped when his mother pleaded for no more. Someone should send *her* a get-well card.

Bookplates

The day after books were invented, friends and neighbors started borrowing them… and forgetting to return them. What to do? Our ancestors came up with the concept of *bookplates* to remind the borrower of the book's original home. It's more subtle and elegant than putting a homing device or heavy chain on a book.

A *bookplate* is a small rectangle of paper that book owners paste on the end-paper or the first page of the book to show that they own it. The custom of using bookplates began in Europe in the 17th century, when only the upper crust owned books. The early plates were much more than ID, however. Bookplates allowed the owners to express their family status, individuality, and deep pockets. Plates were often engraved on copper, silver, or wooden plates. Some were even hand-drawn by such noted artists as Albrecht Dürer and his buddies.

The first bookplates traveled across the pond to the colonies with their Dutch and English owners.

Connoisseur
The plates that bring the highest prices are those drawn by 16th-century artists like Albrecht Dürer and those once owned by *Time* magazine cover boys such as JFK. Pretty book-plates also sell at a brisk pace. Be careful: there are lots of reproductions masquerading as authentic antique bookplates.

Nathaniel Hurd was the earliest American bookplate engraver; examples of his work date back to 1748. Other artists, including Paul Revere, produced bookplates for America's newly hatched nouveau riche. Prices range from a few dollars all the way up for especially desirable examples.

It's Your Deal: Playing Cards

Playing cards are almost as old as yesterday's news. In the 14th century, the French King commissioned three packs of cards in "gold and diverse colors ornamented with various devices." In the days before malls and multiplexes, card games caught on fast.

But such idle fun was an anathema to the religious right. As soon they seized power, Cromwell and his Puritan killjoys trashed the cards. The games survived nonetheless, and eventually the English settled on a style of suits based on a French patterned pack created in the 1300s.

Today, it's almost impossible to find any playing cards that date before the 1800s. And in case you're looking, before that time, cards had full-length pictures of kings and queens, not the two-headed variety we're used to dealing. An 1890 Russell & Morgan deck is valued at $468; a deck from 1910 will set you back $72. A recent Delta Airline deck? $3. TWA's cards go for $2.

Some collectors buy full sets; others prefer single cards. It's your call, but superstition dictates that you shun the ace of spades. Here's why. Before the 1800s, playing cards were taxed. A special stamp was put on the ace of spades to show the tax had been paid. Anyone found guilty of forging this stamp—"Old Frizzle," as the design was called—could have his nostrils slit, his ears cut off, or his body branded with a red-hot poker. This kind of fun-and-games could make a card somewhat unpopular....

Postcards

Quick—what's "Deltiology"? Stumped? It's what postcard aficionados call their special variety of collecting. And *you* thought it was something piggy.

Postcards are the number one collectible in the U.S.—they even beat stamps and coins. The first postcards appeared in the 1870s as advertisements. Souvenir view cards came into being in the United States in 1898.

Before you go hunting for postcards, decide on one or two subjects that interest you. Search out a collector's club in your region. You can get leads by asking at antique shows and shops where postcards are sold. Postcard conventions provide an excellent source of collecting possibilities for what's hot and what's not. You can also get the inside skinny on pricing and trading.

As with other paper collectibles, condition is crucial. Postcards must be mint to be valuable. That's not to say you can't have a lot of fun amassing a pile of dog-eared postcards, but if you want to be a collector and not a Collier brother, go for cards in the best possible shape. To protect your collection, mount your postcards in albums or protect them with glycine coverings and file them in boxes.

Price ranges? A 1940 Imperial Airlines card fetches $35; a 1919 card showing a midget girl is worth $15. Figure on spending $7 for an 1850s card from the Silver Slippers Saloon in Las Vegas. Go for name recognition. A 1919 card signed by the Revolutionary John Reed is worth $800.

Theater Memorabilia

Shakespeare declared that "the play's the thing," but for collectors of theater memorabilia, it's often the playbill—not the play. Dedicated collectors of theater memorabilia hunt down every scrap of paper linked to their favorite performer, playwright, or play. Sought-after items include programs, scripts, photographs, props, cigarette cards depicting actors, costume designs, scenery, newspaper and magazine reviews, posters, and tickets.

Sign on the Dotted Line

For serious collectors of theater ephemera, autographs are often the crème de la crème. They are so treasured partly because they are rare. Like other paper collectibles, many did not survive; in addition, some theater personalities refused to grant them. George Bernard Shaw, for example, would not give autographs; other stars have been known to demand a donation to their favorite charity or even a personal fee in exchange for their John Hancock.

But there are still plenty on the market. A signed and dated photo of diva Maria Callas is worth about $500; Fred Astaire's scribble will cost you less than $100. Audrey Hepburn's autograph? About $300. Steven Spielberg? $200.

Stage-Struck

Designs for stage sets and costumes are also in great demand by collectors. In part, the appeal arises from the fame of those who tried their hand at stage design: Picasso and Braque, for example, both drew stage sets. Drawings linked to famous performers or artists are the most highly treasured. If you're looking, shun pristine sketches. Go for drawings marked up with notes to costume and prop departments.

Get with the Program

Programs are another important collectible in this specialty. The first programs, issued in the 1850s, were small playbills or posters. The programs that have theater buffs panting are those distributed on opening night (also called "first night"). It's the cachet of being the first.

Movie Memorabilia

The field of entertainment collectibles is enormous, including everything from tickets, posters, and scripts to costumes, props, and the films themselves. For example:

Tricks of the Trade
It's very hard to find programs that headline the Broadway superstars of the past. With some luck, however, you may be able to find a past biggie listed at the bottom of the cast list, before he or she made the marquee.

➤ In 1989, Herman J. Mankiewicz's scripts for *Citizen Kane* and *The American* sold at auction for $231,000.

➤ A 1932 Universal poster for *The Old Dark House*, starring Boris Karloff, went for $48,400 in 1991.

➤ Judy Garland's ruby slippers from *The Wizard of Oz* netted $165,000 at a Christie's 1988 auction.

So much to collect. So little time. Let Mama help you. Here's a list of the most desirable movie collectibles.

Cels

Cels are hand-painted scenes that are shot in sequence to make up a cartoon film. Cels are painted on *celluloid*, hence their name. My mother, a skilled artist, painted some of the earliest cels. Wearing thin white cotton gloves to prevent smears on the celluloid, she carefully filled in figures with tempera paints (today acrylics are used). As a young child, I remember pawing through stacks of old cels on rainy afternoons. I also remember helping my mother throw them all out when we moved from New Jersey to New York. In 1991, just one of the 150,000 color cels from *Snow White* (1937) sold for $209,000; two years earlier, a single black-and-white cel showing Donald Duck in the cartoon *Orphan's Benefit* (1935) fetched $286,000. Ah, had I saved just a handful of those old cels!

Poster Girl

In the era of silent films, movie companies often hired the finest commercial and graphic artists to design their posters. Visual appeal was vitally important in an era without radio or television ads. The movie poster, long a pariah, has become a hot collectible. The biggest stars get the biggest prices: For example, a poster of Humphrey Bogart in *Casablanca* is valued in the thousands. Use these four guidelines when you search for posters:

➤ **Age.** Many old posters disintegrated; others were destroyed in wartime paper drives. A noble end for the paper, perhaps, but a calamity for collectors.

➤ **Visual appeal.** Beauty is in the eye of the beholder, but visually appealing posters can be judged as you would any other work of art. They blend color, light, shading, and form to create a stunning whole.

➤ **Marquee madness.** Posters featuring films that have become part of the American psyche, such as *Gone with the Wind, The Wizard of Oz, Citizen Kane,* and *King Kong* are the hottest. There is a small but steady market for posters of quirky films such as *Night of the Living Dead,* a low-budget Philly shock flick.

➤ **Stars.** Big names bring 'em out. Look for posters featuring such head turners as Clark Gable, Cary Grant, Katherine Hepburn, and Marilyn Monroe. Cartoon characters, rock stars, and advertising logos are also popular poster stars.

> **Caveat Emptor**
> Reissues and Repros. Reissue posters are not worth nearly as much as the originals. Look for a small *R* or *r* on the bottom margin. Avoid posters that appear to have had their lower margins sliced off. Also watch for reproductions. Check for pinholes and creases—they're a sign the repro was made from a damaged original.

Which posters will be worth the most? The ones that combine all four factors. A Buffalo Bill poster from 1907 is worth $4,000; a 1925 Houdini goes for $8,500. But you can get Bert & Harry of Piels Light Beer fame (1975) for $7 and Garfield in a 1978 Halloween pose for a dollar less. A Donald Duck poster designed by Disney for the Food and Nutrition Committee California War Council is worth $275 in good condition.

> **Big Deals**
>
> It's not just theater and movie posters—posters in general are hot. What to buy? First and foremost, the artist's name determines the value of a poster. The ranking poster boy is French painter Toulouse-Lautrec, who created 31 posters from 1891 to 1900. In a 1989 auction, *Le Moulin Rouge,* advertising a cabaret, went for $220,000.
>
> Savvy art lovers try to snap up today's posters as they appear with an eye to tomorrow's trends. Commemorative posters are popular. For example, abstract expressionist Robert Motherwell created a poster for the Mostly Mozart festival in 1991. Then, the poster sold for $100. Motherwell died later that year. Five years later, the same poster was worth $1,000.

Loose Paper

Dedicated movie memorabilia collectors are a broadminded lot: They'll collect Dixie cup lids, sugar packets, and scripts as well as autographs, stills, and magazines. What makes a seemingly innocent sugar packet a hot item? It's *association* and *visual appeal*. Let's start with association.

Collectors want items linked to famous stars and films. A script for *The African Queen* is worth a bundle more than one for *Amazon Babes at the Bowl-a-Rama*... although *Amazon Babes* did have its moments.

Second, collectibles are sexy. There's a certain frisson of excitement a desirable collectible sends off. How can you pick up the vibes? Haunt the collectible shows to find out what pieces turn collectors on. Look at the paper items to see which ones are flying off the floor... and which ones are wallflowers at the dance.

A Striking Example of Collectibles: Matchbooks

"Got a match?" Not anymore. Since war was declared on tobacco and disposable lighters became so affordable, matchbooks have been about as welcome as a pit bull with an impacted molar. Twenty years ago, there were about 20 matchbook makers in America. Today? Only three matchbook companies remain. But even these three companies cannot sustain their business on matchbooks alone, so they all produce buttons, plastic mugs, and T-shirts in addition.

Connoisseur

Ed Haberman of Indiana collects grease rags. I could make this up? His interest was sparked in the 1950s, when an ice machine in the family dairy farm sprang a leak and the family bought an oil rag for 8¢ to keep the floor clean. Haberman has never been known to pass up an old rag. He has more than 10,000 rags, all washed and neatly stacked in his garage and basement. Amazingly, Mrs. Haberman does not share her husband's enthusiasm.

The sorry state of the matchbook industry has not deterred serious matchbook collectors. The American Matchcover Collecting Club boasts about 700 members who feel a burning urge to save beautiful examples of the genre. Avid collectors underscore the historical value of their quests.

One matchbook from World War II, for example, has a picture of Hitler. Each match is shaped like a bomb; the striker is Hitler's backside. The sentence reads: "Strike at the seat of trouble." The matchbook sells for about $75, making this a most affordable collectible. There are scores of collectible matchbooks available for less than $10, too.

The Least You Need to Know

➤ *Ephemera* are paper items meant to be discarded. As a result, ephemera is the only collectible that can offer you something for nothing.

➤ Paper falls apart. Don't try to fix it yourself.

➤ Buy all paper collectibles—cards, posters, scripts, and so on—in the best possible condition.

➤ Bookplates and playing cards are popular collectibles.

➤ Baseball cards, theater ephemera, and movie memorabilia are extremely desirable collectibles.

➤ You won't strike it rich with matchbook covers, but they may strike your fancy.

Chapter 8

Truth, Justice, and the American Way: Comic Books

In This Chapter

➤ Learn the history of comic books

➤ Find out how to start your collection

➤ Discover how to grade comics

➤ Learn the lingo

What's faster than a speeding bullet and more powerful than a locomotive? What can leap tall buildings in a single bound? Not that guy with the bulging biceps in blue tights. He's fast, but a seasoned comic book collector running toward a box of fresh finds is faster still. Watch out; these collectors are a swift and sturdy lot.

Historically, people saved books out of reverence for the printed word—but that reverence didn't extend to comics. That's a good thing for comics collectors. If people *had* saved their comics from the 1930s and 1940s, we'd all have copies of the super-valuable 1938 *Action Comics #1*... and it would be worth about as much as a last month's issue of *Action Comics*.

Comics, like most high-priced collectibles, are desirable because they are beautiful and rare (not unlike me). Comics from 1933–1940, for example, are very scarce in any condition, especially those from the mid- to late 1930s. Near-mint to mint condition copies are virtually nonexistent—known examples of any particular issue are limited to a handful of copies or less. For example, fewer than 20 copies of *Action Comics #1* are known to have survived. Old comics are almost as rare as people who admit to inhaling during the 1970s.

This chapter starts with a stroll down memory lane, where you will discover how comic books got their start. Then you'll find out how to start a comics collection of your own. This chapter also describes why the condition of a comic book is so important to its value. Next, you will learn the terms unique to comic book collecting so you'll know what the pros are talking about... and you can become a pro yourself. Then I'll teach you which books are the most valuable—and why. Finally, I'll talk about comic art, the newest offshoot of comic book collecting.

Bam! Pow! Zap! A Short History of Comic Books

The comic book industry began in the mid-1930s when M.C. ("Max") Gaines decided to compile a collection of newspaper comic strips in magazine form as a premium giveaway. Max's first comic book was a series of reprints given away to people who bought Ivory soap. Other companies quickly saw the popularity of such magazines, and very soon all the usable strips were being reprinted.

In stepped Major Malcolm Wheeler Nicholson, a man with a paper supply and a printing contract. This pulp fiction writer/cavalry officer/sportsman/adventurer started his company, National Allied Publications, by printing *New Comics* and *New Fun Comics* using all new material. Thirty-two tabloid newspaper-sized pages long with a full-color cover, the 1935 comic established many of the features of the modern comic book: humor, adventure, sports, and the extended continuity story.

In 1936, Wheeler Nicholson folded his package in half, creating the format that became today's standard. The following year, Wheeler Nicholson started another new title, *Detective Comics*, the first comic book devoted to a single theme. It was an instant hit and gave the company its name: DC Comics.

It's a Bird, It's a Plane...

In 1938, looking for a lead feature to launch another new title, Gaines, an editor at DC, settled on a strip that had been created five years earlier and unsuccessfully offered as a newspaper strip by two teenagers from Cleveland. The character was faster than a locomotive and could leap tall buildings in a single bound. He even had a sexy secret identity. The character? Superman. The comic book? *Action Comics*. Nineteen-year-olds Jerry Seigel and Joe Shuster had created an American icon. Superman was the first of the costumed super-heroes who would define the medium in the coming years. It took only four issues for *Action Comics* to sell 500,000 copies a month, more than twice the industry average at that time.

This lucky collector has a rich trove of highly collectible comics.

As quickly as they could, other publishers (and DC itself) sought to make economic lightning strike again and again. Costumed heroes arrived by the busload, including Batman, The Flash, Green Lantern, and Wonder Woman from DC; Captain America, the Human Torch, and Sub-Mariner from Timely; Captain Marvel and the Marvel Family from Fawcett; and Plastic Man and The Spirit from Quality. It was an age of heroes that lasted through the second World War and into the late '40s.

By the end of World War II, super-heroes were yesterday's news. Publishers started looking for new hooks to reel 'em in. Crime comics, western comics, war comics, and romance comics all started appearing. MLJ Publications started a back-up feature about "America's Typical Teenager"… Archie. The freckle-faced lad and his sidekicks Betty and Veronica are still popular today. And at EC Publications (which Max Gaines had started after leaving DC and which was now being run by his son Bill), horror comics were crawling out from the writers' fevered imaginations.

The Horror, The Horror

With such titles as *Tales from the Crypt* and *Weird Science*, Bill Gaines and his crew set the industry scrambling in a new direction, one that eventually spawned a parental uproar and a Congressional investigation. With each new rival publisher going for more and more gory material, it was an easy task for psychologist Fredric Wertham to gain notoriety by blaming all the ills of society on comic books. (*We* know it was rock music.)

In an attempt to forestall Congressional action and public backlash, the larger publishers banded together and formed the Comics Magazine Association, with a Comics Code to label appropriate comic book material. Virtually overnight, Gaines and his schlockmeister competitors were forced to abandon comics. Only Gaines continued on the fringe of the business, publishing a highly successful comic book turned magazine: *MAD*.

Big Deals

Like Gaul, the development of comics can be neatly divided into three stages. The first stage is called the "Golden Age," from June, 1935 to 1955. Next is the "Silver Age," September, 1956 to the early 1970s. Finally, we have the "Modern Age," 1980s to the present. Collectors use these terms to distinguish among production eras.

They're Back...

Comics languished throughout the early and mid-'50s until 1956, when DC editor Julius Schwartz proposed bringing the super-heroes back for another try. He revised and re-vamped The Flash and met with enthusiastic response. He followed his success with Green Lantern, Hawkman, The Atom, and the Justice League of America.

Meanwhile, over at Atlas (formerly Timely) Comics, publisher Martin Goodman salivated over the success of his rivals at DC and suggested to his editor that they should start publishing super-hero comics as well. The editor, a long-time writer of comics for Timely/Atlas named Stan Lee, took a shot and created the Fantastic Four, Spider-Man, the Incredible Hulk, and the X-Men.

It was not long before a new age of super-heroes was upon us. The early 60s saw almost as many new characters as the 1940s had, in a frenzy then further fueled by the *Batman* TV series in 1966.

In the early 1970s, the comic book industry became aware that their audience was changing. Instead of losing all its readers around age 14 (when boys discovered girls and girls discovered telephones), these readers were staying on, looking for more diverse and challenging material. Coupled with the growth of a direct market (in which the publishers could supply books directly to comic book shops), and the utilization of new printing technologies, the industry went through its largest expansion. Record numbers of titles were produced every month.

A new generation of horror comics, many produced by fans-turned-professionals from England, began to appear, aimed at an adult audience. Far more graphic than those of the '50s, but also with far more complex storylines, these books in particular have led former readers back into the comic book fold.

In leaps and bounds, the comic book industry dove into computerized color and art, bringing it up to techno-speed… and in some cases ahead of the curve. New printing techniques were utilized. Types of paper were reformulated to best show off the subtleties of the artwork.

Comics Today

Which brings us to the present… when it would cost over $2,000 to buy a month's worth of titles. Super-heroes still rule the day, but there is room for much, much more. Today's comics provide something for every taste… for every reader.

Taking the Plunge

In 1995, a copy of *Action Comics #1* in very fine condition sold for $137,500. The same year, *Action Comics #78* (restored) in very fine condition fetched $75,900. A few years earlier, *Detective Comics #27* sold for $96,000.

Caveat Emptor
Beware of reprints of classic comic books sold as originals. Check the cover carefully to distinguish the new from the old.

So you want to be a comic collector, too? With the stratospheric value of investment-grade comic books, it's not hard to explain their appeal. But collectors are also passionate about the art, artists, and storylines in their favorite comic books. Today, slick paper makes the colors burst from the page. Computers allow dazzling special effects. There are brilliant covers. In all, comics are collectibles that give immediate as well as lasting pleasure. They can be read for fun or hoarded as an investment—or both.

For example, check the attic. See if any of the Top Ten comics listed in the following table are playing hide-and-seek. If so, nab 'em fast. They're worth a bundle.

The Most Valuable American Comic Books

Title	Date	Significance
Action Comics #1	June, 1938	First appearance of Superman
Detective Comics #27	May, 1939	First appearance of Batman
Superman #1	Summer, 1939	First comic devoted entirely to Superman
Marvel Comics #1	October, 1939	First appearance of the Human Torch
New Fun Comics #1	February, 1935	First DC comic book
Detective Comics #1	March, 1937	First in a series
All-American Comics #16	July, 1940	First appearance of Green Lantern
Batman #1	Spring, 1940	First comic book devoted to Batman
Whiz Comics #1	February, 1940	First appearance of Captain Marvel
Captain America Comics #1	March, 1941	First appearance of Captain America

If you don't find a collectible comic in the attic, luckily, comic books are one of the most easily available collectibles: You can purchase prepackaged bundles of new comic books in nice plastic bags at monster warehouse stores, and single issues are sold at grocery stores, drug stores, card shops, and comic shops. If there is no comic store in your region, mail order is easy to arrange. Or, call 1-888-Comic Book to get the location of the comic shop nearest to your home. Just don't let the mail carrier read your comics before you do.

Most collectors start by buying new issues from their nearest shop. That way, they can decide which titles appeal to them the most. But there is more to buying comics than taking a few books from a rack and plunking down some bills. You can arrange your collection in almost limitless ways. Three of the most common methods are collecting by artist, company, numbers, title, and character.

➤ **Collecting by artist.** Many collectors follow the career of a favorite comic artist as he or she migrates from company to company like salmon spawning upstream. Today, some artists have even approached the ranks of superstars, complete with eager groupies, flashy automobiles, and impressive egos. Original art work from such fan favorites as Todd McFarlane, Rob Liefeld, Frank Miller, John Byrne, and Jim Lee brings record prices at auctions.

➤ **Collecting by company.** Some collectors latch on to a particular company and collect only the titles that it produces. This method can help you specialize in a huge market, but if you pick a large company, it can still leave you with stacks and stacks of comics. DC Comics, for example, produces over 80 titles a month!

➤ **Collecting by numbers.** All numbers are equal, but some numbers are more equal than others. With comics, it's number one that counts. For years, comic collectors have sought out first issues. It's hard to go astray with number ones: They may introduce new characters, start a new storyline, or underprint to create an instant rarity. An "underprint" is a small print run, which results in far fewer comics than buyers.

> **Caveat Emptor**
> Does it sound easy to collect by title? Remember that some titles run for decades... and decades... and decades.

➤ **Collecting by title.** This is an especially popular way to build a collection. Pick a title and try to nab the entire run.

➤ **Collecting by character.** Collecting by character means saving all the particular issues that feature the super-hero (or villain!) that you have selected. Spider-Man, for example, appears in his own comic as well as in several other issues where he teams up with other characters. Collecting by character presents intriguing bookkeeping chores as well as fun reading.

Don't Step on Superman's Cape

Even the most minor blemish lowers the value of a comic book. Before you buy a comic to add to your collection, look it over carefully. The cover should be on correctly; the colors should be bright and crisp. The corners and staples should be straight, too.

Making the Grade

You thought your junior high math teacher was picky? You remember, the one with the ruler. She was a mastodon, but she can't hold a candle to comic book collectors. Serious collectors grade comics by a very rigid set of standards. Study the following table to see whether your comics make the grade. It's enough to make you wear white gloves when you read the comic book you just bought. (Not a bad idea.)

> **Tricks of the Trade**
> Serious collectors often buy two—or more—copies of a new sure-fire hit comic: One to read and one to store. Speculation is always a gamble, of course, so check carefully before you start snapping up boxes of current issues. It may not be a wise investment, for example, to stockpile comics that are part of a four-million-issue print run.

Comic Condition Grades

Condition	Abbreviation	Description
Mint	M	As close to perfect as perfect can be. The cover is flat; the ink bright. Staples are centered; the spine tight.
Near Mint	NM	Only minor imperfections, such as a few very tiny flecks of color. The bindery tears (small rips that occur during binding) are less than $1/16$ of an inch; the corners are square with ever-so-slight blunting allowed.
Very Fine	VF	Excellent copy, but the spine may have a few barely perceptible transverse stress lines (small wrinkles). A $1/4$-inch crease is allowed, if the color is not broken. Pages and covers can be off-white, but not brown.
Fine	F	The copy shows minor wear but is still flat and uncreased. A fine comic has been read a few times and handled with consideration.
Very Good	VG	This is the average used comic book: It usually has a center crease, a rolled spine, and some discoloration. A staple may be loose, but the cover is still attached— at least partially.
Good	G	The comic has all its pages and its cover, but some pages may have chunks missing. To make the grade, no missing piece can be larger than $1/2$ inch. This is the lowest acceptable collectible grade because comics in lesser condition are usually missing pages and covers or disintegrating.
Fair	F	The book is soiled, ragged, and may be missing large pieces. This is what happens to a comic when you cut the coupon for sea monkeys from its back cover.
Poor	P	These books are badly stained, mildewed, ripped, and defaced. Often, the books are so brittle that they fall apart when you handle them.

A Nip and a Tuck

Judging by what I see at the gym, few of us hesitate to have a little taken off here or added on there. A bit of liposuction down below, a touch of the scalpel under the eyes. No one's *ever* going to convince me that people of a certain age look that good without the aid of a pricey plastic surgeon, no matter how many sit-ups they do.

But the aging comic book collector who easily submits to a little personal refurbishing is likely to recoil in horror at the idea of making his prize books endure the same process. And with good cause. Professionally restored comic books do have a place in the collectible market, but only under three conditions:

1. The work has been done by a professional.

2. The seller discloses complete information about the restoration.

3. The resulting book is priced fairly, based on demand and condition.

Nonetheless, all things being equal, a professionally restored book will rarely be worth the same amount as an unrestored book in the same condition. For example, an unrestored copy of *Incredible Hulk #6* in Very Good condition will be worth more than a Fair copy of the book restored to Very Good condition. To determine a fair price, consult the standard price guide in the field, *Overstreet's Comic Book Price Guide*.

The latest trends at comic book auctions suggest that unrestored rare books in Fine or better condition will be better investments than restored books in the future. This is because there will be fewer unrestored pieces. Conclusion? Save restoration efforts for comic books graded less than Fine. And don't worry so much about your love handles.

Walk the Walk and Talk the Talk

Every collectible has its buzzwords, and comics are no different. How can you learn all the jargon so you sound like a real fanboy? Study this handy-dandy crib sheet:

Term	Meaning
Adult material	Sex, violence, naughty bits
Adzine	A magazine that advertises comics and collectibles
Annual	Published once a year
Arrival date	A dealer or distributor hand-pencils the date when he places the comic for sale. This date is usually a month or two before the cover date.
Ashcan	Dummy title prepared to show advertisers or to copyright a trademark and title. The inside pages are often blank.
B&W	Black-and-white art
Bad girl art	Depicts women in sexually explicit ways
Bi-monthly	Published every two months
Bi-weekly	Published every two weeks

continues

continued

Term	Meaning
Complete run	All issues of a given title
Con	A comic book convention
Crossover	When a character appears in another character's story
Debut	The first time a character appears in a comic
Double cover	An error in binding that results in two covers being bound into the same book; not a defect, and makes the book very slightly more valuable
Fanzine	A non-professional fan publication
Foxing	Orange-brown spots caused by mold
Gatefold cover	A cover that folds out, usually an additional page width
Indicia	Copyright information; usually on the inside front cover or page 1
Logo	The stylized title of the comic or character as it appears on the cover or title page
One-shot	The only issue of a title published
Pedigree	A comic book from a famous collection
Printing defect	A defect that occurs during the printing process, such as wrinkled paper or a misfolded spine
Provenance	The source of a comic book, such as a person's collection
Quarterly	Published four times a year, every three months
Rolled spine	Damage to a comic book caused by folding back the pages while reading
Semi-monthly	Published twice a month
Spine	The edge of the book that is folded and stapled
Spine roll	A defect that occurs during binding. It results in uneven pages.
Splash panel	The large panel on the first page of a comic
Stress lines	Small wrinkles along the comic book's spine
Sun shadow	A serious defect caused by the sun
Swipe	Art in a comic copied and modified, after changing the characters shown, from previously-published material

Art for Art's Sake

In addition to the actual comic books, some collectors lust after original comic art. These black-and-white inked drawings are usually 50 percent larger than the printed pages. Because each piece of comic art is unique, it is highly valued and often difficult to find. There is no definitive guide for pricing comic art. However, Overstreet has a highly respected price guide in this field, separate from his comic book price guide.

In the past, few comic book companies returned the art panels to the artists and so there was little available for sale. Since the 1970s, however, most companies now give the art back to its creators. The artists, in turn, are free to sell their pages to dealers and at conventions. As with comic books, the value of original art depends on four factors:

➤ Popularity of character

➤ Popularity of artist

➤ Rarity

➤ Skill

Connoisseur
Remember when your date's mother used to tell you that character counts? She knew her comic books. Which character is on a page of original art matters. A page of a story that shows Superman is worth more than a page that shows Clark—even if it's the same story.

The Least You Need to Know

➤ The comic book industry began in the mid-1930s. The most valuable comic books date from these early "golden" years. Many Marvel books from the 1960s and DC books from the mid-'50s are hot, too.

➤ Rarity and condition determine the value of a comic book.

➤ Original comic art is a smokin' collectible.

➤ Comic books did not corrupt America's youth. Blame it on the bossa nova.

Chapter 9

Lick That: Stamps

In This Chapter

➤ Learn what each part of a stamp is called

➤ Discover the different types of postal stamps and stamp-like things you can collect

➤ Find out what tools you need to get started with stamp collecting

➤ See where the money is—and isn't—with stamp collecting

In 1863, two crestfallen English sailors walked into a small stamp shop in the English port of Plymouth. The shop owner, Stanley Gibbons, was astonished when the limies dumped thousands of triangular stamps on the counter. The stamps had been issued in the Cape of Good Hope between 1853 and 1863. The sailors disgustedly explained that they had won the stamps in a raffle in a South African pub and just wanted to get rid of them. They were delighted when Gibbons gave them a few pounds for the lot. Gibbons went on to sell the stamps for a profit of £500. Today the stamps are valued at $20 to more than $100,000 each. It should happen to all of us. In this chapter, you will discover what the odds are that you will hit the stamp collecting jackpot.

The colorful bits of gummed paper that move the mail may not look like much, but stamps have excited the passion of collectors for generations. Here, I'll teach you all about the different parts of stamps, lay out the tools you need to become a collector, and describe the best places to get the stamps you need to build your collection. Speaking of collections, this chapter also covers the different ways to collect stamps.

Stamp Collecting 101

In the days before stamps, the recipient, not the sender, paid for the postage. As a result, delivery was never guaranteed. The system had its pros and cons: On one hand, it made it easier for a rejected suitor to delay the inevitable Dear John letter; on the other, if you didn't have the cash, you didn't get your mail. Further, you paid by weight, so heavier letters cost more than thinner ones. Long-winded writers often strained the pocketbooks of their less verbose friends.

> **Learn the Lingo**
> Any hobby poten-
> tially worth a lot of
> money has a fancy
> nickname. Stamp
> collecting is no excep-
> tion. Stamp collecting is called
> **philately**; a stamp collector is
> called a **philatelist**.

The world's first lick-and-stick, prepaid stamps were intro-duced in Britain on May 6, 1840. Only two denominations were issued: the penny black and the two-penny blue. America issued her first stamps seven years later. Five cents bought you Ben Franklin's likeness; for a nickel more, you got George Washington's sweet puss. The stamps had to be cut apart because no one had thought of perforations.

Getting Your Feet Wet

Let's not waste any time. You want to acquire stamps, so here's what you do:

1. Take the canceled stamps off your mail.

2. Ask your friends and family for their old stamps.

3. Go to the post office. Buy new stamps.

4. Put your stamps in a shoe box.

Congratulations! Now you know how to *accumulate* stamps. But that's not the same as *collecting* them. What's the difference? An *accumulator* likes stuff for stuff's sake. An accumulator of stamps hoards piles and piles of stamps. A *collector*, in contrast, wants specific stamps because they have specific meaning and value. Since this is a book about collecting and you're too smart to be an accumulator, let me teach you the basics of stamp collecting.

Getting to Know You, Getting to Know All About You

You look at a stamp and it looks like a stamp. Like all stamps, it has a few thingies and a couple of whoosies. There is even a whatchamacallit it or two. Each of those thingies has a name. Use this diagram to break the code:

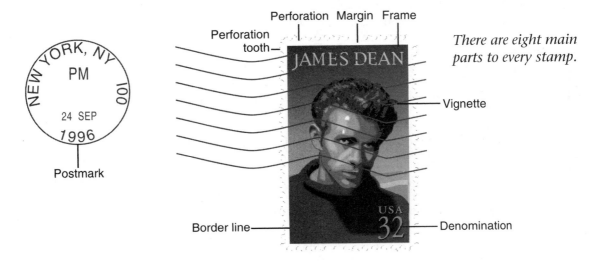

There are eight main parts to every stamp.

Form and Function

Stamp and stamp-like substitutes come in different formats. Different collectors fancy different formats. It's your call. Here's the low-down:

➤ **Sheet format.** This is a perforated sheet of stamps.

➤ **Plate blocks.** This is a block of stamps that includes on the selvage the number of the printing plate used to print the stamps. A block of stamps can be four stamps or more; the "selvage" is the white edge around the outside of the stamps. Some plate blocks contain four stamps. Stamps printed by the flat-plate method are collected in blocks of six; multicolored stamps can have as many as 10 or 20 stamps per block. Stamps with "floating plate numbers" may contain almost half a sheet of stamps per plate block.

➤ **Coil format.** The stamps are issued on a roll. Coil stamps are perforated on two sides only, usually the left and right sides. They are generally collected in pairs.

➤ **Plate-number coils.** The Postal Service started putting plate numbers on coils in 1981. Collectors usually save plate-number coils in strips of three or five. The plate number is printed in the middle of the strip.

➤ **Booklets.** A complete booklet is referred to as an *unexploded booklet*. A page of stamps from a booklet is called a *pane*.

➤ **Self-adhesive stamps.** The stamps are peeled from their backing; they don't have to be licked. They were first issued in 1974.

➤ **Souvenir sheets.** It's a small sheet with one or more stamps, with a commemorative inscription or special artwork surrounding the stamp or stamps.

Tricks of the Trade

If you get an envelope with a canceled stamp you like, don't soak it off the envelope so fast. Sometimes the entire envelope may be worth more than the used stamp alone because of the postmark. Check the value with a dealer or in a stamp price guide.

➤ **Covers.** A *cover* is any kind of envelope that has traveled through the mail. It's called a "cover" because it covers the message—the letter—inside. No one ever said the post office was subtle in labeling its services.

➤ **First-day covers.** First-day covers contain a postmark for the first day the stamp was put on sale. Usually, only one lucky city gets first crack at selling the stamp. The next day, every other post office can offer the stamp for sale. Many first-day cover collectors prefer their covers unaddressed. They send away for them and write their name on a removable label. When the cover arrives, they peel off the label.

A sample first-day cover.

➤ **Postal stationery.** There are three types: *prestamped envelopes, aerogrammes* (letter sheets for foreign postage), and *postal cards* (not the same as picture postcards; these are blank cards with the stamp already printed).

➤ **Postage meters.** These are legal substitutes for stamps, used primarily by businesses.

➤ **Permit imprints.** These are used when you are mailing more than 200 pieces or 50 pounds at one time.

Stop the Presses! How Stamps Are Printed

There are many different methods that are used to actually manufacture stamps. Here are the most common methods:

➤ **Engraving (a.k.a. intaglio).** The most detailed of the printing methods, engraving involves making a photographic reduction of the stamp's original artwork on a master die, transferring the image to a printing plate, and inking and printing.

➤ **Typography (a.k.a. letterpress, surface printing).** After the master die is made, the area not used as a printing surface is cut away.

➤ **Photogravure (a.k.a. rotogravure).** The image is photographically transferred to a special metal plate in many tiny dots.

➤ **Lithography.** The stamp's design is created on a printing plate using an oily material. The portions of the plate that won't be printed have water on them. Since oil and water don't mix, the ink is forced to the oily parts of the plate.

Big Deals

So, you want your cute face on a stamp? Different countries have different rules. In America, it's a little hard to lobby on your own behalf for stamphood, because you have to be dead for at least 10 years before you can appear on a stamp. (If you were the president, you only have to be dead for one year. Yet another reason to run for president.)

Significant events are commemorated only on anniversaries in multiples of 50 years. Only events and anniversaries of widespread national importance are eligible for consideration. Stamps are not issued to honor fraternal, political, sectarian, or service organizations whose main raison d'être is to solicit or distribute funds. Ditto on commercial ventures and religions. If you have an idea for a stamp, send your suggestion to this address:

Citizens' Stamp Advisory Committee
Stamp Information Branch
United States Postal Service
Washington, DC 20260-6352.

And don't forget to stamp the envelope before you mail it.

Stamp-o-Rama: Acquiring Stamps

Notice that I said "acquiring" stamps rather than "buying" them. There are many ways to get stamps, and buying is just one of the methods. How you acquire stamps depends on what stamps you want, where you live, and how much time and money you have to devote to your collection. Always consult a reputable stamp guide before you buy anything; there are several excellent guides available. Select the guides that feature the stamps you collect. Here are the methods; take your pick.

Used, Not Abused

Used stamps have filled their life's work: They have helped a letter get somewhere. As their reward, they have been cancelled to prevent reuse. Don't sneer at used stamps. Some collectors will seek out only used stamps; virgin stamps, they argue, are nothing more than fancy labels. There are two big advantages to collecting used stamps:

➤ You don't have to worry about the gum being pristine. It ain't. As a matter of fact, it's all gone. You soaked it off to get the stamp off the envelope.

➤ Used stamps usually are cheaper than new stamps.

Since some cancellation marks are valuable, always check a guidebook before you soak a stamp off its envelope. Better safe than sorry!

Big Deals

Soak a stamp to get it off an envelope. Do not fully immerse the stamps in water, because the inks may run. Instead, place the stamp in the water so the paper becomes moist—not the stamp. Use cool water, never hot. Always peel the paper from stamps, not the stamp from the paper. Lay the stamp face down on blotting paper. Bend a small edge of the paper with your tongs. Store the stamp between pages of clean blotting paper.

Never cut it off or try to pry it up. They drum you out of the stamp collecting corps for that.

Some used stamps are valuable because of the cancellation they bear. But except for the cost of neato cancellations, used stamps are inexpensive. They can even be free, if you soak them off your own mail and hit up your near and dear kinfolk for their used stamps.

Mixtures and Packets

Stamp mixtures are just what they sound like: piles and piles of assorted stamps. They can be used or new. They are sold in large quantities—even by the thousands—as well as by weight. You can buy them *on paper* (with part of the envelope) or *off paper* (soaked off). I recommend that you buy packets labeled *all different* as opposed to *assorted*. The former term means that every stamp will be different; the latter means that you may get duplicates. Packets are very easily available at stores and through the mail.

Buying mixtures is not like playing the lottery. You won't find the prize in the Cracker Jack box, either. Say the mixture label reads, "1,000 stamps! Total catalog value $50—for only $5!" This means that you have bought 1,000 stamps for $5. Doing your division shows that each stamp is worth 5¢, the minimum value assigned to a stamp in *Scott's Catalog*, **the** stamp catalog. Trust me; there's no needle hidden in this haystack—you won't find a $5 million stamp—or even a $5 one. But it's even a bit more grim. While it is true that the catalog value is $50 for the lot, you won't be able to get that. The 5¢ per stamp ($50 total) represents the dealer's time more than the stamp's actual value.

So why would anyone buy mixtures? They help you acquire a lot of stamps quickly, cheaply, and easily, so you can learn about stamp collecting and decide how to limit and refine your collection.

Dealers

Cozy up to a neighborhood stamp dealer. How can you find a good local dealer? Look in the Yellow Pages and speak to your fellow collectors to see who they recommend. Dealers are the most knowledgeable stamp mavens you can find. Most stamp dealers are fair and ethical people, savvy to the reality that only by establishing a steady, repeat clientele are they going to retire happily.

But this is a quid-pro-quo relationship. They teach; you buy. You cannot hang around the store and pick the stamp dealer's brain without buying enough stamps to make it worth his or her time. You most especially cannot pick Dealer #1's brain and then buy from Dealer #2 because his prices are better. Tacky, tacky.

Try to find a dealer who will be your mentor and help you learn what you need to know to be a successful stamp collector. But a good stamp dealer can help you with more than stamp education. Say you want to collect stamps related to zeppelins, but your dealer doesn't have any particular interest in the Hindenberg. Nonetheless, your dealer probably knows another dealer or several collectors who do groove on blimps, and so can help you network.

Mail Order

Mail order is not for those of you who require instant gratification. But ordering stamps by mail does allow you a much wider range of possibilities. It's also the best way to buy if you don't have a stamp store within reach. You can find mail-order houses listed in stamp magazines. Also consider looking through the Internet—it's the latest way to connect with other collectors.

Keep careful records of stamp mail-order transactions. I suggest that you photocopy your letter. That way, if there is ever a dispute, you have proof of your requests. Also be sure to include your address on the letter; envelopes and letters have a way of getting separated from each other. It's not a bad idea to include your telephone number, too.

Here are two ways to use mail order:

➤ **Approvals.** *Approvals* means that you can see the stamps before you buy them. On your request, a dealer will send you a selection of stamps for your approval. You keep the stamps you do want and return payment for them along with the stamps you reject. However, if any stamps are lost or damaged while they are in your possession, you are responsible. So lock up your stamp-eating iguana when the approval package comes.

➤ **Wanted: stamps.** Here's the scoop: You send the dealer a list of stamps you want. This is called your *want list.* The dealer goes over your list, reviews his or her stock, and lets you know what you can get at your price. You do not have any obligation to buy anything, but you must respond to the dealer's offer with an acceptance or refusal.

> **Caveat Emptor**
> It costs very little to print a stamp, so many small countries issue reams of stamps every year. These stamps are colorful, attractive—and usually worthless. There is even a term for these no-account stamps: *wallpaper.* Most collectors look upon these money-making gimmick stamps with contempt, but it's your money.

Auctions

You can attend a stamp auction in person or bid by mail. Some auctions may only be by mail. Since this method of buying stamps normally involves some serious money, it's important to know and understand the terms of sale, listed in the auction catalog. Usually, you will even have to sign a statement agreeing to abide by the terms of sale. That way, in case of a disagreement, you cannot claim that you did not know or understand the terms of sale.

You must also make sure that you are bidding correctly and accurately. Suppose, for example, that you bid for lot 43 instead of the lot you wanted—34. Tough noogies. If you win lot 43, it's yours.

In some cases, very rare stamps are available only through auctions. If you intend to become a major player in Stampland, it's important to familiarize yourself with this method of buying stamps.

Another Opening, Another Show: Stamp Shows

Stamp shows (also known as Philatelic Exhibitions) are a good way to dive right into the world of stamps. They offer you a way to see a lot of stamps at one time. You'll also get a chance to scope out stamps you might not otherwise get to see—especially those that cost as much as a week in the south of France. Stamp shows are advertised in newspapers and stamp magazines.

Some stamp shows have a *bourse,* where dealers have come to sell rather than play show-and-tell. Like a good consumer, you can comparison-shop and schmooze new dealers. Stamp shows are also great places to meet representatives from stamp clubs and see whether they offer what you need. You might be able to find a club that's right for you.

Some large shows also feature a temporary U.S. Postal Service station where you can mail letters and buy stamps. Convenient postage is nice, but the zowie part of the kiosk is the special postmarks, usually pictorials. The letters you mail from the show will bear these special pictorials. Don't want to mail it? The show's sponsors usually sell a special envelope, which you can decorate with a stamp of your choice and have it canceled with the show's postmark. You can take the envelope with you. Makes a nice souvenir.

Big Deals

The world's most valuable stamp is a one-cent black-on-magenta British Guiana (now Guyana) printed in the capital, Georgetown, in 1856, when supplies from Britain failed to arrive. Yet the young colonial collector who found the only known copy among some old stamps in 1873 sold it for the equivalent of a few pennies because he thought it was dull and uninteresting. In 1934 it sold for $32,000; by 1980, the price had skyrocketed to $850,000.

The stamp is now believed to be a true one-of-a-kind, but there is a story that while it was owned by the American millionaire Arthur Hind, around the turn of the century, a British merchant seaman called on him with another genuine one-cent black-on-magenta. Hind is said to have paid the seaman a huge sum for the second stamp—and then burned it. He told his friends, "Now there is still only one."

Conversely, the most worthless stamp ever issued—taking only face value into account—was a 3,000-pengo stamp issued in Hungary on February 5, 1946. At the time of issue, one U.S. penny would have bought 25 billion of the stamps.

Even-Steven: Trading

As you have learned in previous chapters, many collectors trade rather than purchase collectibles. The same is true of stampmeisters. Often, trading allows you to get the stamps that you want without you having to fork over cash. It's a great way to solidify a collection, too.

You can meet potential trading partners through stamp clubs or at shows. Dealers are often willing to trade as well. Over a period of time, you can trade up to quality stamps you could otherwise not afford to buy.

Tools of the Trade

A stamp collection is one of the cheapest types of collections to start. The cost can be as low as saving the stamps from mail you have received or hitting up friends and family for their cancelled stamps. But a few basic tools will make it easier for you to build your collection. Here's what I recommend:

➤ **Tongs.** Tongs are flat-bladed tweezers. Use them when you examine and mount stamps to lessen the risk that you will damage the stamps with the oil, dirt, or perspiration from your fingers. Remember that stamps are paper and paper is fragile. Save regular tweezers for splinters and stray eyebrow hairs: *Never* use tweezers in place of stamp tongs.

Caveat Emptor

Whether you are pro- or anti-hinge, under no circumstances should you mount stamps with anything else—no rubber cement, tape, or (shudder) staples. You'll make the stamp as worthless as you would by burning them off with a blowtorch.

➤ **Hinges.** Stamp hinges are specially designed adhesive attachments meant for mounting stamps in an album. They peel off when dry and cost very little. To use a hinge, moisten the tip of the smaller end, place the hinge on the back of the stamp near the top, moisten the larger end, and stick it on the album page.

Hinges spark an ongoing debate among stamp collectors. One side sees hinges right up there with mother's milk and voting Republican; the other side recoils in horror at the very idea of hinging a stamp. The pro-hingers argue that hinging doesn't damage a stamp in any way; the anti-hingers snort in derision.

➤ **Stamp mounts.** Hinges remove some of the gum, and mint stamps are usually worth *lots* more with full gum. As a result, stamp mounts are popular alternatives to hinges. Stamp mounts are clear plastic sleeves that are gummed on the back. Since the gummed part of the mount does not touch the stamp, the gum on the stamp is safe. Safe gum is a good thing.

➤ **Albums.** Most collectors put their stamps in albums, binders with pages specially designed for storing stamps. There are more types of albums than Quaker has Oats. The two general types are *printed* and *blank*. *Printed* have pictures of the stamps and you're supposed to place the stamp over the picture. *Blank* allows you to place the stamps where you want in the album.

To begin, you might want to try a general world album. Then you can look to specific albums as you develop special interests.

AUTHORS ON STAMPS

PAUL LAURENCE DUNBAR

Dunbar, Paul Laurence. 1872–1906. American poet, b. Dayton, Ohio, son of an escaped Negro slave. Elevator boy, Dayton (1891–95). Volume of poems, *Majors and Minors* (1895), received favorable notice by William Dean Howells; a second volume, *Lyrics of Lowly Life* (1896), with an introduction by Howells, established his literary reputation. Other works: *Poems of Cabin and Field* (1899), *Lyrics of the Hearthside* (1899), *Candle-Lightin' Time* (1902), *Lyrics of Love and Laughter* (1903), *Lyrics of Sunshine and Shadow* (1905), and four novels, *The Uncalled* (1896), *The Love of Landry* (1900), *The Fanatics* (1901), *The Sport of the Gods* (1902).

RALPH WALDO EMERSON

Emerson, Ralph Waldo. 1803–1882. American essayist and poet, b. Boston, Mass. Grad. Harvard (1821), taught school. Studied for ministry; licensed to preach (1826); minister of Second Church of Boston, Unitarian (1829–32); resigned because of doctrinal differences. Visited Europe, meeting Wordsworth, Coleridge, and Carlyle, with last of whom he maintained friendship and correspondence for over forty years. Settled in Concord, Mass. (from 1834); formed circle of friends, including A. B. Alcott, Margaret Fuller, Thoreau, Jones Very, and Hawthorne. Preached in various churches during next several years; meantime began delivering public lectures, material for which he drew from the *Journals* he had been keeping for many years. First published work, *Nature* (1836), contained gist of his transcendental philosophy, which views the world of phenomena as a sort of symbol of the inner life and emphasizes individual freedom and self-reliance. His address to the Phi Beta Kappa society of Harvard on "the American scholar" (1837) and another address to the graduating class of the Cambridge Divinity College (1838) applied his doctrine to the scholar and the clergyman, the second address provoking sharp controversy. Edited *The Dial* (1842–44). His two volumes of *Essays* (1841, 1844) made his reputation international. Lectured in England (1847). Slowly drawn into participation in national issues and delivered many antislavery speeches; welcomed beginning of Civil War. After 1866 gradually declined in mental powers. Other works: *Poems* (1846, but dated 1847), *Representative Men* (1850), *English Traits* (1856), *The Conduct of Life* (1860), *May-Day and Other Pieces* (poems, 1867), *Society and Solitude* (1870), *Letters and Social Aims* (issued 1876), *Natural History of Intellect* (1893). The centenary edition of his works was edited by his son Edward Waldo (1844–1930), who also edited his *Journals* and his correspondence with John Sterling, and who wrote *Emerson in Concord* (1889).

ROBERT FROST

Frost, Robert Lee. 1874– . American poet, b. San Francisco. Educ. Dartmouth (1892) and Harvard (1897–99). Professor of English, Amherst (1916–20; 1923–25; 1926–38); professor of poetry, Harvard (from 1936). Awarded Pulitzer prizes for 1923, 1930, 1936, 1942. Author of *A Boy's Will* (1913), *North of Boston* (1914), *Mountain Interval* (1916), *New Hampshire* (1923), *West-running Brook* (1928), *A Further Range* (1936), *From Snow to Snow* (1936), *A Witness Tree* (1942), etc.

JOEL CHANDLER HARRIS

Harris, Joel Chandler. 1848–1908. American writer, b. in Putnam County, Ga.; on staff, Savannah *Morning News* (1870) and Atlanta *Constitution* (1876–1900). Fame rests on his creation of Uncle Remus, as in *Uncle Remus, His Songs and His Sayings* (1880), *Nights with Uncle Remus* (1883), *Uncle Remus and His Friends* (1892), *The Tar Baby* (1904), *Uncle Remus and Brer Rabbit* (1906), *Uncle Remus Returns* (1918), etc.

Many stamp albums, such as this one, allow collectors to design individual pages.

➤ **Stock book.** This is a blank book with pockets for you to insert stamps. The biggest advantage of a stock book is that you do not have to use hinges or mounts on your stamps. Stock books are unprinted. They are a good place to store duplicate or unsorted stamps.

➤ **Magnifying glass.** A magnifying glass can be a great help when you study individual stamps. To start, you can buy a perfectly adequate magnifying glass in a drug store.

➤ **Stamp catalog.** Stamp catalogs provide a list of all the stamps issued, by country. *Scott's* stamp catalog is the most famous one.

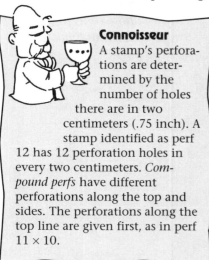

Connoisseur

A stamp's perforations are determined by the number of holes there are in two centimeters (.75 inch). A stamp identified as perf 12 has 12 perforation holes in every two centimeters. *Compound perfs* have different perforations along the top and sides. The perforations along the top line are given first, as in perf 11 × 10.

➤ **Perforation gauges.** The difference between a stamp's perforations—its holes—can make the difference between a valueless stamp and a valuable one. Since counting holes is a drag at best, treat yourself to a perforation gauge, a ruler that measures stamp perforations. They come in cardboard, metal, or plastic and are very inexpensive.

➤ **Watermark tray and fluid.** *Watermarks* are designs that can be seen when you hold a stamp up to the light. Watermarks help prevent counterfeiting and have a major effect on a stamp's value. You can find the stamp's watermark by putting a special liquid called *watermark fluid* on the back of a stamp without altering its gum. Place the stamp in the watermark tray to help the watermark stand out more clearly.

What to Collect?

You can collect any stamps you like: individual issues, plate blocks, first-day covers, and so on. The simplest collection is the general one; it is also dauntingly large. Monstrous, even. As a result, some collectors specialize in the stamps of a particular country. That's still a big. Topical themes narrow down a collection nicely and many collectors favor them. The following list lays out some possible topical themes for a stamp collection. Any of these themes set your pulse a-racing?

Advertising	Fish	Orchids
Animals	Flags	Paintings
Art	Flowers	Royalty
Authors	Horses	Scientists
Aviation	Insects	Scouting
Baseball	Judaica	Seashells
Birds	Maps	Ships
Butterflies	Marine life	Soccer
Cars	Medicine	Space
Cats	Movie stars	The United Nations
Chess	Movies	Trains
Christmas	Music	Whales
Costumes	Nuclear energy	Women
Countries	Nudes	World's Fair
Dogs	Olympics	

Like any paper collectible, the condition of a stamp is very important. Stamps are graded *Mint* (never used), *Extremely Fine, Very Fine, Fine, Very Good, and Good.* How can you assess a stamp yourself? Here are ten factors to consider:

1. How even is the gum on the back?

2. Are there any creases or tears?

3. In what condition are the perforations?

4. Are the colors vivid?

5. How much fading has occurred?

6. How brittle is the paper?

7. Has the stamp been regummed?

8. Is one area thinner than another?

9. Has the stamp been repaired?

10. Has the stamp been singed when someone tried to iron out a crease?

Here are some other terms you will see used to assess stamps:

Label	Meaning
NH	Never Hinged
OG	Original Gum
LH	Lightly Hinged
HR	Hinge Remnants

Don't Bet the Ranch: Stamps as Investments

The scene: Anywhere, USA.

The plot: A stamp collector is trying to sell his collection to a reputable dealer.

Dealer: (examining the piles and piles of stamps) "You've got postage here. It can be used to mail letters. It's worth 80 percent of face value."

Collector: (incredulous) "What?! Less than face value?"

Dealer: "Yes, that's its value."

Collector: "How can that be? Stamps are supposed to be good investments." (Pause.) "I don't want to sell at a loss. Someday they will be worth more. What do you think?"

Unfortunately, time alone will not cause mint postage (unused stamps) to rise in value. Rising prices are created when increased demand exerts force on a limited supply. Demand is the key factor; rarity comes next. Age, by itself, has little to do with value. In order for a sheet of post-1945 mint stamps to increase in value, the collectors (demand) must absorb the vast hoards (supply).

Stamps are generally considered super investments. As is the case with any collectible, some stamps are—and some stamps are not. The vast majority of all stamps—the new issues, the packets, the mixtures, the approvals, the new commemoratives you get at the post office, the designer first-day covers, and so on—are not good investments. But they were never intended to be.

Stockpiles of commonplace stamps will not pay off your mortgage, send your kids to college, or finance your retirement. The math is easy enough for even me to do: If one person puts aside one extra sheet of each new commemorative, there is a supply of 50 stamps (assuming 50 stamps per sheet). That will make 50 new collectors of that stamp happy campers. But if you put aside five or 10 sheets of every new stamp, you have enough to satisfy hundreds of new collectors. If *every* collector squirrels away sheets and sheets of new stamps, the vast supply will far outstrip the demand and saturate the market. And that is what is going on now.

Ironically, the most valuable collections tend to be those created over many years by knowledgeable collectors with little thought to profit.

Caveat Emptor
The following stamps are *not* investment-grade collectibles:

➤ Modern designer first-day covers

➤ Mixtures

➤ Low-priced approvals

➤ Packet material

➤ Post-1945 accumulations of mint postage

This is the most highly collectible stamp of all.

A Little Face Time

"You can't go wrong at face," the time-honored stamp-collecting mantra goes. People who subscribe to this maxim argue that the logic of buying new mint sheets at face value is the same as buying Disney stock at its original issue price. Would that it were so; it's not the same thing at all.

Buying new mint issues at face value is the same as buying shares of *every* new penny stock issued. For every one that becomes a blue-chip, thousands and thousands will be

Caveat Emptor
You can avoid having to sell your stamps at a discount from face value by not buying too many new issues in the first place. Because of their genuine scarcity, earlier, better stamps offer the best potential for rising in price.

losers. Buying new issue stamps willy-nilly at the post office is not picking winners. It's buying piles and piles of stamps.

Mindless buying does not a collector make. It makes a person with a lot of postage to store.

Try this instead. If you collect single stamps, buy *one* stamp of each new issue. If you collect plate blocks, buy *one* plate block... and so on. Advantages: You will spend only a few dollars. The money you would have tied up in duplicates can be better spent acquiring more valuable, earlier stamps.

The Least You Need to Know

➤ Stamp collecting requires relatively few tools—but a whole lot of knowledge.

➤ There are many different ways to arrange a stamp collection, such as single issues, first-day covers, plate blocks, and themes.

➤ With stamps, go for quality, not quantity. More stamps are not better.... they are just more postage.

Chapter 10

Gilt Trip: Collecting Coins

> ## In This Chapter
>
> ➤ Learn the history of coin collecting
>
> ➤ Discover what you need to start your own coin collection
>
> ➤ Grade coins
>
> ➤ Find out how to turn coin collecting into coin investing

The ancient Greeks placed a coin in the mouth of a human corpse as payment to the ferryman Charon who rowed newly dead souls across the sacred river Styx. Business tycoon John D. Rockefeller tossed dimes at passersby. Holding up a silver coin of the Emperor Tiberius, Jesus said, "Render unto Caesar the things that are Caesar's, and unto God the things that are God's." Pirates buried "pieces of eight"; modern beachcombers search for them with metal detectors.

Coins have been an integral part of life since ancient days. They fascinate us with their glitter; please us by their heft. They are also a whole lot easier to trade than salt, seashells, ivory, beaver skins, metal rings—the barter of other societies and ages. The word "coin" comes from the Latin *cuneus* ("wedge"), because ancient coin dies looked liked wedges. In this chapter, you will first learn the history of coin collecting. Then I'll teach you what you need to start your own coin collection, including how to grade coins. Finally, you'll discover how to turn coin collecting into coin investing.

CoinAge: The History of Coins

The first coins were made in the 7th century B.C. in Lydia and Ionia in Asia Minor (now Turkey). The size wasn't standard, so for every business transaction with these "coins," the stamped metal ingots had to be reweighed. Merchants finally had enough of the extra work so they pushed for standard coin weights and the use of obverse and reverse coinage dies, which caused the metal to flatten out into a circle. Voilà! The coin shape we know and love was created. So what if they were uneven and off-centered. You want everything?

Learn the Lingo
An **obverse** die creates the front or "head" side of the coin; a **reverse** die creates the back or "tail" side of the coin.

It's Greek to Me

Ancient Greek coins are revered for their beauty. Typically, ancient Greek coins show the head of a mythological being such as Athena or Hercules on the front, and an animal or deity on the back. The so-called "owls" of Athens, a coin first minted in the 6th century B.C., soon became legal tender throughout the Athenian world. Athena appeared on the front; an owl on the back. Moderately heavy silver coins, they are obviously much in demand by collectors.

Connoisseur
The familiar Latin phrase "E Pluribus Unum" is Latin for "One Out of Many," or "From Many One." So now you know what it says on every U.S. coin in circulation.

When In Rome... Get Some Coins

The first Roman coins, produced around 300 B.C., were bronze. Unlike our modern coin makers, the Romans had no problems honoring living people. Women as well as men made it to coins; in fact, the first coins to picture living women were Roman. The engravings were very realistic, making it easier for us to know what these ancient people looked like. Latin was used on coins (because it was spoken at the time), a custom that continues to this day.

Coin of the Realm: Medieval Coins

The Middle Ages are defined as the period of time from 476 A.D. (the fall of the Roman Empire) to around 1450 A.D. (the beginning of the Renaissance). Collectors of medieval coins seek out samples from the Byzantine Empire, the Crusades, the coinage of the Popes, the *florins* of Florence, and the gold *ducats* of Venice.

Coins were first produced by machines in Europe in the mid-16th century. The moneyers' guild greeted this invention with a notable lack of enthusiasm, since they correctly predicted that it would eventually put them out of a job.

Colonial Coins

The first coins to circulate in the Colonies came from England, Spain, and France. These foreign coins were legal tender in America until 1857. The first colonial mint was established in Boston in 1652; some cranky coin purists insist that the first coins anywhere were these Massachusetts silver pieces. Among the most popular coins from this era are the colonial *coppers* from Vermont, Massachusetts, New Jersey, and New York; the pewter and *silver Continental Dollars* of 1776; and the *"Washington"* tokens.

Bad Spellers of the World Untie: Modern Coins

The first U.S. Mint was established at Philadelphia in 1792. We have Thomas Jefferson to thank for the decimal system adopted for our coins, which replaced the pounds, shillings, and pence of the British system we had used previously. President Washington was too modest to have his face plastered on the coins, so we ended up with the goddess Liberty instead.

Among the first coins were some 10-cent pieces. A bad speller somewhere in the Mint struck 1,500 silver "half disme"; today, even a badly worn specimen goes for several thousand dollars. And your English teacher made you learn to spell.

Regular mintage began in 1793 with copper *Half Cents* and *Large Cents*; this was followed in succeeding years by silver *Half Dollars*, *Dollars*, silver *Half Dimes,* gold *Half Eagles* ($5 pieces), gold *Eagles* ($10 pieces), silver *Dimes* and *Quarter Dollars*, and *Quarter Eagles* ($2.50 gold pieces). All of these coins are scarce, especially in good condition.

This handsome gold Eagle coin is a worthy addition to any collection.

New U.S. coin designs were introduced in the 20th century: the *Lincoln Cent*, the *Buffalo Nickel*, the "Mercury" *Dime*, the *Liberty Standing Quarter Dollar,* and the *Peace Dollar*. Next came the *Washington Quarter Dollar* (1932), the *Jefferson Nickel* (1938), the *Roosevelt Dime* (1946), the *Franklin Half Dollar* (1948), the *Kennedy Half Dollar* (1964), the *Eisenhower Dollar* (1971), and the wildly unpopular *Susan B. Anthony Dollar* (1979). Currently, coins are struck at four U.S. Mints: Philadelphia, San Francisco, Denver, and West Point.

Many collectors start with familiar coins, like this Buffalo Nickel.

Don't Take Any Wooden Nickels: Starting a Coin Collection

In 1933, then-President Franklin D. Roosevelt passed legislation making it illegal for anyone to hoard gold. Too bad he didn't include copper. Today, over 30 billion pennies are "hiding" somewhere. In an attempt to coax some of them out of hiding, in 1974, some banks offered five to ten percent over face value for anyone turning in rolls of pennies. There are still millions of pennies missing. Most of them are probably under my sofa cushions and car seats.

Learn the Lingo
Coin collectors and scholars are called **numismatists**.

Coin collecting (in contrast to misplacing pennies) is an ancient hobby. Ancient Romans collected coins from even more ancient Romans; Popes in the 1200s and 1300s were avid coin collectors. The famous Flemish painter Rubens collected coins; so did John Quincy Adams and King Farouk of Egypt.

According to some estimates, about five million Americans collect coins today.

Heads or Tails? Learning the Parts of a Coin

Before you can start a collection, you have to know what you're collecting. Learn as much about coins as you can—it's the key to a successful collection. Let's start with a typical coin. Next is a list of the different parts of our average coin:

➤ **Obverse**—the front of the coin, the "heads" side.

➤ **Reverse**—the back of the coin, the "tails" side.

➤ **Device**—the major part of a coin's design.

➤ **Edge**—the thin, curved surface of a coin.

➤ **Rim**—the slightly raised border, just inside the edge.

➤ **Field**—the flat surface of a coin, between the ridge and devices.

➤ **Legend**—lettering (also called "inscription").

➤ **Exergue**—the area that contains the value and date.

➤ **Motto**—religious/patriotic phrase, such as "In God We Trust."

➤ **Mint mark**—letters or another symbol that shows where the coin was made.

➤ **Date**—the year, which does not have to be the date when the coin was struck.

➤ **Designer's initials**—optional, indicating the coin's designer.

Tools of the Trade

There *is* a cosmic balance in the world: A coin collection can cost a lot, but the tools you need to create it won't. Here are the basics to assemble for your coin collection:

1. Coin holders and albums for storage.

2. Magnifying glass to help you examine coins. A cheap magnifier may be worse than none at all, because it can cause distortions and color shifts. Go for a good one.

3. Cotton gloves, good for handling uncirculated coins.

4. Soft pad and coin trays. These make it easier for you to handle coins without causing damage.

5. Caliper, to use for measuring the diameter of a coin.

6. Gram scale or balance, used to weigh coins accurately.

Grading Coins

There is no universally accepted standard for grading coins, because grading is an art rather than a science. However, the following categories of currency grades are generally accepted in the industry. Knowing this system can help you assemble and refine your collection.

Grading	Meaning
Proof coins	The coins have a mirror-like finish and are struck from polished dies especially for collectors.
Uncirculated	Mint condition, apart from marks caused by the coins rubbing together.
Extra Fine	Almost perfect.

continues

continued

Grading	Meaning
Very Fine	Shows slight wear.
Fine	Shows signs of wear.
Very Good	The design shows clearly, but the detail is worn away.
Good	The coin is very worn, but the outline of the design is still visible.
Fair	A coin can just about not be identified.

A Penny Saved Is a Dollar Earned: Sources for Coins

You can get pennies from heaven, but there are more reliable sources. I recommend circulation, other collectors, and coin dealers. Let's take a look at the advantages and disadvantages of each method of getting coins.

Pennies from Heaven: Circulation

Circulation is the most convenient way to get coins. The drawback? Many coins are no longer circulated. For example, pre-1965 U.S. dimes, quarters, and half-dollars no longer circulate because their silver content (bullion value) is worth more than their face value (fiat value).

But it can be difficult even to get commonplace coins that have only face value. For example, "wheat cents," Lincoln pennies made before 1959, are rarely seen. Since billions of these pennies exist, their value is low, so hoarding them is irrational.

Want an easy entry to the world of coin collecting? Assemble an album of *Lincoln Cents* by date and mint mark. Start with 1959 coins. It's the least expensive set you can make and it will teach you a great deal about putting together a coin collection.

Coin Dealers

Coin dealers are the number one source of coins for serious collectors. Dealers have the knowledge and the coins. There is no shortage of coin dealers, so keep looking until you find someone you feel comfortable dealing with.

You can find reputable coin dealers by asking your fellow collectors who they like. I recommend that you first check out your local coin shop (listed in the Yellow Pages). It's convenient and you're more likely to develop a professional relationship that will help you in many ways. You'll get better discounts, hints, and perhaps even supplies, as your dealer will know what you need. In addition, a local coin dealer who knows you is more likely to buy back coins as you trade up. He or she may even be willing occasionally to buy less-desirable coins from you to keep your business.

Other Collectors

Network via the Web or work to find other people who share your interest in coin collecting. Tap into coin collectors' clubs; check the local community bulletin boards for news about coin collector clubs. Coin dealers can often put you in touch with other collectors; in fact, you may meet collectors at coin shops. Try attending some local conventions and coin shows, too. Many of the collectors you meet will be willing to trade coins with you and share their knowledge.

> **Tricks of the Trade**
> Feel free to bargain when you're buying big-ticket coins, but it's tacky to try to get a price reduction on a coin that costs a few dollars.

Taking Care of Your Collection

Since they are made of metal, coins are a lot less fragile than stamps, paper money, and the like. That's not to say that you can toss your coins around, however. Follow these guidelines for handling coins:

➤ Wash your hands before you handle your coins.

➤ Wear clean, white cotton gloves when you handle uncirculated coins.

➤ Handle only one coin at a time.

➤ Handle coins over a soft, clean surface, in case they slip and fall from your hands.

➤ Store coins in protective holders, either soft or hard plastic. Albums are also acceptable.

➤ Always handle coins by their edges, never by their flat surfaces.

➤ Keep coins in a cool, dry place. Coins may tarnish when they are stored in direct sunlight or by a heater. Plastic holders may damage coins that are exposed to heat.

> **Caveat Emptor**
> I have just one word of advice to you if you're thinking of cleaning your coins: Don't.

➤ Don't buff, rub, or puff on your coins.

The March of Dimes: Collection vs. Investment

If we could see into the future, we'd all have bought AT&T stock and given up red meat. (Well, maybe not the meat.) Who can tell which coins will be hot... and which ones will be stinkers? Remember this mantra: Age, rarity, and demand. And follow these guidelines:

➤ Remember to use common sense and evaluate your dealer's reputation and reliability *before* you send money or authorize a credit card transaction.

➤ Comparison-shop: visit at least three dealers before making any major purchase.

➤ Check prices in leading coin publications to make sure that you are not being overcharged.

➤ Beware of any "coin investment" promotion that promises "guaranteed profits," "limited quantity," "lowest price in the world," "limited sale time," or "guaranteed grading."

Caveat Emptor
Be especially leery of coins sold by telemarketing. Reputable coin dealers with high-quality goods don't have to smooth-talk you over the phone while you're trying to eat dinner.

You can check the value of a coin in the annual *A Guide Book of United States Coins* by R.S. Yeoman. Called the "Red Book" by those in the know, it is the standard U.S. coin catalog for determining retail coin prices, mintages, and popular collectible coins. Since the *Guide Book* is published only once a year, there will sometimes be a time lag if the coin market is changing rapidly, as it did during the 1970s.

Plunking Down Your Spare Change

OK, so your mother calls you up. She's at a garage sale pawing through a pile of coins. She wants to know if she should buy the nickel marked 1912D. It's only a dollar. The answer is an enthusiastic "Yes."

Connoisseur
In 1990, a woman searching through a potato field in East Hampton, New York, found a 1652 coin, with the simple "NE" design. She sold it for $75,000. I'll race you to the field. Worst-case scenario, at least we'll have some fresh spuds for dinner.

Below are some other coins to consider learning more about as possible investments. There are many, more; these are just a few suggestions. It's not likely that Mom will find these in a garage sale, but you never know.

➤ Scarce 20th-century coins such as *Mercury Dimes,* in uncirculated condition.

➤ *U.S. Bust* coins in high grades.

➤ *Indian Head* cents with low mintages, in uncirculated condition.

➤ Ancient coins in silver and gold (I know, this is a no-brainer; you already figured this one out for yourself).

➤ Nineteenth century European silver *crowns* or gold coins with small mintages, in uncirculated condition.

➤ "Key dates" in popular coin series, such as 1877 *Indian Head cent,* and an 1895 *Morgan Dollar.*

➤ *U.S. Pioneer* gold coins.

➤ Nineteenth century U.S. proof sets in uncirculated condition.

➤ *U.S. Half Cents* and *Large Cents* in uncirculated condition.

➤ Popular U.S. classics, such as *Barber coinage, Liberty Seated*, preferably in uncirculated condition.

> **Caveat Emptor**
> Coins are often and all-too-easily counterfeit. Beware. Check and double-check before you buy. Your best defense is doing your home-work.

A (highly collectible) penny for your thoughts?

The Least You Need to Know

➤ Repeat after me: Age, rarity, condition.

➤ Don't be penny-wise and pound foolish: Buy quality coins.

➤ Knowledge is power: Learn as much as you can about coins before you invest in them.

➤ Beware of fraud and counterfeit coins.

Chapter 11

~~Love~~ Money Makes the World Go 'Round

In This Chapter

➤ Learn the history of paper money

➤ Find out how to start and maintain a paper money collection

➤ Get to know each part of a bill

➤ Discover which U.S. and foreign issues are hot

It's been called *moolah, cash, bread, dough, lettuce, clams, bills, folding money, fins, ten-spots, C-notes, travelin' money, bucks,* and *greenbacks.* But no matter what we call it, we know what we mean—paper money. The word *money* comes from the Latin *moneta* (from *moneo,* "to warn"). Since ancient times, money has fascinated people like few other tangibles.

Compared to coin collecting, paper money collecting is a relatively recent hobby. People in the past looked upon paper money as something to spend, not admire—and besides, who had extra money to *collect?* The purchasing power of bank notes from the 1800s and earlier was so much greater than today's money that few people could afford to "hoard" any paper money at all, much less be crazy enough to collect it. Hoarding would lose you bank interest. If this wasn't bad enough, banks went under so fast—and so invalidated their paper money issue—that smart people spent their banknotes rather than collecting them.

In this chapter, you will learn the history of paper money. You'll find out which country invented the first paper money and when. Then we'll get a little cozy with some folding money, so you become familiar with each part of a bill. Next, I'll teach you how to start and maintain a paper money collection. Finally, you'll discover which U.S. and foreign issues are hot. Along the way, I'll show you how to take care of your collection, including storing, displaying, and insuring.

If These Bills Could Talk: A Brief History of Paper Money

Paper money is any type of currency printed on paper. Besides the traditional wood pulp and cloth rag, "paper" money has also been made from tree bark, leather, and silk. Paper money itself has no intrinsic value—after all, you can't eat it or wear it—but it can be converted (or *redeemed*) for metals that people perceive as valuable, such as gold and silver.

Connoisseur
Sweden was the first European country to have issued Bank Notes (bank-issued paper money, payable on demand, freely transferable, and non-interest bearing). The date was July 16, 1661.

The First Money

The world's first true paper money originated in China, but scholars argue over the specifics. Some claim that the first paper money was created as early as 650 A.D., during the Tang Dynasty, but none of those notes survive. Others contend that paper money was not freely circulated until the 9th century A.D., during the T'ang Dynasty, and they can buttress their claims with actual paper money from the era. Tang or T'ang: take your pick.

We're in the Money: The Development of Money in America

Visiting our shores in the early 19th century, Frenchman Alexis de Tocqueville commented on the relationship of Americans to their greenbacks: "I know of no country, indeed, where the love of money has taken stronger hold on the affections of men," he said. He was on to something.

Connoisseur
From the term *Bills of Credit* we got our slang term "bill"—a piece of American paper money.

American paper money dates from 1690, when the Massachusetts Bay Colony printed *Bills of Credit* to pay military expenses for the soldiers sent to fight against the French colonists. Other states quickly followed suit.

Colonial Currency arose from a constant shortage of coins and insufficient British paper money. In 1775, the Continental Congress issued its own paper money, in $1 to $30 denominations. Over $240 million in *Continentals* (as the money was called) was in circulation by 1779. Rising inflation and rampant counterfeiting made the bills virtually worthless; at the end of the Revolutionary War, they were redeemed at the rate of one cent on the dollar.

Alexander Hamilton organized the First Bank of the United States in 1791, and it soon issued its own notes. The bank was liquidated in 1811, leaving the country flooded with paper money from private, state-chartered banks. The Second Bank of the United States was founded in 1817. It was soundly managed and brought a uniform paper currency to the country by the 1820s.

The South Will Rise Again—But Its Money Won't

When South Carolina seceded from the Union in 1860, there were 3.5 million enslaved people living in the 11 states that would become the Confederate States of America. About 22.3 million people lived in the North. The Confederate government found it impossible to pass up the reckless printing of unbacked paper money to finance the war and so issued over $2 billion in Confederate Notes. Not a good move. By the end of the war, the money was so worthless that some Confederate soldiers refused to accept their pay in Confederate money, insisting on being paid in Union currency!

Big Deals

Want to collect *Confederate currency*? All types are available, making it easy to plan a long-term collecting strategy. Here are some guidelines:

1. Get to know which notes are rare and which ones are commonplace.

2. Buy notes that are in good condition.

3. Go for notes that give you a matched color set—all bright or all faded, for example.

4. Collect by issue (there are seven issues), denomination, type, variety, engraver, or vignette.

5. Watch for counterfeit Confederate notes. They make an interesting collection, if you are so inclined.

Dollars and Sense: Why Collect Paper Money?

There are so many things to collect—so why collect paper money? Here are my top five reasons.

Learn the Lingo
Collectors of paper money and banknotes are called **notaphilists**. The slang term "rag picker" is used by those philistines who can't spell **notaphilist**.

1. *It's beautiful.* A finely made banknote is a work of art.

2. *It's historic.* You can chronicle the rise and fall of empires on their paper money.

3. *It's valuable.* Nearly all paper money is worth something aside from its collectible value. Drop a few twenties on the sidewalk and you'll see what I mean.

4. *It's interesting.* You meet fascinating people through this collectible.

5. *It's fun.* Everyone likes money.

The Almighty Dollar

Quick—without looking—can you name the different parts of a dollar bill? In case you've been spending your time collecting (shudder) credit cards, here are the parts of a modern U.S. bank note:

➤ *National identification:* The issuing country's name. Our bills say "The United States of America" at the top of the note, on both sides.

➤ *Denomination:* The face value of the note. It appears on our money both in lettering and in numerals.

➤ *Vignette:* The scene portrayed on the note. It includes the portrait on the front and the central design (such as the building) on the back.

➤ *Portrait:* The picture of the famous American on the bill.

➤ *Treasury seal:* The seal of the U.S. Department of the Treasury.

➤ *Federal Reserve seal:* The seal of the Federal Reserve District Bank.

➤ *Signatures:* The written names of the authorizing officials. Modern bills are signed by the Secretary of the Treasury and the Treasurer of the U.S.

➤ *Serial numbers:* The official set of letters and numbers that designate the individual number of each note. The serial number is printed twice in green on modern Federal Reserve notes.

➤ *Series:* The year when the bill's design was adopted. It does not have to be the same year that the note was printed. When a small design change is made, a letter is added after the date.

➤ *Back plate number:* The small, green number on the back that is used to identify the printing plate. It is in the same shade of green as the entire reverse design.

➤ *Check letter, letter plate letter, quadrant number:* Identifies the printing plates and plate positions of the note.

➤ *Legal tender clause:* Wording that states that the money is legal. U.S. notes have this legal tender clause: "THIS NOTE IS LEGAL TENDER FOR ALL DEBTS, PUBLIC AND PRIVATE."

➤ *Type of note:* The words "Federal Reserve Note" in white letters at the top of the face.

➤ *Scrollwork:* The elaborate designs on the note's borders. Scrollwork is done to make it more difficult to counterfeit the note.

➤ *"Fort Worth Letters":* These are the "FW" letters that appear before the check letter and face plate number on notes made at the Fort Worth, Texas, Bureau of Engraving.

➤ *Inscribed security thread:* This is the clear polyester thread embedded in the paper. "USA" is printed on the thread, visible when you hold it up to the light. The security thread cannot be reproduced on modern color copiers.

➤ *Motto:* "IN GOD WE TRUST."

➤ *Microprinting:* This is the lettering "UNITED STATES OF AMERICA" printed over and over outside the portrait oval. You can see it only with a magnifying glass.

Big Deals

The Federal Reserve removes worn and mutilated notes from circulation. Every year, about six billion bills, weighing 7,000 tons and having a face value of $60 billion, are trashed. Between 1960 and 1990, about $474 billion in paper money was burned, shredded, or compacted because it was unfit for circulation.

Know Your Money

Before we go any further, here's a crib sheet for the most common circulating notes today. How many of these portraits and back designs can you name?

Denomination	Portrait	Back Design
$1	Washington	Great Seal of U.S.
$2	Jefferson	Signing of Declaration of Independence
$5	Lincoln	Lincoln Memorial
$10	Hamilton	U.S. Treasury Building
$20	Jackson	White House
$50	Grant	U.S. Capitol
$100	Franklin	Independence Hall
$500	McKinley	FIVE HUNDRED DOLLARS
$1,000	Cleveland	ONE THOUSAND DOLLARS
$5,000	Madison	FIVE THOUSAND DOLLARS
$10,000	Chase	TEN THOUSAND DOLLARS

Building Your Collection

Whether you collect rare bills or commonplace ones, domestic or foreign, old or new, some guidelines stay the same. Here they are:

- ➤ **Go for quality, not quantity.** You can learn a lot from a box of cheap bank notes, but you'll never lose sleep from buying the best.

- ➤ **Know the market.** This can help you avoid overpaying or getting stuck with a stinker.

- ➤ **Go for variety.** Avoid duplication, whenever possible. Variety helps you reduce risk.

- ➤ **Specialize.** Build your collection around a logical theme.

- ➤ **Avoid damaged money.** Don't shell out for notes that are severely damaged. There's a reason why they're cheap; they're not worth anything.

Top U.S. Notes for Collectors

You can start a collection of U.S. notes by reaching into your wallet, but if you wish to collect notes that are obsolete (no longer in circulation), you will have to get them from dealers or other collectors. Speak to fellow collectors to get the name of a reputable dealer. You can attend paper money shows and club meetings to find other collectors. The collector's rule holds here, too: Your cost will depend on the bill's rarity, condition, and demand. What follows is my list of the most popular types of U.S. bills for collectors.

1. **Colonial and Continental Currency.** The most valuable specimens are bright, flawless notes with broad margins.

2. **Broken Bank Notes.** Also known as *obsolete currency, wildcat bank notes, state and local currency,* and *private bank notes,* the bank notes from the 1800s are collected by time period, design, denomination, locale, etc.

3. **Confederate Currency.** Collected by state, denomination, vignette, locale, and so on, Confederate and Civil War currency affords a wide variety of collecting opportunities.

> **Connoisseur**
> Criswell's *Confederate and Southern States Currency* is **the** reference text for collectors of Confederate currency. It is available at most public libraries.

4. **U.S. Fractional Currency.** "Fractional Currency" refers to notes issued from 1862 to 1876, when people hoarded coins because of Civil War hysteria.

5. **Large Size Notes.** "Large Size Notes" refers to those notes issued from 1861 to 1929. Nicknamed "horse blankets" because of their larger size, these notes come in many different varieties, including Compound Interest Treasury Notes, Interest Bearing Notes, and Treasury Notes.

6. **Small Size U.S. Currency.** These are the bills we see everyday, first issued in 1929. There are over 1,000 different varieties, so specialization is the way to go unless your pockets are very deep.

7. **Rare American Colonial Notes.** All Colonial notes issued before 1755 are rare; so are Delaware notes from 1729 to 1739. Check with guidebooks and dealers for many other examples.

8. **Rare Obsolete Currency.** There is much commonplace obsolete U.S. currency available, but some collectors seek out only the rare notes. See a guidebook for specific examples.

9. **Rare U.S. Military Payment Certificates.** The real rarities are *Replacement Notes.* They do not have a suffix letter at the end of the numbers.

Hot Foreign Money

Does your taste run to French wines, Italian leather, and Swiss chocolate? Then foreign notes might be for you. You can collect foreign currency in many ways, including by country, region, political party, ruler, and chronological order. Some of the most popular notes are Australian pounds/shillings pre-1966, anything Fiji pre-World War II, and Russian notes from the Czarist empire. Below are some other foreign issues that are popular with collectors. There are many, many more hot issues, but space doesn't permit me to list them all.

1. **Canada.** Anything worth more than face value.

2. **China.** There are over 10,000 basic notes available. Be selective.

3. **France.** Notes from 1900–1950.

4. **India.** British colonial issues from the 1800s–1947 (the date of Indian independence) are desirable.

5. **Mexico.** Hot areas include provincial bank issues, revolutionary bank issues, and modern government issues.

6. **Norway.** Notes from the 1800s and earlier are very pricey; as a result, most collectors focus on modern issues.

Connoisseur
Hell's Notes are fake Chinese currency burned at a funeral to provide the deceased with money in the afterlife. The notes are *not* prized by collectors.

7. **Portugal.** Many collectors favor notes from 1900–1910, which show historical scenes.

8. **Switzerland.** All the money is valuable; what else would you expect from Europe's most stable country? Trilingual notes are expensive and much sought-after by collectors.

9. **Tibet.** Notes from 1912–1950, before the Chinese Communists seized control.

10. **Yugoslavia.** Notes from the 1920s–1930s for their beauty.

Money Matches Everything... Or, You Can't Go Wrong with Money

A 1985 Federal Reserve study concluded that about 75 percent of the circulating U.S. money (coins and paper money) cannot be located—amounting to $154 billion. Possibilities include foreign hoarding of American money, tax-evading cash transactions, and illegal drug deals. Numismatic collectors have very little of it.

Nonetheless, the 1970s saw a collecting boom in paper money. As speculative fever reached a pitch in the 1980s, paper money that had sold for $100 just a decade earlier was up to $1,000. How can you get into the action? First, let me teach you how to grade paper money.

Making the Grade

There is no universally accepted standard for grading money, since grading paper money is an art, not a science. Nevertheless, the following categories of currency grades are generally accepted. Knowing this can help you get your collection together.

Grade	Meaning
Gem Crisp Uncirculated	As fine as a newborn baby's bottom.
Uncirculated	May have a few smudges or bent corners.
Extremely Fine	Three light folds or one major crease, but no major stains or tears.
Very Fine	Several creases, some dirt and limpness.
Fine	Many folds and creases; some wear and tear.
Very Good	Shows much wear, but no missing pieces.
Good	As limp as a wet noodle; missing small pieces.
Fair	Missing large pieces, big holes, filthy.
Poor	Severely damaged—missing large pieces, stained, may be torn in half.

Cash on the Barrelhead

Now that you know how paper money is graded, how can you discover which bills are available to collect? Use the following list to see how dealers and collectors classify the availability of paper money. These classifications can help you locate the bills you want for your collection.

Classification	Definition
Unique	One of a kind
Very Rare	Offered for sale very infrequently, perhaps every five or ten years
Rare	Offered for sale a few times every year
Scarce	Missing from most routine collections, but usually available from major paper money conventions
Common	Easy to find—but may be very pricey!

151

Pass the Bucks: Handling and Preserving Money

Store your collection in protective plastic holders. You can get individual soft plastic holders for pennies each. Sealed on three sides, they are open at the fourth side so you can insert the bill. They come in many different sizes.

Prized notes belong in hard plastic holders. These holders consist of two clear panels fastened to each other with plastic screws, so that you can see both sides of the note. They are more expensive, but hey, your finest pieces deserve the best.

Tricks of the Trade
Collectors sometimes iron their money to smooth out wrinkles. Ironing can scorch the paper or make it as shiny as a cheap pair of pants. Ironing can also make your bills brittle. If you cannot resist the urge to press, place the bill between two smooth pieces of cloth or blotting paper. Iron both sides, but never touch the iron directly to the money. Or you could come and do my shirts. They are really piling up.

Wash and Wear Money

Should you clean your money? When in doubt, don't. Unless you're a professional paper cleaner and restorer, less is more. You can always do more, but it may be impossible to undo what you have already done.

Further, make sure that everything you do can be reversed—that the bank note is not permanently changed by your actions. I recommend that you practice your cleaning and repairing techniques on pocket currency (you know, the stuff we use every day) before you try it on a collectible. You may even wish to practice on a less valuable note of the same period before you try your technique on an especially valuable piece.

Start small. For example, you may wish to try to erase a small pencil mark before you attempt to tape a large hole. Not that I think you should repair anything large. Leave it to the experts. They have to make a living, too.

Strut Your Stuff... Not

Many old paper notes are delicate because of chemically-destructive inks, thin paper, and wear and tear. Even notes in good condition can be damaged in many ways. Follow these guidelines to keep your collection in optimal condition:

1. As you learned in previous chapters, humidity spells danger for all paper collectibles. Don't stash your paper money collection in the freezer in an old head of lettuce. Instead, store your collection away from high humidity sources.

2. Keep your collection away from direct sunlight, because light causes inks to fade.

3. Critters love the taste of money. Termites, silverfish, mice, and bookworms will eat up your money faster than inflation. If you are prone to creature features, invest in a quality exterminator.

4. Store paper money above the floor, away from sources of dust: heaters, windows, bookcases. Dust off your albums before you handle them.

5. I know your money never seems to stretch far enough, but avoid tug-of-war with your bills. Be gentle when you pass a note to someone else. Also, don't force notes into holders, and store currency albums upright.

6. Air out your collection on a regular basis to prevent mold and mildew from forming.

7. A great deal of money has been destroyed by fire. To prevent this from happening to your collection, store your paper money away from fireplaces and heaters. You may also wish to store valuable specimens in fire-resistant containers or a bank safe deposit box.

8. Wash your hands before you handle your money. The natural oils on your hands, combined with lotions, dirt, and cosmetics, spell trouble for paper money. Of course, paper money was meant to be handled, you protest. Yes, I answer, but when you collect valuable examples of paper money, you want to protect them.

Penny Wise, Pound Foolish

You've invested considerable amounts of time and money in your collection, so it would be foolish not to store it properly. It is neat to have your paper money at home to show off to friends, relatives, and the occasional burglar. Resist the temptation to flash your wad. Paper money is easy to hide, but if you keep valuable notes at home, consider insuring them or storing them in a safe.

All safes are not safe. Know that a burglar-resistant safe is not the same thing as a fire-resistant safe. A burglar-resistant safe has thick walls, a tough combination lock, and is often bolted to the floor. But it may not be fire-resistant. Some fire-resistant safes have heat-resistant walls, but others spray chemicals or water that sounds the death knell to valuable paper money. Consider fully insuring your collection and storing it in a burglar-resistant safe.

Caveat Emptor
You still need insurance if you store your collection in a bank safe deposit box. The contents of a safe deposit box are rarely insured by the bank.

Bank storage is another option. As an added incentive, many bank vaults are climate controlled, making them the ideal environment for paper money. If you go this route, rent a safe deposit box large enough to comfortably accommodate your collection and perhaps even leave a little room for growth.

The Least You Need to Know

➤ When selecting bills to add to your collection, follow the collector's mantra: *rarity, condition, demand.*

➤ Like any paper collectible, money requires special handling and storage.

➤ A fool and his money are soon parted.

Part 3
Hot Stuff

Thimble Collectors International (TCI) recently held its 10th Biennial Convention in Bloomington, Minnesota. The convention featured seminars on a wide variety of topics as well as a sales mall where conference attendees could shop for that special addition to their collection.

Thimbles don't do it for you? How about toothpick holders? The annual convention of the National Toothpick Holder Collectors Society was held this summer in Eugene, Oregon. Is glass your thing? Then consider dropping by the Westmoreland Glass Society's annual meeting. They promise glass and a good time.

Thimbles, toothpick holders, glass, books, china, toys, beer bottles, household items, clocks, quilts, radios, records, tools—collecting offers myriad fabulous everyday objects. Take your pick. So let's go shopping already.

Chapter 12

Book Learnin'

In This Chapter

➤ Learn the history of books

➤ Discover which books make the best collectibles

➤ Find out how to build a book collection

I remember the time I snagged what I gleefully assumed was a treasure trove of early 19th century books. My source was a garage sale, no less. Certain that the books were extremely valuable, I called an expert book dealer, made up a list of the books, and planned for my retirement in Barbados. The dealer was gentle when he broke the news that my "treasure" was trash. He was right—no one wanted my old books. I couldn't even recoup my initial (admittedly modest) investment. I finally ended up donating the books to the library. And I'm sure they only took them because I'm on the Board of Trustees.

This experience taught me that as with any antique, age is not enough. Desirability and the law of supply and demand set the price for old books. With the exception of *incunabula* (books printed before 1501), a book must have much more than age going for it to be a valuable collectible.

Book and manuscript collecting is an area that requires a whole lot of studying if you want to keep up with the latest and greatest. That's what this chapter is for. Here, you'll get a capsule summary of the development of printing. Then I'll tell you all about Bibles, the highest profile book ever printed. Nothing like a little good press.

Next, you will learn all about first editions, one of the most potentially rewarding areas of book collecting. Along the way, I cover children's books, atlases, and other intriguing collectible types of books. Finally, I'll explain how you can build your own book collection. You'll find out what books to collect and what books to avoid—like those with dry rot, fading, and mold.

This original copy of Mark Twain's Life on the Mississippi *features 14K gold leaf on the cover.*

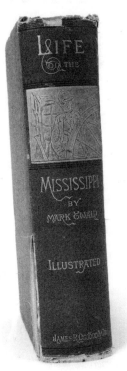
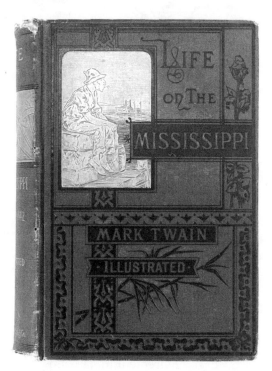

Book 'em, Danno

The success of printing, mass production at its most noble, has led to the survival of a vast body of collectible materials. The printing revolution of the mid 1400s was the result of the invention of movable type, a method of mass-producing individual metal letters that could be rearranged into any combination and used over and over again. Movable type made it vastly easier to edit and correct texts. Its big buzz, however, was its speed at printing pages. Johann Gutenberg, a German who lived from around 1399 to 1468, gets credit where credit is due.

As you learned earlier, books produced during the first 50 years of printing are called *incunabula*, which literally means "in swaddling clothes." Most of these books look very much like the manuscripts from which they had been copied because of the style of the type.

Soon, printing presses were established in all the important commercial centers. Vellum, calfskin, lambskin, or kidskin treated for use as a writing surface, cost too much to use to feed all these presses. As a result, the paper makers put the pedal to the metal to keep the presses rolling. In 1400, about 20 percent of all books were produced on paper rather than vellum; a century later, the number had risen to 50 percent. The durability of early paper has ensured that many examples of early printing still exist. Fortunately, some still go uncollected because they have yet to be sufficiently regarded as valuable. Which ones are they? I can keep a secret.

It's What's Inside that Counts

In the early years, most books were of a religious nature. By the middle of the 1600s, however, historical, scientific, and fictional works became far more popular. Along the way, printing became publishing and an industry was born. Book reviews, book advertisements, book catalogs, and many related products were offshoots. By the early 19th century, the entire printing process had become mechanized and production soared.

Increased literacy and disposable income resulted in the beginning of the throwaway age: Cheap, discardable books became the rage with the masses. In 1935, Allen Lane founded the Penguin paperback series in England, making quality books available at little cost. The paperback revolution followed on its heels.

How Not to Get Rich Quick Collecting Books

For some odd reason, Americans think that more is better. This is especially noticeable at salad bars and diners, but it spills over to book collecting as well. Here's the faulty reasoning I hear all the time: "If a specific book is a best seller, it must be a hot collectible." Say it ain't so, Joe. It ain't. More copies published is not better, especially when it comes to collecting books.

Kid 'n' Play

For example, take an especially fertile field of book collecting: children's books. Books specifically for children were rare until the 1750s, and those that were published tended to be overly educational and didactic in tone. Many were *chapbooks*, little illustrated books sold by itinerant peddlers.

In 1744, John Newberry began publishing children's books lite: more entertainment, less moralizing. The 1800s saw a slew of children's books, including English translations of the Grimm Brothers' fairy tales (1824), Hans Christian Andersen's *Wonderful Stories for Children* (1846), and Lewis Carroll's *Alice in Wonderland* (1865). But many people see the early 20th century as the golden age of children's books. Glittering examples include Beatrix Potter's *The Tale of Peter Rabbit* (1901), Arthur Rackham's gorgeous illustrations for *Peter Pan in Kensington Gardens* (1906), and Edmund Dulac's magnificent pictures in *Fairy Tales* (1910).

Picture books for small children are among the most difficult items to locate in fine condition because their young owners were rarely wearing kid gloves when they did their reading. As a result, *some* types of children's books are eagerly sought by collectors. Note that the word *some* is in italics.

Here's a list of the top ten best-selling children's books of all time:

Title	Number Sold
1. *The Tale of Peter Rabbit*	9,000,000
2. *Green Eggs and Ham*	6,500,000
3. *One Fish, Two Fish, Red Fish, Blue Fish*	6,200,000
4. *The Outsiders*	6,000,000
5. *Hop on Pop*	5,900,000
6. *Dr. Seuss's ABCs*	5,800,000
7. *The Cat in the Hat*	5,600,000
8. *Are You There, God? It's Me, Margaret*	5,500,000
9. *The Wonderful Wizard of Oz*	5,200,000
10. *Charlotte's Web*	4,900,000

This list doesn't even include earlier kiddie best-sellers that have long been out of copyright, such as *Little Women* and *Tom Sawyer*. Zillions of them are in circulation.

If this many copies of each book have been printed, how can any one copy be worth much? It can't. And it never will be. That's why specialization was invented. Let's take a look at a very special book: the Bible.

A Good Book—But Not a Good Investment: Bibles

The Good Book has many things going for it, but collectible value isn't one of them. There are two factors working against making the Bible a collector's item. First, the Bible is the most frequently printed book, which keeps the price down. The Bible has been published in more editions and in more countries than any other book. Second, millions of copies survive because no one is willing to destroy any. Thus, large supply equals low collector value. However, there is a ray of hope: early Bibles. Some of these are very valuable. The following tips may help you if collecting Bibles is your area of interest.

➤ **Age.** Rule of thumb: To be of interest to a book collector, a Bible must go back to the 18th century, when the early presses and wooden type were still used. An older, handwritten, and hand-illuminated Bible is of much greater value, of course.

➤ **Photo op.** Bibles with woodblock pictures are valuable, more for the pictures than the Bible itself. If the pictures were colored by hand, the value is even greater.

➤ **Illumination.** Among the most valuable Bibles are those with hand illumination done by painting and gilding, painstaking work most often undertaken by monks. "Illumination" includes elaborate illustrations of initial letters, page borders, and the like.

➤ **Bible Bonanza.** A Bible that has been both hand-written and hand-illuminated is the Holy Grail of all Bibles. Even single pages from such Bibles sell for staggering sums, which is unfortunate because it causes the Bible to be torn apart.

➤ **Errata.** Other rare Bibles include those that have errors in print. For example, there is the so-called "Place Makers Bible" that states, "Blessed are the place makers, for they shall be called the children of God." (If I have to explain the error, you don't deserve to find the Bible.) The "Place Makers Bible" is otherwise known as the Geneva Bible, second edition, published in England in 1561–62. You might chance upon the Vinegar Bible ("The Parable of the Vinegar" instead of "The Parable of the Vineyard") and the Basket Bible, which had a whole basketful of errors.

Caveat Emptor
Religious books in general are poor collectibles and usually sell for only a few dollars each.

Leader of the Pack: First Editions

An *edition* is all copies of a book printed at any time from one setting-up of type; an *impression*, in contrast, comprises the entire number of copies of that edition printed at any one time. The distinction seems picky but it's crucial for the collector. Say that a mistake is found while a book is being printed. The mistake is corrected on the spot and the printing and binding continues. The first books to roll off the presses will have the mistake—*but the other copies won't.* Ironically, a collector will prefer the first edition over the second, even though the first contains an error. Since it's the first, it's more valuable to these collectors. First place works in families, too. I'm the oldest of all my siblings; that's why mom always loved me best.

First editions of books by noted authors are a "must have" for some book collectors. "First edition" alone is not enough to make a book a collectible—especially since the first edition might very well be the last edition. The author must be famous, the book important, and its condition excellent. Here are some notable examples of pricey first editions:

➤ F. Scott Fitzgerald's *The Beautiful and the Damned* (1922)

➤ William Faulkner's *The Wild Palms* (1939)

➤ Theodore Dreiser's *Sister Carrie* (1900)

➤ George Orwell's *1984* (1949)

Each of these first editions is special in some way. For example, the first edition of *Sister Carrie* is valuable because it was suppressed by the publisher on the grounds of obscenity. Dreiser was forced to rewrite the book and change the ending. Only recently has the original version been republished.

Let's assume that you're at a garage sale or a flea market, nice places to find (potentially) valuable first editions. How should you go about determining whether the books you've grabbed from that poor little old lady have any collectible value? Ask yourself these four questions:

1. Is it a real first edition?

2. Is the author or illustrator hot?

3. Is the book in collectible condition (including the dust jacket)?

4. Are there other features that make the book a desirable collectible (such as being a limited edition/print run)?

Identifying a First Edition

How can you tell a first edition? First editions, like a ripe melon, are not always easy to distinguish. On a very lucky day, you might get a break because the copyright page will actually say "first edition." If this happens, go and buy a lottery ticket right away. Sometimes, the date is clearly printed on the title page—and it matches the copyright on the reverse side. In these instances, buy another lottery ticket. Hey, you never know.

There are other clear ways to identify first editions. Some publishers will often indicate which print run the book came from by a code. Some publishers use the numeral system to denote the run, printing numbers 1 to 10, for example. As each successive printing is done, a numeral is dropped to indicate which printing the book comes from. In the past, though, some editions were not marked. Others have been found marked with the first year the book was published, although they may have been issued years later from a new print run.

With many books, however, you have to do some serious detective work to identify the edition. A detail about the color of the binding or a misspelled word (not corrected until the second edition) can help you authenticate a first edition. Bibliographies are available that list these important points.

Who's Hot... And Who's Not?

First editions by well-known authors such as Nobel laureates Saul Bellow, Ernest Hemingway, William Faulkner, and Toni Morrison are desired by some collectors. But how about the lesser-known writers whose books may be far more valuable because they are suddenly politically correct? Unfortunately, there's no substitute for hitting the books. You have to study dealers' catalogs and get to know your authors. Once is not enough, either. You have to keep up with the trends here; an author who's hot one year may very well be tepid the next.

> **Learn the Lingo**
> Book dealers and collectors refer to the characteristics that identify a first edition as **points**.

> **Caveat Emptor**
> Authors love selling their tomes to book clubs because they bring in big bucks, but collectors shun these editions as worthless first edition wannabees. If you see the logo from the Literary Guild or the Book-of-the-Month Club, pass the book on by.

While there are many 20th-century illustrators popular with the book collecting crowd, the following lists notes some of the most popular ones. I make no claims for completeness; and remember, the list changes with shifts in public taste.

Edwin Abbey	W.W. Denslow
Thomas Hart Benton	Maynard Dixon
Pierre Bonnard	Edmund Dulac
Frances Brundage	Harrison Fisher
Marc Chagall	Thomas Fogarty
Warren Chappell	A.B. Frost
Howard Chandler Christy	Edward Gorey
Walter Crane	Kate Greenaway
Salvador Dalí	Thomas Hanford
Edwin Deakin	Maude Humphrey

Peter Hurd	Norman Rockwell
Rockwell Kent	Charles M. Russell
Robert Lawson	Frank Schoonover
Henri Matisse	Maurice Sendak
Alfred Miller	Kate Sewell
Gerald Nailor	Ernest Shepard
Maxfield Parrish	Jessie Wilcox Smith
Edgar Samuel Paxson	Ben Stahl
Pablo Picasso	Arthur Szyk
Beatrix Potter	Garth Williams
Howard Pyle	Andrew Wyeth
Arthur Rackham	N.C. Wyeth
Frederic Remington	

Memorize the preceding list so you know which book illustrators are the most highly collectible.

You can find out more about collectible books by consulting one or more of the reputable price guides. I recommend *The Official Price Guide to Old Books* (House of Collectibles, Florida). As with all price guides, get the most recent edition possible. This guide has a 1994 copyright.

Dressed for Success: Collectible Condition

The presence of the original dust jacket often makes the difference between a book being a collectible or just another (dusty) old book. Without a dust jacket, a 20th-century first edition is worth only a fraction of its dust-jacketed value.

Also check the book for signs of wear. Is it ripped, stained, damaged? Does it look like it's been through the Crimean War? Check the hinges and spine, too. Are they overly worn? About to give up the ghost? Did Johnny write in the book? Unless Johnny happens to be John Steinbeck, John Fitzerald Kennedy, or John the Baptist, the book's a goner.

Collectors expect first editions published after 1950 to be in very good condition because they are not that old.

Gilding the Lilly

A first edition signed by the author is one of the book collector's ultimate trophies. Signed books are especially valuable if they are signed by an author reluctant to autograph books—even if the book isn't a first edition. Autographs by J.D. Salinger and Vladimir Nabokov, for example, are highly prized by collectors because they are so rare.

First editions that contain manuscript emendations in the author's own handwriting are highly prized. So are books with presentation inscriptions ("Mary— Never forget Paris—Ernie").

> **Tricks of the Trade**
> When you buy a new book today, try to have the author sign it whenever possible. This enhances the value of the book immediately, and may even elevate it to collector's status down the road.

Hot Tip: Old Atlases

One area of book collecting that commands steady interest is atlases produced in the 1800s. Invaluable as a means of researching American history, old atlases are of special interest to the residents of the areas covered in the books. Lawyers also seek out old atlases for the regions in which they ply their trade, since genealogies, property lines, and past ownership of items are often revealed in these books.

Old atlases also have the advantage of being easy to collect since you can learn all you need to know fast. After all, there are usually a very limited number of old atlases produced for each region. Keep in touch with your local book dealer to find out what atlases are in demand. With this collectible, age helps value because not many copies of a specific printing survive.

> **Caveat Emptor**
> Be sure to find out which old atlases are bring reprinted, since reprinting seriously lowers the value of this collectible.

Building a Book Collection

Savvy collectors know that some books are more desirable than others. Next is a list of the five most expensive books and manuscripts ever sold at auction.

Book or Manuscript	Price
The Gospels of Henry the Lion, c. 1173-75 Sotheby's, London, December 6, 1983	$10,841,000
The Gutenberg Bible, 1455 Christie's, New York, October 22, 1987	$5,390,000
The Northumberland Bestiary, c. 1250-60 Sotheby's, London, November 29, 1990	$5,049,000
Autographed manuscript of nine symphonies by Mozart, c. 1773-1774 Sotheby's, London, May 22, 1987	$3,854,000
Audubon's *Birds of America*, 1827-38 Sotheby's, New York, June 6, 1989	$3,600,000

Look for copies of these books the next time you clean the attic.

In the meantime, here are some collectible books you can afford:

➤ *Little Red Riding Hood*? An 1857 edition is about $300.

➤ A signed first edition of James Kelman's *How Late It Was, How Late* goes for under $25.

➤ A 1979 edition of R.L. Stevenson's *Treasure Island*, *Kidnapped*, or *The Black Arrow* sells for under $10.

➤ Want to get in on the cutting edge of book collecting? Consider the *Dr. Who Annual* and a *Lion King* book and tape set. Both are under $10.

➤ How about a set of bookbinder's brass letters and numbers made in the 19th century? They will set you back less than $100.

If These Books Could Talk (and Some Can)

You're a grownup. That means you can stay up past 10:00 (if you can keep your eyes open), eat ice cream before dinner, and collect whatever books tickle your fancy. Some collectors buy books they want to read; others look for investment-grade books. Valuable books do share some common traits: They tend to be rare, limited, old, and in great condition. But what can you do if your tastes are rich but your purse is poor? Below is a list of some collectible categories of books that are still affordable—around $100 to $400—but likely to rise in value with time.

➤ Old books on art

➤ Old books on antiques

➤ Old auction catalogs

➤ Books about native heroes

➤ Diaries

➤ Sailors' logs

➤ Captain's logs

➤ Nonfiction books on hunting

➤ Nonfiction books on fishing

➤ Nonfiction books on the military

➤ Nonfiction books on sports

Caveat Emptor
In general, avoid old school books. They have very little value to most collectors. There's a lesson here somewhere.

Whatever books you buy, remember your collector's mantra: *condition, condition, condition.*

To Each His Own Taste

Book collectors generally limit their collection by concentrating on categories, such as genre, author, illustrator, or period. The most popular genres are as follows: horror, biography, science fiction, crime, fiction, fantasy, history, and erotica.

Serious Shopping

Where you shop for books depends on your collection. Lower-priced collectible books are readily available at garage sales, flea markets, estate and tag sales, and library book sales. Most of the real finds have probably already been located by savvy collectors who zipped through the sale before you were even in the shower, but you may still find something to your liking. Avoid first editions that were library books because the library stamps and card jackets make the book far less valuable.

If your collection is more upscale, consider shopping through mail order or from a reputable book dealer. Most book dealers feel that if they cannot charge at least $25 to $50 for a first edition, it is not worth listing in their catalog. Secondhand book stores are usually stocked to the rafters, but the condition of the books is often a problem. The books have usually doffed their jackets and may have been annotated by previous owners.

Big Deals

Some 19th-century books are collected for the woodblock prints they contain. In some cases, the prints are cut out and individually framed because they are worth far more money than the book. Some of these woodblock prints or steel engravings are the only record of certain scenes executed by famous illustrators. Look for prints by Winslow Homer and Frederick Remington.

The Least You Need to Know

➤ Age alone does not make a book valuable to a collector.

➤ Bibles and other religious books are rarely hot collectibles.

➤ First editions are valuable only if they were written by a hot author or illustrator, still have their dust jackets, and are in good condition.

➤ When you are collecting books, round up the usual suspects: rarity, condition, and age.

Chapter 13

The China Syndrome

In This Chapter

➤ Get a brief history of china

➤ Discover the similarities and differences of earthenware, stoneware, bone china, porcelain, and ironstone

➤ Learn which china is collectible and which is not

➤ Find out about fakes, reproductions, forgeries, and absurd mistakes

German alchemist Johann Bottger (1682–1719) was imprisoned in Albrechtsburg fortress in 1703 by August the Strong, elector of Saxony, because he had failed in his promise to make gold. Bottger won his freedom by promising to make porcelain instead. At that time, porcelain had to be imported at great cost because only the Chinese knew how to produce it.

By 1708, Bottger had the recipe perfected and so began producing high-quality, marketable porcelain at Meissen, near Dresden. Today, the town remains a center for the production of porcelain. Now the most valuable Meissen pieces, dating from the early years of production, fetch more than $200,000 each.

The first objects made entirely by people, ceramics are still one of the most valued of all collectibles. Because the basic materials—clay and water—were readily available, ceramic objects are found in virtually all cultures.

This chapter starts with a brief history of china. Then I'll teach you everything you always wanted to know about earthenware, stoneware, bone china, porcelain, and ironstone but were afraid to ask. Next, I will list and describe the hottest china collectibles. You'll learn what manufacturers and pieces are the most eagerly sought-after. Finally, you''ll discover how to sort out china fakes, frauds, reproductions, and dopey errors. I''ll even explain why china is called "china."

Shards of History

The first ceramic pieces were pots, made by coiling tubes of clay around a center base. Fired (or baked for hardening) at a low heat, they were as fragile as a teenager's ego. As a result, only shards survive. The potter's wheel, invented in Egypt around 1500 B.C., called for better clay and firing techniques, resulting in sturdier pots. Pottery was manufactured extensively through the ancient world.

As you learned in the opening of this chapter, it was not until the early 18th century that Europeans cracked the china code. Americans were too busy building a country to make fine plates: As a result, until the mid-1800s, almost all china in America was imported. But even after American china gained a foothold on our shores, French, English, and German china remained so popular that Americans never really became big names in the china biz. Even today, most fine china collected in America is imported.

Kissing Cousins: Earthenware, Stoneware, Bone China, Ironstone, and Porcelain

The type of ceramics is determined by the composition of clay and the way it is prepared, the temperature at which it is fired, and the glazes used. Each of the most common types of ceramics is described next.

Salt of the Earth: Earthenware

Earthenware is porous pottery, usually fired at the lowest kiln temperature (900°–1200°C/ 1652°–2192°F). To be made waterproof, it must be glazed. Nearly all ancient, medieval, Middle Eastern, and European ceramics are earthenware—as are most of our everyday dishes.

American art pottery runs the gamut from hand-made one-of-a-kind treasures to mass-produced items with the look of individually crafted pieces. Like many sizzlin' collectibles, some art pottery that is highly valued today sold for very little when it was first produced. As it emerged from attics and basements, it was dusted off and promptly flew into the eager arms of collectors. Museum exhibitions and scholarly articles in glossy antiques magazines have alerted all but the most obtuse collectors to the value of fine art pottery.

You can still get small art pottery bowls for around $50, but prices rise steeply after that. A 5-inch vase with a matte green glaze goes for $1,870; a pair of 6-inch signed Rhead candlesticks sell for around $1,430.

Be aware that many long-established potters and workshops have keen local followings but may not be known across the country. In addition, regional potters who are starting out today may soon be highly regarded.

Next is a small list of American art potters whose work is actively collected. The list is meant as a guideline to get you started; there are far more potters whose work is remarkable but space limitations prevented their inclusion here. Since collectors of art pottery often favor examples from their region, I have listed the potters by their state.

➤ Arkansas: Niloak

➤ Colorado: Van Briggle

➤ Louisiana: Newcomb

➤ Massachusetts: Dedham Pottery, Grueby

➤ Minnesota: Red Wing

➤ New Jersey: Fulper Pottery

➤ New York: Buffalo Pottery, Deldare Ware

➤ Ohio: Cowan Pottery; Hull; Knowles, Taylor, and Knowles; McCoy; Rookwood; Roseville; Shawnee; Weller

Tin-glazed earthenware (earthenware with a white glaze) dates from the 700s; by the early 1200s, it was being produced in Spain. Here are the most common types of tinware:

➤ **Delft.** Italian immigrants settled in the Netherlands in 1508 and within a few years began producing a tin-glazed earthenware in Antwerp. Many towns, including Delft, had factories making this earthenware. In the early 1600s, two ships arrived in Amsterdam groaning with piles and piles of Chinese blue-and-white porcelain. Unlike many other types of ceramics discussed here, several Delft factories actually stopped production in the early 1800s, and Delft was not revived until the late 1800s.

The difference in value between 18th century Delft and later Delft is astonishing—an early Delft piece is worth more than six times the value of a modern piece of the same size and design. For example, a modern Delft ashtray shaped like a shoe sells for under $10; a modern butter dish with a lid is valued at $16.50—but a signed 9-inch 1750 Delft bowl sells for $3,450. The 18th-century pieces are extremely valuable, even in imperfect condition. Pieces marked with the word "Delft" or "Holland" are modern vintage and thus far more affordable.

➤ **Faience.** Faience, characterized by a wide variety of highly colored designs, took off in 1661, when a group of Dutch religious refugees in Germany opened the first faience factory. There, it was called "fayence." A 4-inch, two-handled bowl made in France is valued at $55; a 10-inch figurine sells for $195.

➤ **Majolica (or "Maiolica").** In Majolica, painting over a white glaze was further developed, in yellow, orange, green, black, turquoise, blue, and purple. Many times a transparent overglaze was then added, as well as incised and molded-relief decoration. These wares were widely exported via Majorca (hence the term "Majolica") to Italy. They are distinguished by their bright colors and intricate patterns. A small shell-shaped bowl fetched about $170; a signed cake plate, $625.

➤ **Quimper.** First made in the 1600s, pieces frequently seen now date from the present day. You can identify Quimper ware by its bright paintings of French peasants and farm animals. Quimper is more popular today than ever; older Quimper commands top dollar, depending on condition, design, and the specific piece. Be aware that there is a "reproduction" line of Quimper that imitates the peasant motif. A small Quimper ashtray will set you back a mere $15; a pair of coasters, $58; a large signed platter, $3,250.

Stoneware

Stoneware, fired at higher kiln temperatures, is water-resistant and much more durable than earthenware. It was developed toward the end of the 1300s in Germany. It does not need a glaze. Some of the earliest stoneware was manufactured at Siegburg. Marked by an elegant form and distinctive, light color, this type includes slender jugs and pewter-covered tankards. Cologne was an important center of production in the 1700s, noted for its bulbous jugs decorated with a bearded face. One of the most famous types of stoneware is Wedgwood.

Josiah Wedgwood is considered the founding father of industrial English pottery, and rightly so. Born in Staffordshire in the mid-18th century, Wedgwood stoneware was inspired by a revival of ancient classical Greek and Roman art. Today the term "Wedgwood" is associated almost exclusively with blue-and-white jasperware (hard, fine-grained stoneware). Nonetheless, he also perfected Queenware (a creamware), variegated ware, pearlware, black basalts, cane ware (straw-colored) and all kinds of colored and plain stoneware. Fortunately for collectors, he marked his products clearly. A Wedgwood ashtray is valued at around $38; an 18th-century black basalt bowl, $290. Signed, a 1925 bowl is worth $3,700.

Roll 'Dem Bones: Bone China

In the mid-18th century, English potters invented *bone china*, a somewhat harder ware that gained whiteness, transclucency, and stability through the inclusion of calcium phosphate in the form of calcined (fired, chemically altered) oxbones. Below are some of the most highly collectible types of bone china:

➤ Anysley

➤ Wedgwood

➤ Lenox

Always a Bridesmaid, Never a Bride: Ironstone

Ironstone (a.k.a. semiporcelain) used to play Betty to china's Veronica. But with rare porcelain (such as patterns decorated with rich cobalt blue and gold borders) out of reach of the average collector, ironstone has become a hot collectible. Extremely fine 19th-century English ironstone such as Mason's is much sought-after, especially the large serving pieces. The following quality rankings can help you rank the value of ironstone pieces:

Excellent Quality	Fine Quality	Good Quality
Dansk	Fiesta	Homer Laughlin
Coalport	Franciscan	Hull Pottery
Mason's	Metlox	Johnson Brothers
Villeroy & Boch	Russel Wright	Mikasa
Wedgwood	Vernon	Pfaltzgraff
		Sango

American ironstone varies greatly in quality and rarity. As a result, there is a wide range of value and desirability. For the purpose of collecting, buy what you like and enjoy it. For the purpose of investing, buy items of the finest quality in the best condition that you can afford. Check in two or three price guides to get an idea of the current value of each piece. Here are some of the most popular English and American varieties of ironstone.

➤ **Lusterware.** Lusterware originated in the ancient East, and the technique spread to Italy and Spain in the 1300s and 1400s. Today, most collectors are familiar with

English lusterware from the 1800s. Luster is created by applying a thin layer of a precious metal to pottery. Using gold results in a "luster" of copper to pink. Platinum yields a silver luster. Figure on spending around $150 for a good-quality piece of lusterware.

The market was flooded with cheap copies, so if the real thing tickles your fancy, check the bottom to see if the piece is marked "England" or "Made in England." That's a good sign that you may have the real McCoy. Older luster tends to be more translucent and thinner; in comparison, the newer stuff sometimes looks like it was slapped on with a trowel.

➤ **Staffordshire.** Staffordshire is a region in England where pottery factories abounded in the 1700s and 1800s. Originally, the term "Staffordshire" was used to refer to the ironstone produced by Ralph and Aaron Wood. Now, however, the term is used to indicate any English figurine or decorative ironstone that looks vaguely "19th-century," or at least our idealized version of bucolic British life. Historical view plates are a perennial winner; people must like to get a glimpse of jolly ol' England under their oatmeal.

Caveat Emptor
American china companies freely stole (oops… *reworked*) European names and hallmarks. For example, the Chelsea Pottery Company of West Virginia adopted its name from the famous 18th-century Chelsea porcelain manufacturer in England. American companies also used European hallmarks such as the lion, crown, horse, and unicorn. Check your guidebooks carefully to identify pieces of china.

➤ **A Potted Portrait: Toby jugs.** The common toby jug is thought to immortalize a legendary drinker, Harry Elwes, who was said to have downed 16,000 pints of beer without eating in between. An unlikely tale, but when Elwes died in 1761, the beer industry and Staffordshire potter Ralph Wood began making portrait jugs. He named the jugs "Toby Fillpot," which may have been Elwes's nickname and is a character in the ballad "Little Brown Jug." The true toby jug was a fat, old man seated on a chair and holding a pint pot. A "Frowning Man" Toby jug is valued at $24; a jug showing Mamie Eisenhower goes for $50.

Now there are hundreds of varieties of toby jugs with portraits of famous people, such as Ben Franklin and Winston Churchill. Scads of fakes were produced.

Putting on the Ritz: Porcelain

The discovery of *kaolin* (china clay) in the 7th century A.D. enabled people to make a hard, white, translucent china that has a musical ring when tapped: porcelain. Collector alert: There are two kinds of porcelain: *hard-paste* (porcelain made with kaolin as its main ingredient) and *soft-paste* (largely bone ash). The term "porcelain" is used interchangeably with "china" to mean high-quality and expensive dinnerware. This what you put on the table when you want to impress the in-laws—or what they use when they want to impress you.

Porcelain is translucent—light can pass through it. The usual way to test it is to put your hand on the back of the plate, then hold the plate in front of a strong light. If you can see the outline of your hand, the plate is most likely made of porcelain.

Here are some of the most-collected varieties of porcelain:

➤ **Belleek.** Belleek is fragile, popular, and valuable Irish porcelain. It is ivory with delicate yellow or green decorations. Prices range from $30 for currently produced smaller pieces to thousands of dollars for antique pieces. *Willets Belleek* is an American china. Although very similar to Irish Belleek in appearance, it is generally not as valuable as Irish Belleek. A creamer is valued at $80; a 6-inch bowl is worth $295. Figure on spending $1,400 for a 59-piece dinner set.

➤ **Bing & Grondahl.** Established in the 1850s, Bing & Grondahl is a Danish china best known for its porcelain figurines, Christmas plates, and other commemorative items.

➤ **Capodimonte (also spelled "Capo-di-Monte").** Very popular in the 19th and early 20th century, Capodimonte pieces have raised designs in Italian or Mediterranean designs. It is still being produced today. A square 6-inch ashtray is worth $45, a 10-inch box, $220.

➤ **Dresden.** "Dresden" figures—as well as copies—were made in almost every country and in every different quality. Their value greatly depends on their condition and details (such as meshlike crinoline lace skirts). Today, a Schumann open-work compote is valued at $195, but a 5-inch dish will set you back a mere $15.

Learn the Lingo
Porcelain was first made in China—hence its common name, *"china."*

➤ **Haviland.** Haviland china is thought to be extremely valuable because it was extremely popular in the 19th and early 20th centuries. Be very careful; you can find a lot of Haviland modestly priced in fine antique shops, which suggests that it is not as valuable as some collectors would like to think. Haviland is still being made today. Budget $8 for a 5-inch berry bowl, $185 for a 5-piece set, and $875 for an 1890s 7-piece ice-cream set.

Learn the Lingo
Nippon means *Japan*. Much of the china marked "Nippon" was made by the Noritake company. Most pieces only cost a few dollars. Truly exceptional pieces range in the low hundreds.

➤ **Hummels.** Almost every home has at least one of these figures. Regardless of my long-standing personal revulsion for cute china, coveys of collectors eagerly gobble this stuff up. There are clubs devoting to collecting Hummels; like music groupies waiting for a new CD, Hummel fans line up at the shop when a new figurine is about to be released. Figure No. 4, the "Little Fiddler," is worth $195-$200; No. 8, a bookworm, $250.

Value is based on subject, age, size, and condition. Values generally range from $75 and up. You can break the code by studying the marks on the bottom of the figures. This will tell you the age and help you deduce the rarity of the piece. See Hummel guidebooks for more information.

To be sure that your cutie pie is indeed a Hummel, check for the impressed "M.I. Hummel" marking on the base. Hummel figures were also made into ashtrays, candlesticks, and lamps, if the figures weren't enough. Also be aware that not all Hummels are colored; the religious figures, for example, are white.

Sometimes you feel like a Hummel; sometimes, you don't.

➤ **Imari.** Imari is a deep orange-red color and cobalt blue, highlighted with gold. Patterns include flowers, birds, and symbols of Japanese life. Imari china was first made in Japan in the 1600s, but the Imari offered for sale today is 19th and 20th century vintage.

Imari bowls and plates are widely collected, but the less frequently seen items— candlesticks and vases—are more valuable. A single plate can cost more than $100.

➤ **Limoges.** Limoges is actually a town in France where Haviland and other brands of china were manufactured. Thus, you can find Haviland Limoges, Elite Limoges, etc. In general, this is a middle-range fine china.

➤ **Lladro.** These are a line of very popular china figurines, characterized by pale, anemic colors and elongated lines. You can find them in fine stores in America, Europe, and in the Caribbean islands. A 1987 Christmas bell is valued at $35; Figurine No. 1495, "A Lady of Taste," goes for $625.

➤ **Meissen.** Meissen china was first produced in the early 1700s. Although it is very fine, its value depends on pattern, design, quality, age, and condition. The good stuff, though, is so good that if you have any, you should insure it—fast.

➤ **Sèvres.** Sèvres is a town in France, just as Dresden is a town in Germany. Sèvres is perhaps the most famous name in china—although it is not very different from the rest of the high-end china produced in Europe at the time. As a result, "Sèvres" has become a greatly misused name. If that wasn't bad enough, fakes abound.

For instance, Sèvres china was imitated in East Liverpool, Ohio, when a china firm calling itself "Sevre China Company" marked its products with the distinctive and famous Sèvres' fleur-de-lis. Few people blinked when the fleur-de-lis appeared on American-made dinner sets, bowls, and plates, but when it showed up on a china toilet seat, people took a closer look.

> **Tricks of the Trade**
> Many modern collectibles are aimed at different markets. Lladro, for example, produces many figurines only for its domestic market, or their European market, or their duty-free stores. Americans find these items while traveling abroad and come back convinced they have discovered something rare and enormously valuable. They haven't.

> **Caveat Emptor**
> Any china marked "Occupied Japan" was made between 1945 to 1952, when the Allies occupied Japan immediately after World War II. Although highly collected, it is considered an inferior product and is worth very little. The market is flooded with it.

Aside from dopey copies like these toilet seats on the market, there are some very good copies available. To distinguish between the real and not real takes close study of museum pieces. The basic distinguishing characteristic is the quality of the painting. Depending on the size of the piece, the difference between a real Sèvres and a good copy can be thousands of dollars.

In Your Dreams: Building a Collection

By now, I've hammered it home that you should collect whatever gives you pleasure. For example, let's say the china guidebook says that New England salt glaze and slip crocks are hot this year. But you think crocks are as clunky as clogs. Solution? Don't collect 'em. Pick what you like and can live with. That way, you'll never be saddled with pieces you selected for investment because someone said they would be the latest and the greatest. Check the extensive list of guidebooks in Appendix B for additional information.

But no matter what type of china you collect, you must know how to authenticate it. That's what the following section discusses. I've also included some useful guidelines that can help you get the best value for your money. So read on!

Dating Porcelain

Even though you may have a tough time getting a date, take heart; it's relatively easy to date china. Worst-case scenario, you can always take a soup tureen to the office party.

Here are the two dates you need to know: 1891 and 1914.

If the name of the country appears on the china, it was made after 1891, in accordance with the McKinley Tariff Act. If the additional words "Made in" appear, the china was produced after 1914. China made before 1891 is much harder to date; if the china does not have a date marked on it, do not assume that it is "antique." It may indeed be valuable or—it may simply be unmarked, breakable dreck.

Even when you buy cheap china at a flea market or antique store, take the time to look at the back or bottom of the piece for identifying marks. Look for the words "Made in" or the country where the china was made. Compare this to what you just learned—and with what the seller tells you.

The marks on the back of your china can help you identify the piece.

Good, Better, Best: Condition

Easy rule: Only buy china in the very best condition you can afford. You can sometimes find a small, hairline crack by ringing the porcelain with your finger. Porcelain has a clear ring. A dull thud indicates that the piece has been patched.

MacCollectibles: Limited Editions

In recent years, collectors have become more knowledgeable and cultivated. There are also more collectors—and they have more money. As result, the availability—and affordabilty—of prime collectible ceramics decreased. In response, "limited-edition collectibles" are born. Like take-out and drive-thru, it was an instant hit.

Today, there are more than seven million registered collectors of "limited-edition collectibles"—and that's only the people who have *registered*. Millions more are collecting these articles. Limited-edition collectible clubs have sprung up around the world, laced together by national and international conventions and a tower of publications. Limited-edition collectors have their own subculture, fueled by producers, distributors, and dealers. If you like these items, buy them to grace your home. I do not recommended them for investment.

Tricks of the Trade
If possible, use a black light to see if a piece of china has been repaired. Often, repairs—even big ones—will not show up under normal light.

Something's Rotten in China: Reproductions, Forgeries, Fakes, and Just Plain Stupidity

The artful forgers' tricks and the more honest efforts to create reproductions can be equally hard to detect—especially by china collectors eager to unearth the find of a lifetime. In this section, I'll teach you all about reproductions, forgeries, fakes, and astonishingly idiotic errors.

Reproductions

Ceramics collectors are bedeviled by a wide range of copies. Most of them are honest reproductions, made without any attempt at deception. In fact, they were often made at the same time as the original, such as Chelsea copies of Meissen figures. Advertisements exist from more than a hundred years ago touting "inexpensive reproductions of Spode, Copeland, Wedgwood, and Mason china."

All things being equal, this is not a problem—as long as you know that your reproduction is a reproduction and not an original… and pay accordingly.

Forgeries

But some copies were deliberately made to deceive buyers into thinking they were getting originals. These forgeries can be very hard to detect. If you are considering investing in a valuable piece of china, I suggest that you study as many original pieces as possible and check with trained appraisers to make sure that the piece is not a forgery.

Fakes

Fakes are a subclass of forgeries, genuine objects altered in some way. Most fake china pieces come out of Japan, some from Germany. Wedgwood is one of the most frequently and blatantly faked types of china. A very popular gift item, Wedgwood is decorated with classical scenes in white on blue, green, yellow, or lavender backgrounds. The correct spelling is *Wedgwood*; many fakes are easily identified by their misspelling: *Wedgewood*.

In other instances, the identifying marks on the bottom of china pieces have been removed with a grinding wheel or hydrochloric acid. You will find this most often with 19th- and 20th-century china pieces that are being fobbed off as "antiques." The inverse con is also common: Marks are added to make newer Japanese china seem like antique English, French, or German china.

Stupidity

Sometimes china is sold for something that it's not. In these cases I like to give the seller the benefit of the doubt and ascribe the error to idiocy rather than a deliberate intention to deceive. Otherwise there's no hope for the world.

Be very careful if you try to buy fine china or china collectibles at flea markets, garage sales, tag sales, or antique shops because it is so often wrongly marked. The mistakes are so egregious they can only be explained as stupidity. For example, at a New York barn sale I saw supermarket giveaway dinner plates marked "collectibles." My set of the same ugly plates was only a few years old. Since most of the free world had the same plates, how could they be collectibles? The market must be expanding much faster than I imagine.

Another time, at an antique store I found ironstone plates marked "dishwasher safe" also labeled "genuine antiques." They had mechanical dishwashers a hundred years ago?

Dresden is a town in Germany where the Meissen factory was located. Many uninformed china collectors use the term "Dresden" to describe the flowers that often appear on Meissen china. From this misunderstanding, it's just a short hop, skip, and jump to the stupidity that any china with this flower decoration is Meissen china. Actually, what you have here is china with flowers on it. Flower-power china was very popular in the 1930s, and so many companies turned out loads of it.

The Least You Need to Know

➤ The type of ceramics is determined by the composition of clay and the way it is prepared, the temperature at which it is fired, and the glazes used.

➤ *Delft, Faience, Majolica*, and *Quimper* are all tin-glazed earthenware.

➤ *Wedgwood* is a type of stoneware.

➤ *Lusterware* and *Staffordshire* are ironstone.

➤ Porcelain is the same as china. *Belleek, Bing & Grondahl, Capodimonte, Dresden, Haviland, Hummel, Imari, Limoges, Meissen, Sevres*, and *Lladro* are all types of porcelain.

➤ Avoid buying "limited-edition" china collectibles for investment.

Chapter 14

Fun and Games

In This Chapter

➤ Find out why kids' toys aren't for kids anymore

➤ Learn all about dolls—including that plastic bombshell, Barbie

➤ Take a tour of doll houses and miniatures

➤ Cast your vote for cast-iron toys

➤ Learn about fuzzy wuzzies, especially teddy bears

➤ See why it's important to keep all your marbles

Collecting toys, games, and dolls is a relatively recent activity, one which has evolved in the past thirty years. At first, many antique mavens refused to take toys seriously. "Kid's stuff," they sneered. "Give us real antiques and collectibles like china, art, and jewelry."

Now, however, toys are widely regarded as a bona fide area of serious collecting. International auctions are devoted to selling rare and beautiful toys; special appraisers deal with pricing dolls, mechanical metal banks, and teddy bears. Some antique toys are even selling for more than traditional antiques and collectibles such as paintings and furniture! Who's laughing now?

In this chapter, you will find out all about dolls, doll houses, and miniatures. Then comes detailed information on die-cast toys. It will help you understand why these intriguing toys captivate collectors far and wide. In addition, you will get the scoop on teddy bears, those adorable follicularly-endowed playthings. You'll learn why increasing numbers of toy collectors are turning their attention to modern toys rather than antique ones. By the end of this chapter, you will know which toys are hot collectibles and why. Let the fun begin!

Not for Kids Anymore

Toy making was a well-developed industry in southern Germany in medieval times. It flourished with equal success on the continent in the 1600s. Nonetheless, until very recently, the vast majority of toys were either the product of humble rural craftsmen or made at home by parents to placate bored offspring. Some were even made by children themselves.

Along with a few railroads, steel foundries and assorted factories, the Industrial Revolution marked an enormous mass-production of toys. The "Golden Age" for toys was the late 19th century and early 20th century. Rich Victorian families gave their little sweetums miniature trains powered with steam and fragile china dolls dressed in the latest designer outfits. Fine workmanship was not confined to expensive play things, however.

> **Learn the Lingo**
> Avid doll collectors are called *plangono-logists*. They are sticklers for perfection in their dolls, studying specimens like prospective lovers on a first date.

Even the reasonably priced toys of the past are notable for their craftsmanship and design. Sounds like an ideal collectible, no? Hold the phone. Because of their very nature, toys are subject to wear and tear. You can get collector's angst trying to find toys from the past that are in good condition. Partly as a result of this, many toy collectors are becoming increasingly interested in modern toys. More on that later—now, on to dolls!

All Dolled Up

There are dolls in every material—terra-cotta, glazed stoneware, alabaster, rags, leather, papier-mâché, wax, and even gold. Dolls are known to have existed in ancient Egypt and ancient Greece, where they served as religious artifacts rather than as children's toys. Antiquarians eagerly hunt for these ancient dolls, but today's hard-wired collectors want only children's dolls, dating from the 1600s onward. In the past two decades, collecting dolls has reached new heights. See Appendix B in the back of this book for resources you can consult to get price ranges on collectible dolls. Judging from the prices they get in auction houses, dolls are sound investments. Here's the lowdown on dolls.

Block Heads: Wooden Head Dolls

Perhaps 17th-century woodpeckers were a particularly assertive lot, much taken with wooden dolls. More likely no one thought to save their daughters' wooden dolls. Whatever the reason, few wooden dolls made it through the 1600s to the present. The best of the lot that survived are known as "Queen Anne" dolls and date from the 18th century. The earliest ones are more finely carved and painted than later specimens. Wigs made of flax or real hair are perched on their plastered head. If you're lucky enough to find one of these dolls, you can do an approximate dating from its eyes: the early dolls had dark eyes spaced far apart; later dolls had blue eyes, more closely set.

Bisque Heads

During the last quarter of the 19th century, Parisienne or *poupee* dolls made their appearance. These French dolls had bisque (fired but unglazed) ceramic heads. Among the most beautiful and highly prized of all dolls, they were made for daughters of the uptown set. As with all other French bisque dolls, you can usually (but not always) find the mold number and/or the maker's initials carved into the back of the doll's head or stamped on the body. Reproductions are common, so identification is very tricky. A 20-inch bisque-head doll with a kid body and cloth legs made around 1900 sells for $975, but you can find lesser-quality bisque-head dolls from the same time for as little as $100.

Also look for bebe dolls, luxury dolls with large eyes and open or closed mouths. Those with closed mouths are more desirable, which shows that some people have always preferred that women be seen and not heard…

By the 1800s, the Germans had become the preeminent makers of bisque-head dolls. The early German dolls look like the French ones, but have thicker bodies. The top manufacturers include Armand Marseille, Kammer and Reinhardt, Gerbruder Heubach, Cuno and Otto Dressel, and Max Handwerk.

Papier-Màché Heads

Ludwig Greiner, America's first doll maker, worked in the mid-19th century. Greiner made only the doll's head; the consumer made the body to suit her specifications. Look for a gold or black label inside the head to clinch identification and distinguish Greiner's American papier-màché dolls with painted eyes from the glass-eyed babies produced in Germany during the same time.

Another type of papier-màché doll was called a "milliner's doll" because of its wild hairstyles, often arranged in bunches of ringlets like grapes. They are much sought-after by today's doll collectors.

185

German dolls from this period were often dipped in wax to make the papier-mâché bodies soft and lifelike. "Wax over composition" dolls, as these are known, have aged poorly. All-wax dolls were even more fragile.

Paper Dolls

Nearly all old paper dolls are super collectibles. Marilyn Monroe paper dolls in particular are as hot as the star was herself. The trick is to find the paper dolls uncut and in good shape. But paper dolls go back much further than the blonde bombshell, at least to the 1800s. You can date paper dolls easily by looking at their hairstyle. Study the following table.

Dating Paper Dolls

Date	Hairstyle
1840s	Hair curled on the neck
1850s	Short curls
1860s	Chignons

Although most old paper dolls are behind glass in museums, you might still find some examples from the 1930s and later. Beware of very good reproductions that are sold as antiques. A 14-inch uncut Amy Carter paper doll sells for $25, a 1943 uncut Ann Southern, $75. Poor Carmen Miranda—her 1940 uncut paper dolls go for only $5! The South will rise again: An uncut 1940 Gone with the Wind paper doll set is $275.

Date with a Doll

In 1891, Congress passed a law requiring dolls be marked with their country of origin. This makes dating a doll much easier. From 1891 onward, any dolls marked "German," for example, were made or at least imported after 1891. If a doll has no marks of origin, check the cloth body. If she is machine stitched, she dates after the invention of the sewing machine in 1850.

Caveat Emptor
Beware of overly restored dolls. Perhaps only one arm is original… which severely decreases the doll's value to a collector.

Unlike many other collectibles, you don't have to pass up a valuable doll because it is missing a key part, such as an arm or leg. There are doll hospitals all over the country waiting to perform medical miracles.

Barbie: The Plastic Bombshell

When Barbie was introduced in 1959, the buyers didn't like her, and the parents didn't either. It wasn't until Mattel started running commercials for her during *The Mickey Mouse Club* that she started selling. And selling. According to Mattel, two Barbies are sold every second, worldwide. Even Barbie's critics—those who claim that her body is unrealistically perfect, or that she's a poor role model for girls—cannot deny that she's made great strides. For example, Barbie no longer has holes in her feet (used to secure her to a doll stand) and no longer comes clad only in a swimsuit. She's much more successful than Ken—he's really no more than an accessory. From her humble start to her icon status, Barbie has become one of the most eagerly collected, sold, and traded modern dolls. A No. 2 Barbie, with the original stand and box, is valued at $5,100; the 1988 Happy Holidays Ken and Barbie special edition, $546.

Character Counts

In addition to Barbie, other hot modern dolls include character movie dolls (Sonja Henie, Snow White, and so on), Chatty Cathy dolls, and many more. To find the exact price for each of these dolls, as well as others not mentioned here, consult one of the scores of doll price guides available. In addition to guide books, many magazines and newsletters specialize in specific kinds of dolls. Check Appendix B in the back of this book for some specific doll price guides you may wish to consult.

Lost in Lilliput: Dolls' Houses and Miniatures

This is no Johnny-Come-Lately collectible: Collectors have been fascinated by scale-sized objects since the 17th century, and very likely before. Artisans in Germany and Holland began producing the forerunners of today's doll houses: elaborate cabinets that opened to reveal miniature furnished rooms. These "doll's houses" weren't houses at all; nor were they intended as playthings. They were simply boxes meant to represent a room with a side or a wall missing. The inside was a like a peepshow, showing a proper room of the era. Some experts believe that these models were used to show young girls what they were letting themselves in for as housewives.

Because every item was made by hand, only the wealthy could afford to trade up into two- or more-room dioramas. By the end of the 18th century, dolls' houses moved from the parlor to the nursery and became the toys we know today. The exteriors became more realistic; the interiors now had staircases to make the rooms accessible to each other.

These adorable play things are no play things; they are serious collectibles for serious collectors. If you like antique miniatures or even well-made pieces from the 1920s and 1930s, be prepared to ante up some real money. Most of the early 1930s furniture, for example, was made in Europe. It's beautifully detailed down to the last dovetailed drawer. Tiny sewing machines sewed; mini-grandfather clocks had swinging pendulums. Japan sent Satsuma vases the size of a thumbnail; China contributed tiny Ming sculptures. Dedicated collectors cherish hand-painted tea sets a quarter-inch high and Venetian glass tumblers. There are thumbnail-sized, leather-covered printed versions of Sherlock Holmes novels... stamped in 14K gold. Look for craftsmanship, scarcity, and the quality of the materials used. Figure on laying out $150 for a 19-inch 1875 set of miniature kitchen furniture—but a 1900 three-story Victorian dollhouse, 56 × 40 × 27, fetches $1,150.

The Magic Kingdom of Collectibles: Disneyana

What is Disneyana? A semi-radioactive mineral? A distortion in the time-space continuum? A new dance craze? No mouse ears for you. Disneyana is actually any item associated with the Walt Disney Company or its affiliates, past or present. People who buy Disneyana fall into four groups:

1. Consumers who buy items such as Disney toys, games, and dolls to be used. The items are then discarded, thrown out, or given away.

2. People who buy a Disney article as a souvenir or display piece.

3. Collectors who buy Disneyana to add to their collection. Motives include personal enjoyment, investment, and an inability to distinguish between art and kitsch.

4. Dealers and investors who buy Disneyana in an attempt to make a profit.

I'm not a fan of Disneyana, no doubt because the perennially cheerful theme park depresses me. But I'm clearly the party pooper when it comes to this collectible. Fans of Disneyana claim it is art. Some even claim it's good art. But then again, there are people who claim frozen bagels are really bagels and mocha latte decaf is really coffee.

Fans of Disney collectibles further point out that Disneyana has been produced in large quantities since the 1920s and it can be found worldwide. The tremendous quantity produced argues against its worth, but some examples of Disneyana do bring high prices at major auctions. Go figure.

So how can you decide what's hot and what's not in Walt's World? Follow these three guidelines:

➤ With Disneyana, rarity doesn't always equate with value. In Disneyana collecting, the strongest demand is often generated by people who want to obtain items of special value. Character popularity, cross-overs to other collecting fields (such as plates, books, and dolls) and the type of item (anything showing Santa Claus, for example) can be strong factors.

➤ Price has regional influences. Prices run high on the coasts; lower in the corn belt.

➤ The completeness of the box or package is a big factor with this collectible. In some cases, the box is more attractive than the item itself. Some boxes include instructions and extra parts, too. A complete box in mint condition can add 20 to 50 percent to the price.

> **Big Deals**
>
> In 1986, a Disney cel and master background estimated to sell for $2,500 brought $20,900 at auction.
>
> Vintage Disney tin wind-up toys, character dolls, and porcelain bisque figures sell in the $1,000 to $5,000 range. Extremely rare examples in mint condition can go for as much as $10,000. That's almost as much as admission and dinner for four at Disney World.

Mechanical Toys

The early makers of mechanical toys were a clever lot. In the 1870s and 1880s, they used flywheels—simple and reliable gizmos. The mechanism could either be set in motion by twirling a knob with your fingers or with a piece of string. Here are some of the most famous examples of early mechanical toys:

➤ The German company Math. Hess was known for its Hessmobile, a model-tin plate car, which used a flywheel to propel the car.

➤ Schuco produced a model Beemer that had a clockwork motor with a clutch, hand brake, four forward gears, and one reverse.

➤ Another German company, Lehmann, is famous for clockwork models such as the "Stubborn Donkey," "Lehmann Beetle," and "Bucking Bronco." Each of these mechanical toys involves some creature acting in character: a horse attempting to throw a rider over its head, a car that won't drive straight, a baby that attempts to escape from its bath.

➤ The American firm of Ives created mechanical rowing men, trains, and dancing figures.

Prices were kept reasonable by using recycled parts and slot and tab fixings. More expensive cars use all-new materials and were soldered. The invention of paper lithography in

Connoisseur
Toys were made from lightweight tin because there was a tax on weight. As a result, American manufacturers were penalized on world markets even though their mechanical toys were of superb quality.

1895 allowed toymakers an inexpensive way to decorate their toys; before that time, everything was hand-painted or stenciled.

Banks and cast toys are widely faked and aged to look old. Many were reproduced 30 to 40 years ago and novice collectors could be taken. Also, high-end banks can and do have repairs that take an extremely well-trained eye to see. Be really careful with these collectibles. This is another area where it pays to consult with an expert before you buy the item.

The Die Is Cast

Die-cast toys are produced by pouring molten lead (normally a lead alloy) into molds and then putting them under pressure. It is an affordable and fast method of production, ideal for mass producing inexpensive toys to satisfy the hoi polloi. Die-cast cars have only recently incited lust in collectors' hearts. Here are some the most collectible ones:

➤ **Tootsie Toys.** Die-cast toys were first produced in the early 20th century by the Dowst Manufacturing Company, an American firm. In 1914, Dowst introduced the Tootsie Toy range of cars, including models of Fords, Chevys, and Buicks.

➤ **Dinkie Toys.** The famous Dinkie toys were first produced in 1933 by the Liverpool entrepreneur Frank Hornby. His "O" gauge Hornby train sets of the 1920s and 1930s were tremendously popular; their accessories gave rise to the Dinkie toy. The Dinkies includes motor trucks, delivery vans, tractors, tanks, and two sports cars.

Caveat Emptor
The early die-cast toys have a dangerously high lead content. As a result, they were—and still are—quite unsafe for handling. But at these prices, who's going to play with them?

But production of die-cast mechanical toys largely ceased after 1945, with the notable exception of a model of a gasoline tanker with POOL (the German term for rationed gasoline) stenciled on its side. Today, Tootsie Toy, Dinkies, and Solido die-cast models are much sought-after by collectors as irreplaceable period pieces.

A Penny Saved Is a Penny Earned: Penny Banks

Once we adopted a coin currency, we needed somewhere to stash the extras. (Remember, this was in the days *before* parking meters.) The first mechanical banks were made in the 1870s. Iron ore and skilled foundry workers were in plentiful supply and people were eager for new products. Here are some of the most important companies and their mechanical toy banks:

➤ **The J. & E. Stevens Company.** This was the first and most prolific company to manufacture mechanical banks; it remained a leader in the field for 50 years. They produced some of the finest mechanical banks: the *Darktown Battery, Girl Skipping Rope, Calamity, Two Frogs, I Always Did 'spise a Mule,* and *Eagle and Eaglets*—as well as various mechanical churches, houses, and toy safes.

➤ **The Shepard Hardware Manufacturing Company.** This early and important mechanical bank maker entered the field in the early 1880s. Notable banks include *Uncle Sam, Humpty-Dumpty,* and *Punch and Judy.*

➤ **Kyser & Rex.** *Roller Skating, Lion and Two Monkeys,* and the rare *Bowling Alley* are their most famous mechanical banks.

➤ **The Weeden Manufacturing Company.** This firm produced such mechanical banks as *Weeden's Plantation, Ding Dong Bell,* and the very rare *Japanese Ball Tosser.* All the Weeden banks are wind-ups.

> **Caveat Emptor**
> Condition is paramount to a toy collector. A crack on the face of a bisque doll, chipped paint on a doll house, metal fatigue in a Dinkie toy, and worn pads and bare patches on a teddy bear lower the value of the toy considerably.

Action and Rarity

Listen up, collectors/investors: There are two criteria that determine the value of a mechanical bank: Its action and its rarity. Regarding action, some collectors value banks that work on a clockwork mechanisms; others seek spring, lever, or sustained action banks. Regarding rarity, banks produced in limited quantities and delicate banks are especially rare and thus desirable. Exceptionally rare (and thus exceptionally valuable banks) include the *Freedman's Bank, Clown, Harlequin, Queen Victoria, Bowling Alley, Girl in the Victorian Chair,* and *Red Riding Hood.* Banks of this rarity and value fetch prices in the five figures. Again, many are fake or have replaced parts. Be very careful with these collectibles. Spend the bucks to hire an expert if you suspect that you have stumbled on a real "find."

Getting in on the Action

You can save your pennies (in a non-mechanical bank) or follow these guidelines for starting (or refining) a penny-bank collection:

➤ **Repaired and repainted banks.** All mechanical bank collectors want banks in mint condition. We all want to look and feel like we're 21, too. Reality check: If you've got the money for the collection, you're probably getting a little long in the tooth. So here's the scoop: A

> **Caveat Emptor**
> Old mechanical banks work smoothly; the parts of recast banks, in contrast, rarely fit together well. Old banks feel silky; recast banks lack the same rich patina.

mechanical bank that has been carefully repaired will not lose all its value. Steer clear of repainted banks, however. A high-end bank will lose a lot of value if it is repaired.

➤ **Recasts and reproductions.** Recast banks are the tricky ones because they can be made from the original pattern or the bank itself. They are often sold as originals, but are worth much less. Reproductions are usually clearly labeled as such and are obviously new.

Caveat Emptor
Restoration of damage to a toy should be undertaken only by an expert and only as a last resort. It is better to have some original rust than a spanking new finish that completely obliterates the original paint.

➤ **Variations.** What happens when you find different versions of the same bank? Often, manufacturers of mechanical banks made changes in the casting, improving the structure or providing a new coin trap. As a result, some variations are authentic, but others are fakes. Check guidebooks carefully to tell if you've got the real McCoy.

➤ **Frauds.** Interesting frauds with this collectible: non-mechanical objects d'art that were converted to mechanical banks. Some were non-mechanical banks, others were toys—and some were even inkstands!

This Punch and Judy mechanical bank, a rare and valuable mechanical bank, was produced in 1884.

Grin and Bear It: Teddy Bears

We have the 26th President of the United States to thank for the invention of teddy bears. On a hunting trip in Mississippi in 1902, Theodore Roosevelt refused to shoot a bear cub. It must have been a slow news day, because the *Washington Post* publicized the incident in a cartoon. An enterprising Boston shopkeeper, Morris Mitchom, cashed in on the publicity by making toy bears and christening them "Teddy Bears." By the way, Theodore hated the nickname "Teddy."

This is the political cartoon that launched the bear known 'round the world.

Other soft toys come and go, but the teddy bear soldiers on. It has proven to be a fertile creature, bearing many progeny. Among its most notable descendants is Yogi Bear, the wily picnic-basket thief of Jellystone Park. There's also Winnie the Pooh, named after the teddy bear that belonged to Christopher Robin Milne. The arrival of the first giant panda to the London Zoo in the 1930s led to a stampede of stuffed panda bears. A few years later we were attacked by stuffed koalas, many created with real kangaroo fur. As Koala Bear slipped in the popularity ratings, the hideous stuffed troll arose from Scandinavian mythology to take its place on the toy shop shelves.

Popular around the globe, Mr. Ted E. Bear resembles the country of its origin. European teddies, especially those made in Germany, tend to be more slender and long-limbed, while British bears are chubby and stubby. Some even squeak, growl, or jingle.

The basic form of the teddy bear has undergone significant changes since 1903. The value of a teddy

Connoisseur
As an American I am duty-bound to uphold my country's claim to the creation of the teddy bear, but it is undeniably true that in Germany at the same time Margaret Steiff was also manufacturing a soft toy bear. Our bear was better than their bear, so there.

bears depends on its age, rarity, and condition. You can use a teddy bear's shape to roughly determine its age, as detailed in the following table.

Use the Teddy Bear's Shape to Figure Out When and Where It Was Made

Year	Body shape
1900s	Long limbs, pronounced snout, prominent back hump, small ears
1920s	Shorter arms, smaller feet, torso the same as bears from the early 1900s
1930s	Rounded heads, softer snout, larger ears
post-1945	Chubbier and less-realistic, stumpier limbs, larger head, no back hump

Big Deals

Arctophily, or teddy bear collecting, is an increasingly serious hobby. The most expensive teddy bear ever sold at an auction was a Steiff teddy bear, named "Happy," made in 1926. It sold at Sotheby's (London) in 1989 for $55,000. Steiff bears are the most prized among collectors.

Here are some sample prices. A 1940s Chad Valley mohair gold teddy bear sells for $395; a 1910 embroidered excelsior stuffed fully-jointed bear is worth $144. You may want to consult the price guides listed in Appendix B.

Losing Your Marbles

Are marbles your bag? Top of the line are only those marbles made before the 20th century. Especially desirable are marbles made by hand in eastern Germany from 1840 from 1926. Sulphide marbles contain metal figures of birds, fish, and so on; the rarest contain numbers and figures. There are also marbles made of clay, china, stone, jade, onyx, and jasper.

Like anything else worth collecting, marbles are being reproduced. Nicks alone don't make an antique. To distinguish authentic marbles from reproductions, hold the marble up to the light. Old marbles will have a greenish-blue tint. In addition, they will be heavier than the new ones. Top-of-the-line marbles start at around $450 apiece. Prices soar into the thousands of dollars per marble!

Modern Toys

As the prices of early toys have soared into the stratosphere in recent years, some collectors have turned their attention to the best of today's toys. In particular, space and TV-related toys of the 1960s have become extremely desirable. As modern toys rise in popularity, the horizon for this collectible seems limitless. Collectors have even gone berserk over metal lunch boxes—the newest hot collectible!

As you learned in the section on Disneyana, it's important to save everything associated with a modern toy, including all boxes and instructions. For example, if Barbie is your doll, be sure to save all those minuscule combs, brushes, and other accessories. The more pristine the toy's condition, the more it will be worth when we're all sporting with Saint Peter.

Connoisseur
The yo-yo, whose popularity swept across America like some medieval plague, originated in China in the pre-Christian era, but did not appear on the scene in Europe until the 1700s. It was originally called an "emigrette."

The Least You Need to Know

➤ Toys are very hot collectibles, whether they are antiques or modern.

➤ Among the most-eagerly collected toys are dolls, doll houses and miniatures, mechanical toys, teddy bears, and marbles.

➤ Age, rarity, and condition determine the value of a toy.

➤ If you collect modern toys, save the whole kit and caboodle: the toy, the box, and the directions.

➤ Toys aren't kids' stuff anymore.

Chapter 15

Home Sweet Collectible

In This Chapter

➤ Find out if you have a fortune hiding in your house—in plain sight!

➤ Learn which beer cans, bottles, clocks, and pens are hot collectibles

➤ Discover which household items, quilts, radios, and tools make collectors faint with anticipation

"The time has come," the Walrus said,
"To talk of many things:
Of shoes—and ships—and sealing-wax—
Of cabbages—and kings—
And why the sea is boiling hot—
And whether pigs have wings."

History does not record what Lewis Carroll's Walrus and Carpenter collected, but if this passage is any indication, this famous literary duo certainly shared the collector's spirit. This chapter is devoted to the little collectibles that mean a lot, things like beer cans and bottles, clocks, and kitchen tools.

We have all spent hundreds, maybe even thousands of dollars, on the little things that make our homes special. This bric-a-brac often expresses our personal taste more than our furniture and big collections do. In this chapter, you will discover which collectibles have emerged from the living room, den, and pantry to the marketplace. I'll teach you the basics of collecting today's hottest household items: beer cans, bottles, clocks, pens, quilts, radios, and tools. You'll learn what factors make these commonplace items a collector's dream come true.

Having Your Hobby and Drinking It, Too: Beer Cans

Do you get weepy when you hear der Bingster croon "White Christmas?" Do Al Capone's escapades send a little tingle down your spine? Do you have a thing about World War II, cone-tops, pin-ups, or the Bicentennial? If so, beer cans may be your collectible of choice. There are beer cans for almost every possible interest. For example:

➤ As many beer cans as evergreens are festooned for Christmas—and beer cans are easier to get into the car.

➤ Scarface Capone once owned the Manhattan Brewing Company.

➤ World War II beer cans were colored a dark brown-black and lettered in dull orange. This kept the cans from attracting the enemy's attention. Since so few of the cans came back to the United States, they are great rarities.

➤ For years, the American Can Company tried to find a way to make a beer can that did not impart a metallic taste to the suds inside. In 1935, the G. Krueger Brewing Company of Newark, New Jersey, finally developed a specially coated can in which to package their product. These "cone-top cans" were widely used until World War II when "flat tops" were introduced. Today, these early "cone-head" cans are out-of-this-world collectibles for brew mavens.

Tricks of the Trade
A series of revolving shelves makes an attractive beer can display.

➤ The Miss Rheingold series made from the 1940s to the early 1960s carries a line of luscious pre-p.c. pin-ups. A variety of Miss Rheingolds—including actress Diane Baker—had their face and figure plastered on the cans.

➤ Falstaff and other companies issued Bicentennial beer cans.

Beer, Here

Considering the popularity of malt liquor, it's no wonder that beer can collecting is such a widespread hobby. Fortunately for those so inclined, a beer can and breweriana collection is easy to start. Most collectors begin by buying as many local varieties of canned beer as they can; others comb dump sites and recycling centers. (Hey, I said it was an easy hobby, not a *clean* one.) You can drink the beer and save the empty can, but if you do drink the beer, open the can from the bottom so the "flip tab" is kept intact. Beer can collectors very much value "perfect" specimens.

You can attend some of the many "canventions" held across the country to get rare varieties of cans. Often, these gatherings of like-minded beermeisters are advertised well in advance in newspapers and beer can collectors' publications. It's not unusual for rare cans to sell for hundreds of dollars at these events. They must be in top condition, however: clean, dent-free, and unscratched. See Appendix B for a list of guide books that cover beer can prices. Figure on spending anywhere from a few dollars for cans such as a 1960 German Löwenbräu München to several hundred dollars for cans such as a perfect Fort Pitt Brewing Company.

Tricks of the Trade
Got a little rust on one of your beer cans? Rub some oil on it to prevent the rust from spreading.

Bottoms Up

The most popular categories of beer can collecting are *brand name, era, region, design,* and *size.* Some collectors specialize on the expensive cone-tops; others seek out beer cans in their travels throughout the United States.

Anything connected in any way with the production of beer is considered *breweriana.* This includes the following items:

➤ Calendars advertising beer

➤ Brewery hardware such as meters and plaques

➤ Beer coasters

➤ Beer barrel plugs

➤ Signs advertising beer

➤ Napkins with beer brand logos

➤ Beer trays

While all of these items are legitimate fodder for the collector of breweriana, some items are more desirable than others. An original beer barrel meter, no matter how unusual, is not likely to fetch as much as a colorful poster advertising a popular brand of beer. The latter has far greater visual appeal and so would likely be a hotter collectible.

Bottle Babies

Bottle collectors, like popsicles, rarely divide neatly into groups. One group includes collectors of bottles made before 1900, when the bottle-making machine was invented. Within this group are those who specialize in handblown bottles, mold-blown bottles, historic flasks, snuff bottles, medicine bottles, and inkwells. There's another group that looks for bottles in the shape of famous people, animals, and objects. A third group collects 20th-century bottles created especially for the collector. Then you have people who seek out Mason jars and those who want barber bottles. There are so many different kinds of bottle collections that you can rest assured there's a place for you in Bottle Collector Land, bunky. Prices range as widely as collector tastes. You can get a New Orleans 7-Up seltzer bottle in a pretty pinkish rose for $30... or spend $750 for a green Crump & Fox "Superior Mineral Water" bottle. See Appendix B for a list of price guides. Here are some of the most popular kinds of bottles that collectors covet:

➤ Avon	➤ Figural	➤ Modern
➤ Barber	➤ Flasks	➤ Poison
➤ Jim Beam	➤ Food	➤ Sarsaparilla
➤ Beer	➤ Fruit	➤ Scent
➤ Bitters	➤ Liquor (miniature and full-size)	➤ Soda
➤ Cologne	➤ Mineral water	➤ Whiskey

Let's look at some of the most collectible bottles in more detail. Here are the top five types of collectible bottles:

1. **Ding, Dong: Avon Calling.** Avon was founded in 1886 by a whiz kid named David McConnell and his wife. Working out of their Manhattan pied-a-terre, they illogically named themselves the California Perfume Company and sent women door-to-door hawking their powders and perfumes, ointments, and unguents. In 1928, they introduced a new line of products called "Avon."

   Avon collectors save anything produced by the California Perfume Company and/or Avon. The most popular collectibles are novelty perfume and cologne bottles in various shapes, such as cars, flowers, and animals. People also collect the boxes and advertisements that came with the products. On the average, bottles range in price from $12 to around $200.

2. **Here's Looking at You, Kid: Whiskey Bottles.** Many different types of whiskey bottles are collected. In general, the most desirable ones were produced in the 19th century. You can roughly assess age by the bottle's size: before 1860, the bottles were both large and small; after, bottles became the standard "fifth" size. Bottles

come in many intriguing colors, including purple, amber, green, and blue. Jim Beam bottles form a sub-genre of collectible bottles. Collectible whiskey bottles range from a low of about $5 per bottle to a high around $250.

In 1880, Colonel James Beam came to work for the Jacob Beam Company. His name became the company's moniker (it should happen to you) and since 1955, the firm has been producing a series of Beam novelty bottles. These are made of china, glass, porcelain, and plastic. To bring top dollar, the bottles should be in excellent condition. Whether or not the bottle still contains the liquor is not important to these collectors. Collectible Beam bottles cost about the same as whiskey bottles.

3. **Medicine bottles.** There are two main categories of medicine bottles to collect:

    Bitters bottles. Bitters were quack remedies that were sold before the passage of the Pure Food and Drug Act in 1907. Their heyday was from 1875 to 1905. These bitters came with wild claims to cure whatever ailed ya: from stomach cramps to headaches, muscle pains to brain fevers. The two main ingredients were herbs and a walloping alcohol base. The herbs gave the "medicine" an exotic taste; the heavy doses of liquor often made gullible consumers more than a little tipsy. True bitters bottle collectors want only those specimens that have the word "bitters" on the glass or label. Most of these bottles are reasonably priced ($25-$50), but some of the rare ones have sold for hundreds and even thousands of dollars. No bitter medicine here!

    Other medicine bottles. The most popular bottles are those produced between 1845 and 1907 that have an unusual shape and a rare color. All other factors being the same, a light red bottle is more desirable than a clear one, for example. Unusual labels, like those for "Barker's Poison Panacea" and "Baker's Vegetable Blood" are also hot.

4. **Soda bottles.** Whether you call it "soda" or "pop," these bottles have collector's cool. Strictly speaking, bottle collectors seek containers for carbonated beverages that date from 1840 on. Because many city water systems were contaminated, the wealthy drank bottled carbonated water. At first (1840 to 1850), the bottles were made of stoneware; later, they were made of glass. Hundreds of different varieties exist, and nearly all are reasonably priced at $10 to $150.

5. **Inkwells.** In 1810, the first inkwells were imported to America. These early varieties were made of ceramic. Soon, American artisans began to produce glass and silver inkwells. Inkwells vary widely in price, depending on age, composition, rarity, and condition. You can find affordable inkwells at flea markets and swap meets ($35 and up), but the finest examples are sold only in upscale venues such as antique bottle shows and auctions. High-end collectible inkwells cost well into the thousands of dollars. If you want to go the high-end route with this collectible, I recommend that you gather as much information as possible by attending bottle shows and auctions.

Study the wares and catalogs. Be especially aware of reproductions fobbed off as authentic articles.

Bottoms Up

Whatever types of bottles send your blood a' tingling, you can find beautiful old bottles in many ways.

➤ **Dig we must.** For the athletically inclined, you can dig for bottles at village, town, or city dumps. Dumpsites that date back 100 years or more are often the most fertile hunting grounds. Mining camps are another rewarding site. I do not recommend this method for those of you who, like me, are convinced that staying at any hotel without that crucial fifth star is tantamount to (shudder) camping.

➤ **Swimming with the fishes.** Forget snorkeling in the warm turquoise waters of the Caribbean. Who wants to look at all those boring fish when you can dive in the icy green North Atlantic for bottles? Seriously, a surprising number of bottle collectors snag their greatest finds in local lakes, rivers, and streams near old hotels and resorts. Talk to town historians and consult old maps and town documents to find promising locations to plumb.

Caveat Emptor
Always get permission before you go on a bottle dig. I also recommend that you bring along a sturdy pair of gloves, a shovel, newspapers, and plastic bags.

➤ **Shoppers of the world, unite!** Couch potato collectors like me go to conventions, flea markets, and antique shops to find neat bottles. Always look for bottles in the best possible condition. Very, very carefully feel the rims for chips and nicks.

Cleaning Bottles

If your hunt in the dump has been a roaring success, you're apt to stagger home with a pile of greasy, mucky bottles. In this case, your best bet is to leave them soaking overnight in a solution of water and gentle liquid washing detergent.

The next day, clean the insides of the bottles with a test-tube brush. Dry each bottle carefully and lay them out on their sides on a towel. Allow several days for the bottles to dry out completely.

Connoisseur
Medicine bottles are most valuable when the label is intact.

Never, never, never soak a bottle that still bears its label, however. The label often adds a great deal to the value of the bottle. To clean these bottles, fill them with warm, soapy water. I recommend that you use a funnel to prevent slops. Let them soak a while. Then empty out half the water and gently shake the bottle. Rinse and repeat until the bottle is clean. If necessary, scrub the inside with the test-tube brush. Wipe the outside with a damp cloth. Be careful not to damage the label.

Whatever Winds Your Watch

Galileo, that old heretic, gets credit for inventing pendulum clocks. Clocks with movements carved from cherry wood and oaks were made in the United States until the mid-18th century, because brass was then both expensive and difficult to obtain in North America. The wooden clocks were invented by two brothers, Benjamin and Timothy Cheyney, clockmakers from East Hartford, Connecticut. In 1806, another clockmaker named Eli Terry, of Plymouth, Connecticut, made 4,000 wooden clocks by fitting standard parts together on an assembly line. In 1836, cheaper brass spelled the end of wooden time, and few such clocks now survive. Sour grapes department: They were not very accurate and the parts wore quickly.

By the mid-1800s, imposing grandfather clocks and more modest mantel and shelf clocks were commonplace accessories in wealthier American homes. These are called "case clocks." By the end of the century, clocks were being mass-produced, and so were found in even modest homes. Take a hike through a flea market some Saturday; you'll find numerous wooden case clocks. Some will be authentic; others, reproductions and fakes.

Prices for so-called "antique" clocks can be staggering... and an astonishingly large number of people pay the going rate. Prices range from $50 (New Haven, art nouveau, small) to $9,000+ (Pierre-Philippe Thomire, Empire, Ormolu mounted, 15–20 inches). Before you invest in an antique or collectible clock, be sure that you are getting what you've been promised. Check a guidebook (see Appendix B) and follow these guidelines before you plunk down your money:

➤ The clock should work. Sounds like common sense, no? You'd be surprised at how many of these clocks are clinkers.

➤ All the parts should be original—even the glass panel and all parts of the case. You may wish to mix and match by creating your own clock with the innards from one and the case from another, but that's a whole 'nother kettle of fish.

Caveat Emptor
Because there are so many clocks from the 1800s and early 1900s, only those clocks that are unusual because of their fine cases or other rare features (such as regulator clocks and calendar clocks) are valuable to most collectors.

Connoisseur
Art deco shelf clocks have been appreciating in value recently, especially those with obvious art deco motifs. Clock/lamps from the 1930s are another up-and-comer.

➤ Beware of banjo clocks. They have been copied for years and are often sold as early 17th-century clocks, when they are 75 years younger! Real period banjo clocks are very rare and very expensive.

Something to Write Home About: Pens

In February of 1988, a Japanese collector paid $2,340,000 for the "Anemone" fountain pen made by Reden, France. The pen is embellished with 600 precious stones, including emeralds, amethysts, rubies, and sapphires. It took more than a year to create.

The most expensive writing pen commercially available is the Meisterstuck Solitaire Royal fountain pen made by Mont Blanc. Made of solid gold, it is encrusted with 4,810 diamonds—the height in meters of the mountain named Mount Blanc. The pen can be made to order for $121,000. For prompt delivery, be sure to place your order six months in advance.

Fortunately, most writing implements are well within the reach of today's collector, but signs indicate that the market is rising. Glass fountain pens, those decorated in art nouveau and art deco style, and early masterpieces of design such as Mont Blanc and Waterman, are among the most desirable collectibles in this category. All types of pens are collected, including ball-point pens as well as fountain pens. A 1967 Monkees pen costs about $3; a ball-point Martin Luther King picture pen, $35. Some collectors also seek out pencils. The most eagerly sought-after ones are automatic pencils of unusual designs. (And let us not forget pencil boxes and sharpeners!)

Big Deals

As of April 29, 1992, Vilma Valma Turpeinen of Tampere, Finland, collected 14,492 different pens. Vilma's collection earned her a place in the *1996 Guinness Book of World Records*.

Domestic Goddess Strikes It Rich!

Slap the bread into the old toaster and drift off into a reverie: A collector of art deco pieces from the 1920s–1940s taps on your screen door and offers you some serious money for your 60-year-old toaster. "OK," you think, "it has a sleek, rounded style, but it's still an old toaster. Who would want an old toaster?"

Think again. Streamlined toasters, irons, and Mixmasters from the 1920s, 1930s, and 1940s are one of the newest collectibles. So are Bakelite radios, metal lunchboxes, and other kitchenware from the past. Collectors of kitchen kitsch look for plastic, chrome, and hand-hammered aluminum items. Bright colors add to the item's value, as does design. Geometric shapes and snazzy silhouettes are most desirable.

Most old kitchen utensils and furnishings have value to collectors. The most popular categories of collecting are *personal appeal, era,* and *purpose.* Below is a list of some of the most eagerly sought household collectibles:

> **Tricks of the Trade**
> Knowing which household bric-a-brac are currently hot collectibles can help you know when to buy, when to sell, and when to hold. Being up-to-date with the market can also help you avoid low-rent fakes, frauds, and reproductions masquerading as high-class collectibles.

➤ Baskets

➤ Butter, candy, and chocolate molds

➤ Caddies and containers

➤ Dishes

➤ Electrical appliances, such as hand-operated washing machines, iceboxes (wooden or metal), irons, Mixmasters, and toasters

➤ Funnels

➤ Jell-O molds

➤ Measuring devices

➤ Milk pails and jugs

➤ Mortars and pestles

➤ Nutmeg graters

➤ Pots and pans

➤ Pressure cookers

➤ Racks of serving spoons and other utensils

➤ Rolling pins

➤ Sausage grinders, stuffers, and so on

➤ Thermometers

➤ Trivets

➤ Waffle irons

➤ Washboards

Now you know what kitchen utensils to look for when you blitz through flea markets, garage sales, and antique shows.

With the exception of items such as books and catalogs, collectors do not require kitchen collectibles to be in mint condition. The item must be in working order, however. This is especially important for things such as cake tins and toasters. Avoid buying items that have rust, holes, or missing pieces.

Living in an Amish Paradise: Quilts

Quilts are three-layer fabric sandwiches: the top (the design), the filler, and the back. The layers are held together by the stitching, called "quilting." In the old days, quilts were filled with wool or cotton; today, many synthetic fibers are used. Below are the four most common types of quilts:

➤ *Appliqué* quilts are made by sewing different pieces of fabric on the top cover.

➤ *Crazy* quilts, made during the Victorian era, consist of random pieces of fabric, flags, and ribbons.

➤ *Patchwork* (or *pieced*) quilts are made by stitching together small pieces of fabric in geometric patterns.

➤ *Trapunto* quilts have stitching spaced to form ridges in the fabric.

The quality of each quilt must be individually determined by its design, the quality of the work, the color, age, and condition. If the quilt is documented with the year and possibly the name of the maker or owner, it will assume much more value. Among the most valuable quilts are the so-called "Baltimore quilts," named for the city where they were made by young women preparing for marriage. These quilts date from the middle of the last century.

Today, collectors can find outstanding examples of contemporary quilting at the annual Mennonite auctions held in Harrisburg, Pennsylvania. This is the largest quilt auction in the world, attracting about 10,000 people every year. No matter where you buy your collectible-quality quilt, figure on plunking down at least $300. Fine examples of this handiwork go for around $1,200 to $2,500.

Valuable old quilts can sell for more than $25,000 each at exclusive auctions.

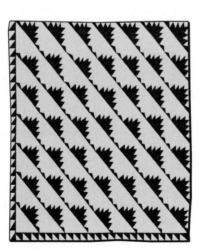

What's the Frequency, Kenneth? (Radios)

Entertainment devices are interesting—and expensive—collectibles. Radios, for example, were manufactured in great quantities after World War I. Examples made during the late 1930s and 1940s are especially popular with collectors. Made of *Bakelite* or *Catalin*, early types of plastic, they are usually about 14 inches long and 10 inches high.

If you're looking for exotic radios, concentrate on early Atwater Kent, Majestic, RCA, and Polle Royal. To some collectors, the most desired of all are the Scott all-wave receivers of the 1930s. They were built on two chrome chassis: the upper tuning section, and the lower amplifying section. These sets contained as many as 30 tubes, guaranteeing superb reception. An especially desirable model is the Philco 690 XX made in 1937. Collectible Philco radios start at $80 to $250. Other collectible radios range from $30 to $4,500.

There is also a growing interest in short-wave reception. If this is your field, look to the early Scotts. Those built today most likely cannot exceed the quality and reception of the earlier models.

Let's Twist Again, Like We Did Last Summer: Records

The scene: A cocktail party. I am nursing a diet cola and minding my own business.

The conversation: A friend of a friend of a friend says to me, "I hear you know something about collectibles. I have a fortune in old opera records. Collectors will give me a bundle for them."

I think, "Not bloody likely. Records are not valuable merely because they are old. There are records from the early 1900s you can't give away... but there are records from the 1960s that are very hot." But for once in my life I say nothing and head for the peanuts. A smart move.

Most of the records that collectors covet today are desirable because they were originally produced in small supply for a limited audience and have since developed a cult following. Records can also become popular collectibles if they were made by certain companies. A record bearing a scarce label will likely be valuable even if the music isn't terribly popular.

Record collectors are especially demanding about the condition of the record. A chipped, cracked, or warped record is as good as worthless unless it is extremely rare. A record that is scuffed is worth less than half the value of the same record in mint condition. The condition of the album cover is also crucial with this collectible. In the case of records from the 1950s, 1960s, and 1970s, the sleeve can be as valuable as the record itself.

Learn the Lingo
Record collectors are known as **discophiles**.

Here are some types of records that are highly popular at this time:

➤ Early recordings of people who later became stars.

➤ Rare record labels.

➤ Original-issue records of the 1950s and 1960s featuring rock and roll stars and bands such as Elvis Presley and the Beatles.

On average, collectible albums range from $10 and up; an autographed *Best of the Beach Boys* album, for example, is valued at $400. Unless exceedingly rare, wax cylinders are not especially pricey; they cost from $6 to around $50.

Tool Time

Tools are a hot collectible at the moment. Especially desirable are tools from the turn of the century up to the 1930s.

➤ **Rarity.** As a rule of thumb, the more unusual the tool, the greater its potential for value. For example, tool collectors scramble for wooden planes and brass-mounted rulers.

➤ **Name recognition.** Well-known names in tools (such as Stanley) add value.

➤ **Condition.** All things being equal, tools in excellent condition fetch higher prices than rusted wrecks, but never assume that a rusted or worn tool is worthless. Just the opposite is often the case.

➤ **Original packaging.** Like many other collectibles, tools are worth more if they are in their original boxes.

The Least You Need to Know

➤ Among today's most desirable household collectibles are beer cans, bottles, clocks, pens, quilts, radios, and tools.

➤ Condition, age, rarity, and design distinguish the valuable from the merely old.

Chapter 16

As Clear as Crystal

Legend has it that glass originated on the shores of the Mediterranean when a group of Phoenician sailors built a fire to cook dinner. Careless campers, they found the next morning that the burning coals had melted the sand underneath the fire to create a rough glass. (Don't try this at home, Scouts: there must have been soda in the sand, since soda acts as a flux to form the melted silica.)

Since that time, silica (sand) has been mixed with various minerals and elements to create different types of glass, each with its own unique qualities. All of them are gorgeous in their own glittering way.

In this chapter, you will learn about the hottest collectible glassware today, including fine crystal, Depression glass, carnival glass, Waterford, Tiffany, Lalique—even those Bugs Bunny juice glasses you thought were worthless. There's also a section on glass paperweights for those of you who favor these lovely baubles. In addition, you'll find out what makes a piece of glass collectible. Finally, I'll show you some of the tricks that the pros use to distinguish authentic period glass from reproductions.

The Cadillac of Glass: Crystal

The secret of clear crystal glass was locked up for most of the 1500s on the isles of Murano in the Lagoon of Venice. But money talks and a hundred years later, renegade Venetians had sold the secret to producing colorless glass. (In case you're wondering, the secret is adding a dash of manganese to the mix. Skilled glass blowing doesn't hurt, either.)

Other countries, especially Bohemia, started setting up rival glassmaking industries, and soon they had outstripped the Venetians with their better techniques. By the 1700s, the Venetian industry had fallen so far behind in the glass biz that in 1730 a Venetian named Briati disguised himself and worked for three years in a Bohemian glasswork to relearn the secrets that his country had lost. Today, a 17th-century Venetian glass goblet in good condition would go for more than $50,000. See Appendix B for a list of price guides that cover Venetian glass.

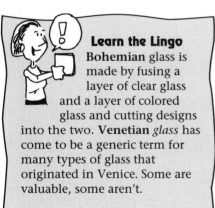

Learn the Lingo
Bohemian glass is made by fusing a layer of clear glass and a layer of colored glass and cutting designs into the two. **Venetian** *glass* has come to be a generic term for many types of glass that originated in Venice. Some are valuable, some aren't.

Glass made in the 1950s and 1960s in Murano, Italy, especially by well-known makers like Vennini, are red-hot collectibles today. These shimmering collectibles are often featured in major auctions. There are still fine samples of this glass available because many pieces were shipped to the our shores 30 to 40 years ago.

Fine crystal is called "lead crystal" because it contains lead oxide, the ingredient that makes the glass clear and gives it the bell-like ring when the rim is tapped or "pinched," a sound not found in other stemware.

Bump and Grind: Cut Crystal

Is there a home in America that doesn't have a piece of cut crystal? This heavily faceted crystal is almost as ubiquitous in the suburbs as TVs and telephones. It went out of favor for many years because it tends to be hefty and can scratch furniture. But in the 1960s, cut glass, like some sparkling Richard Nixon, made a resurgence.

Cut glass made between 1890 to 1915 (the so-called "Brilliant" period") is the most desired by collectors and commands steep prices. About 25 to 28 percent of this cut glass was lead, which gives the glass its brilliance and weight and allows deep cutting to enhance its design. The need for lead to manufacture munitions accounts for the scarcity of cut glass during World War I.

Cut glass decanters like this one are popular collectibles.

Today's cut glass (also called "cut crystal") is comprised of 10 to 12 percent lead, which accounts for its lack of glitter when compared to its ancestors. Items made with cut glass and sterling silver (such as powder jars and pitchers) are also highly desired by many collectors. The value of the piece depends on the following qualities:

➤ **Condition.** Chips or cracks can render a piece valueless.

➤ **Brilliance.** The more sparkle, the more value.

➤ **Rarity.** Unusual shapes are more valuable. A heart-shaped piece will be more valuable than an oval, all things being equal.

It can be difficult to distinguish cut glass from pressed glass. Although the former is made by cutting the glass on a wheel and the latter by pressing the glass into a mold, they can look very much the same. You can tell the difference most easily by letting your fingers do the work. Use the five Ts to help you distinguish between pressed glass and cut glass.

➤ **Touch.** The edges of pressed glass are rounded and irregular, while the edges of cut glass are sharp and irregular.

➤ **Trademark.** *Nucut, Near-cut, Deep cut,* and *Press-cut* are trademarks of pressed glass. These are very highly valued collectibles.

➤ **Tint.** Cut glass is clearer and brighter than pressed glass.

➤ **Timbre.** Cut glass has a higher ringing tone than pressed glass.

➤ **Tonnage.** Pressed glass is much lighter than cut glass.

Connoisseur

To protect their trademark in this country, foreign producers of glass often identify their products with either a small "C" in a circle (copyright), a small "R" in a circle (registered), or a small "TM" (trademark). These marks are sometimes *extremely* small. You will have to look very closely, for example, to find the circled "R" on the Swarovski crystal trademark."

If this is really your lucky day, you might find the manufacturer's signature on your cut glass. This is a long shot, however, since only about ten percent of the cut glass made between 1880 and 1900 was signed. In case you're looking, the signatures are round or oval, and as faint as an adolescent boy's mustache. Look on the uncut side of the glass. Like autographed books, signed pieces are usually more valuable than unsigned ones.

All top-notch *modern* glass collectibles are marked by their manufacturer. Look at the bottom or the base for the trademark. If the crystal does not have the correct trademark, it is part of the "gray market"—a knock-off, a copy, a fake. Unregistered products may cost less, but they will always be worth less.

A Rose By Any Other Name Wouldn't Smell as Sweet: Waterford

It is virtually impossible to tell the difference between the English and Irish crystal made during the 1800s. Better informed collectors call it "Anglo/Irish" glass; the hoi polloi often call it "Waterford." The first Waterford plant closed in 1851; another one with the same name opened in 1951. As a result, if granny got some new wedding glass from England and Ireland, it sure wasn't Waterford. None of the Anglo/Irish glass made before 1851 was known to have been marked, but Waterford glass produced after 1951 is clearly etched with the "Waterford" name. Collectors prize this heavily cut crystal. A modern carafe is worth about $75; a pitcher, about $150; and a 12-inch vase, around $350.

> ### Big Deals
>
> The most famous piece of glass in the world is the Portland Vase, housed at the British Museum in London. The epitome of Roman luxury glass, it is the most celebrated surviving piece of "cameo glass," wherein layers of glass were fused together and then carved. Produced during the 1st century A.D., it was acquired in the mid-1800s by the Duke of Portland, who presented it to the museum. It was smashed, then totally restored.

Steuben (Corning)

Steuben was founded in 1903 in Corning, New York. In 1918, the Corning Glass Works bought Steuben and the company turned from producing fine glass to making light bulbs. Nonetheless, during Prohibition Corning turned out a considerable number of wine and cocktail glasses, which just goes to show how effective Prohibition wasn't.

In 1933, in the beginning of the Depression, Steuben embarked on an unlikely project: to produce the greatest crystal in the world. And they didn't do half bad.

Today, Steuben is considered the greatest continual producer of American glass. Pieces are expensive and quality is exceedingly fine.

> ### Learn the Lingo
> **Aurene** is a type of Steuben glass, similar to **Favrile** made by Tiffany.

Feeling the S-q-u-e-e-z-e: Pressed Glass

When pressed glass was first produced, in the 19th century, it was as popular as a water fountain in the Sahara. Hundreds of pressed glass patterns were made, many in complete sets. There were the everyday cups, glasses, and bowls... but also such unusual items as egg cups and covered compotes. Fashionable hostesses had complete sets of pressed glass, not difficult since the stuff was sold in five-and-dime stores, dry good stores, and through catalogs. Eventually, the craze abated.

By the late 1920s, however, pressed glass emerged from dusty shelves and became one of the most popular items for American glass collectors. The fad didn't last long, however. The market was flooded with reproductions, confusing collectors and debasing the real thing. What goes around comes around: I predict that pressed glass is due for another rebirth. Today, a high-end 8 × 11-inch pressed glass compote sells for about $100, but you can still pick up a 6-inch Georgia pressed glass compote for under $20.

Pressed glass could have unique decorative patterns.

Air-twist stem   Diamond motif   Flared lip   Quarter fan motif

Baluster stem   Etched floral motif   Globe shape   Scroll motif

Faceted stem   Notched motif

Identify the patterns on your pressed glass goblets.

Other 20th-Century Glass

The craft of glass making has continually been refined and adapted to current tastes and needs. It's no surprise that a tremendous amount of collectible glass has been produced in the last century. Let's take a look at some of the best.

Art Glass

American art glass dates from 1880 to 1925. During this time, some of the finest de-signed, colored, and decorated glass appeared. Some are identified by color, such as ruby, black amethyst, and cranberry. Others are known by their names, such as Peachblow, Burmese, Amberina, and Crown Milano. Others were categorized by their finish and decoration, such as enameled or satin finish. Generally, most pieces are referred to as "art glass" when there is no specific name given. They range in price today from a low of about $30 for a tumbler to a high of about $7,000 for a 1925 7-inch bottle made by the designer Maurice Marinot. Figure on spending about $100 for a bowl.

➤ **Tiffany art glass.** The most famous art glass was produced by Louis Comfort Tiffany and Tiffany Studios. Tiffany is especially well-known for vibrant stained-glass windows and beautifully colored lamp shades. *Favrile* is a type of Tiffany glass, recognizable by its iridescent surface and metallic design. The real thing will be signed with initials (L.C.T.) or the name "Tiffany."

215

*Tiffany lamps are a
well-known form of
art glass.*

*Tiffany also made
Favrile glass, known
for its iridescent
surface.*

➤ **Reproductions.** From 1920 to 1940, many reproductions of the early art glass were made. Most were produced by machine, so it doesn't take a rocket scientist to distinguish them from the earlier hand-blown examples.

Carnival Glass: Poor Man's Tiffany

Frank Fenton gets the nod as the first to turn out easily affordable iridescent glass in fancy shapes. The year was 1907: the place, Newark, Ohio. Other glassmakers jumped on the idea and it spread as fast as a chill through a nudist colony. Common designs include fruit bowls, powder jars, and pin trays. On the rarer side you can find banks, jelly jars, and paperweights. At least 1,000 different patterns were created between 1909 and 1929.

This glass earned the moniker "Carnival glass" because it was often given out at carnivals and fairs. It was also used as a freebie by tea and cereal companies. Long regarded as a stepchild in the glass collectors' extended family, the pieces made with more care have become popular collectibles recently.

The top favorites are Northwood pieces, made by the Northward Glass Company in Wheeling, West Virginia. Fortunately, his pieces are easy to identify: They are well marked with a capital N within a circle, usually at the bottom of the piece. The most popular colors (in order of preference) are purple, blue, green, orange, yellow, and marigold. White carnival glass is very rare. Look for deep cut, well-colored quality pieces. Small pieces, such as a tumbler or a punch cup, cost about $20 each, 9-inch bowls fetch about $100, and a fine six-piece set sells for about $1,000.

Crystal on Steroids: Depression Glass

What is Depression glass? No, it's not glass that should be on happy pills. It's America's first mass-produced glassware, as different from crystal as sushi is from donuts. It was made in the Depression years, from the 1920s to the collector cut-off date of 1940. Compared to pressed and blown glass it looks clunky, but at least the pattern names are elegant, such as Raindrops, Oyster and Pearl, Lace Edge, Queen Mary, Royal Lace, and American Sweetheart.

The Hush Puppies of glass, Depression glass was molded and mold-etched, sold in the five-and-dime stores and some chain stores. It was produced in many colors, including clear, black, red, blue, and pearly white. The opaque white is often called *milk glass*. The most common colors were green, pink, amber, and yellow.

Many collectors seek complete sets of dinner, breakfast, or breakfast pieces. This is a daunting task, but not impossible. Pieces that were most heavily used and thus prone to breakage (pitchers, ashtrays, and so on) are especially hard to find. See Appendix B for a list of price guides you may wish to consult.

Since there is still so much Depression glass around, greed can be your worst enemy. Try these guidelines:

1. **Quality.** Concentrate on quality, not quantity. Look for undamaged pieces and unusual items such as gift and decorative pieces.

2. **Category.** Consider specializing in one category instead of trying to find a matching service for twelve.

Connoisseur
Depression glass tumblers with decal decorations of palm trees, nudes, or geometric designs were often sold as containers for processed-cheese spreads. Collectors call those containers used for Kraft Foods "swanky swigs."

3. **Companies.** Collectors of Depression glass often buy glassware made by specific companies. The most popular companies are Cambridge Glass Company, Imperial Glass Company, Jeanette Glass Company, and Fostoria Glass Company.

4. **Colors.** Red is the most prized color, followed by blue. Pink is the least desired.

5. **Styles.** The famous Nuart and Nucut lines from Imperial are especially popular with collectors of this type of glass.

Oo La La: Lalique

Around the turn of the century, French artist Rene Lalique attracted international acclaim for his innovative jewelry designs. In 1920, he formed a glass company in the province of Alsace-Lorraine and began making tableware, bottles, fruit dishes, stemware, and decorative pieces. Most of his statues and figures have a satin finish, highlighted with clear glass. Nearly all the pieces are signed, making them easy to identify. Rene Lalique died in 1945, but the company carries on.

Lalique is highly collectible and even exhibited in museums. One of the finest collections is housed in the Brighton Museum in Brighton, England, if you have a hankering to see a lot of Lalique. Want to buy some of your own? A signed ashtray, made around 1913, recently sold for $400, the same price as a signed 9-inch bowl. A water buffalo figurine, however, is valued at $3,000.

Make Room for Coffeepots: American and European Glass of the 1940s and 1950s

In addition to Levittown, Richard Nixon, and the Man in the Grey Flannel Suit, the 1940s and 1950s saw the creation of some beautiful American glass. Great advances in glass technology were made during this time. New items were resistant to sudden temperature changes, which meant that soup bowls, cups, and coffeepots could be made of glass. In addition, manufacturers learned how to produce larger items, such as foot-long ashtrays (no home is complete without one) and lamps shaped like rearing horses. During this time, glass was hand-made as well as machine-made.

Below is a list of some of the glass manufacturers of this era whose products have attracted the most attention among collectors. Space limitations prevented me from listing all the different glass manufacturers, so don't hold it against me for the ones I couldn't fit in. Check Appendix B for a list of price guides for this glass.

➤ **Crystal Glass.** Produced by the Crystal Art Glass Factory in Cambridge, Ohio, it is also called "Degenhart," the name of the firm's owners. Many of the items were made of rich, opaque slag glass in amethyst and off-white. You can find such novelty items as paperweights, salt and pepper shakers, and toothpick holders.

➤ **Dunbar Glass.** This West Virginia company produced beverage sets, cake stands, animal figures, vases, and tumblers. The firm closed its doors in 1953.

➤ **Heisey Glass.** Heisey produced some of the most popular post-war glass before it closed in 1956; the products were so well regarded that in 1950, pieces were exhibited at the Metropolitan Museum of Art in New York City. To authenticate this glass, look for an H inside a diamond. Rare examples cost hundreds of dollars, but there are still some affordable pieces commonly available. The most desirable Heisey glass is Verlys, frosted in various patterns. Prices start at $20 for a small nut dish, cheese plate, or punch cup, and range up to $250 for large pitchers.

➤ **New Martinsville Glass.** Collectors lust after this firm's black glass, produced in bold modern shapes. In 1944, New Martinsville became the Viking Glass Company, whose products are also collectible.

➤ **Pilgrim Glass.** Pilgrim, established in 1951, made high-quality cranberry glass. They are popular collectibles. To authenticate them, look for paper labels.

➤ **Westmoreland Glass.** Known for its novelty items (such as high hats, pistols, and ashtrays shaped like turtles), Westmoreland Glass comes in black, ruby, and amber. Items made after

Learn the Lingo
Amberina glass has shades of color from light amber to rich ruby.

Connoisseur
Collectible drinking glasses featuring TV puppet Howdy Doody and those with early Disney characters continue to grow in popularity and value. A 1950s Howdy Doody juice glass can sell for as much as $20. A Disney glass at the same price is considered a bargain.

219

1949 are marked with the intertwined letters W and G. Ashtrays run about $15, bowls about $95, and milk-glass cookie jars about $250.

Paperweights

OK, so you use your cat as a paperweight. I don't want to go there. This section is for people who use real glass paperweights, the kind suitable for throwing at the cats who howl outside my window at midnight.

Paperweights first appeared in Venice in the early 1840s and were perfected by the French glass factories of Baccarat, Clichy, and St. Louis by 1848. At first, the French manufacturers created *millefiori* weights, multicolored canes arranged in patterns and encased in a ball of fine lead crystal. This served to magnify the contents. Soon the line expanded to include elaborate flower designs. Today, high-quality paperweights with this design sell for $50 and up.

Paperweights are important glass collectibles; masterpieces of this art form are priced in the thousands of dollars. Weights created by Bacarrat, Clichy, and St. Cloud are the paperweight collector's dream, but American firms also produced some lovely specimens. Look for those by the Boston and Sandwich Glass Company and the New England glass Company. The latter specialized in flowers, animals, letters, and stars. The Pairpoint works in New Bedford and the Millville works in New Jersey produced some elegant samples.

A glass paperweight.

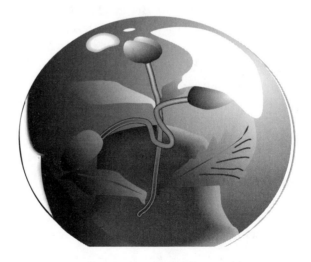

Paperweights first appeared—along with paper—in ancient Egypt. Even Louis Comfort Tiffany tried his hand at paperweights. Look for his initials and the trade name "Favrile""

on the bottom. Paperweights produced by individual artisans such as Domenick Labino of Grand Rapids, Ohio and Charles Kaziun of Brockton, Massachusetts are also fan favorites.

Many of the techniques of the early weights have been imitated in reproductions. The new paperweights are lighter than the old ones and may have flaws in the glass. They may also feel slick, like a politician running for re-election. The real McCoys have pontil marks and convex bottoms. The novelty weights will likely never be worth enough to put your child through college, but they can make an interesting collection to the budget-minded among us. A National Lead Company paperweight with a Dutch Boy logo is worth about $35; a paperweight showing President John Fitzgerald Kennedy is worth $75.

> ### Big Deals
>
> In 1875, the first glass candy containers were produced. Filled with (you guessed it) candy, they were in the shape of the Liberty Bell and Independence Hall and were sold at the Centennial Exposition of 1876 in Philadelphia. By 1920, novelty glass candy containers were popular sellers; now, the "hot" containers made between 1905 and 1935 in great condition will sell for more than $1,000 each. Here are the top companies: Cambridge Glass Company, Jeanette Glass Company, L.E. Smith Company, J.H. Millstein, T.H. Stough Company, Victory Glass Company, West Brothers, and Westmoreland Glass Company.

Collecting Glass

Gotta have it? Memorize these Top Ten Rules to use the next time a yearning for glass overtakes you.

1. **Learn Your Glass.** Remember that many items were not marked, and others may have lost their labels. Some even carry forged marks and faked labels. Visit factories, museums, and other people's collections. If you learn to recognize the Real Thing, you will be much more likely to get great deals that other people don't recognize.

2. **Attend Estate Sales.** Most auction houses will only handle certain types of glass. If you are interested in other types, haunt estate sales. You can often find great examples at excellent prices—because other bidders didn't follow Rule #1.

3. **Rummage Around.** Always check box lots of kitchen and household items for sale at flea markets, swap meets, house sales, and the like. You may find an excellent item buried in a box of junk.

4. **Check Lesser-Known Factories.** Look for products produced by small factories whose products were not widely distributed. These glass pieces can be an excellent value.

5. **Visit Shops in Large Cities.** You can sometimes strike it rich in big city antique shops that specialize in specific items, such as those from the 1930s to 1940s. They are more likely to have exotic types of American and Depression glass, too.

6. **Condition, Condition, Condition.** Do not buy damaged pieces. They have little value.

7. **Check and Double-Check.** Before you buy an item, check it carefully. I suggest that you use an ultraviolet light, which will reveal any cracks or repairs.

8. **Research.** One of the most frustrating aspects of learning about glass is trying to figure out who made it. Much stemware was never marked with the manufacturer's marks. I suggest that you check reprints of manufacturers' catalogs. Both the articles and the ads will help you identify a piece and ascertain its value.

9. **Labels.** Always check labels. Some unscrupulous sellers copy early labels and attach them to unmarked pieces. An original label will be worn and faded.

10. **Fakes.** Look for fake manufacturer's marks. Some reproductions carry the names and marks of defunct glass companies.

Glass Wannabes

Caveat Emptor
Do your homework; check all guidebooks; and use common sense before you invest a hefty chunk of change in a glass collectible.

Of all antiques, glass is among the most often copied and faked. Since glass is so easy and inexpensive to produce and can command such high prices, fakery abounds. Pressed glass, for instance, has been copied for years. Although some companies claim that they use the original molds, they should be trusted about as readily as the telemarketer who promises you a sweet deal on Florida swampland. Even Depression glass is being copied.

The Least You Need to Know

➤ Crystal contains lead, which gives it brilliance.

➤ Depression glass and carnival glass are affordable and popular collectibles.

➤ Learn as much as you can. Glass is especially easy to fake… and fakes abound with this collectible.

➤ Glass breaks. Be careful when you handle it.

Part 4
Master of Arts:
Furniture and Art

"This is not art to me, all these squares and things. Real art has, you know, like a Madonna in it."

—*Unknown (from the guest book at an exhibition of modern art)*

"I'm glad all the old masters are dead, and I only wish they had died sooner."

—*Mark Twain*

No other aspect of the collectibles world is as sexy as the art market. The prices of fine paintings boggle the mind: $51 million for a Picasso, $49 million for a (relatively) minor Van Gogh. The cost of exquisite furniture and rugs is almost as high. It's a world of high-fliers: singer Elton John, for example, collects contemporary black-and-white photographs for his apartment in Atlanta and the portraits of 18th-century artist Arthur Devis for his English country mansion. "No way I could collect fine art and home furnishings," you think. Wrong.

There's plenty of magnificent collectible art, furniture, and carpets—enough to suit every taste and budget. Let me show you how to go from rugs to riches in this part of the book.

Chapter 17

Different Strokes for Different Folks: Collecting Paintings

In This Chapter

➤ Get a quick history of oil painting

➤ Find out how to buy paintings and drawings with confidence and skill

➤ Learn how paintings are valued and priced

➤ Learn about the major schools of painting

Art, like morality, consists of drawing the line somewhere (or so said G.K. Chesterton). In this chapter, I'm going to draw the line—and color in the spaces. When I'm done, you'll be ready to plunge into the exciting world of art collecting.

Of all of the collectible fields, paintings are the most profitable. They are found everywhere. The biggest scores for antiques dealers are found in art.

No other collectible is as glamorous as art. It's where the wheelers and dealers wheel and deal, where the big money changes hands. You'll have no trouble finding paintings and drawings that suit your taste; after all, paintings are as common as vending machines that eat your quarters, green lights that turn red as you approach, and teenagers who think they're overworked.

But there is a tremendous difference between a mass-produced paint-by-number oil painting and a masterpiece. So you have a frame of reference, the first mention of oil painting appears in German manuscripts from the 13th century. The paintings were not very good, because proper solvents had not yet been created. Turpentine and varnish changed all that. Soon, artists were painting with oils on wood or parchment.

In this chapter, I'll help you focus on your goals as an art collector. Then I'll teach you the steps you need to know to collect art. You'll learn where to shop—and where not to shop. I'll teach you the importance of researching before purchasing and how to determine pricing. Along the way, you'll learn all about the major schools of highly collectible art.

Be Art Smart

"I'll have the BLT on white with mayo." If only buying paintings was as easy as ordering lunch! Unfortunately, it's not. For one thing, lunch is cheap and art is expensive. Prices for investment-grade paintings start in the low hundreds and spiral rapidly upward. To make collecting paintings even more complicated, you cannot tell if a painting is priced fairly by just looking at it. Unlike bacon, paintings aren't priced by the pound. Artists don't work by the hour and art dealers don't have set fees. Table 17.1 lists the most expensive paintings ever sold.

Table 17.1 The Most Expensive Paintings Ever Sold

Artist/Painting	Price	Place and Date
Van Gogh, *Portrait du Dr. Gachet*	$75,000,000	Christie's, NY, 1990
Renoir, *Au Moulin de la Galette*	$71,000,000	Sotheby's, NY, 1990
Picasso, *Les Noces de Pierrette*	$51,700,000	Paris, 1989
Van Gogh, *Irises*	$49,000,000	Sotheby's, NY, 1987
Picasso, Self Portrait: *Yo Picasso*	$43,500,000	Sotheby's, NY, 1989
Picasso, *Au Lapin Agile*	$37,000,000	Sotheby's, NY, 1989
Van Gogh, *Sunflowers*	$36,200,000	Christie's, London, 1987
Picasso, *Acrobate et Jeune Arlequin*	$35,500,000	Christie's, London, 1988
Jacopo da Carucci, *Portrait of Duke Cosimo I de Medici*	$32,000,000	Christie's, NY, 1989
Cezanne, *Nature Morte*	$26,000,000	Sotheby's, NY, 1993

The market for American art of every kind is rising; the best portraits and landscapes of the 18th and 19th centuries are rising in value faster than George Steinbrenner's ego. Let's start with the very best paintings produced on this side of the pond. Study Table 17.2:

Table 17.2 The Most Expensive Paintings by American Artists

Artist/Painting	Price	Place and Date
Willem de Kooning, *Interchange*	$18,800,00	Sotheby's, NY, 1989
Jasper Johns, *False Starts*	$15,500,000	Sotheby's, NY, 1988
Jasper Johns, *Two Flags*	$11,000,000	Sotheby's, NY, 1988
Jackson Pollock, *Number 8, 1950*	$10,500,00	Sotheby's, NY, 1989
Willem de Kooning, *July*	$8,000,00	Christie's, NY, 1990
Frederic Edwin Church, *Home by the Lake, Scene in the Catskill Mountains*	$7,500,000	Sotheby's, NY, 1989
Robert Rauchenberg, *Rebus*	$6,600,000	Sotheby's, NY, 1991
Willem de Kooning, *Palisade*	$6,500,00	Sotheby's, NY, 1990
Jasper Johns, *White Flag*	$6,400,000	Christie's, NY, 1988
Roy Lichtenstein, *Kiss II*	$5,500,000	Christie's, NY, 1990

Art 101

Let's hear a chorus of the collector's lament: "So much art, so little time." Here's a cribsheet for the most-often talked about modern art so you, too, can talk the talk and walk the walk:

➤ **Barbizon**—When landscapes came into fashion early in the 1800s, a group of artists began painting scenes in places such as Germany's Black Forest. The French came along for the ride, and the Barbizon School was born. These paintings are characterized by dark foregrounds that frame a lighter middle ground, the central theme. A three-dimensional effect is created by the lighting.

➤ **Impressionism**—Pioneered by Monet, Renoir, and Cezanne, Impressionist paintings are marked by fabulous lighting and atmosphere.

➤ **Cubism**—Pablo Picasso rebelled against Impressionism by breaking down and taking apart the forms of nature. Cubism has a geometric quality that reshapes known forms. Aside from Picasso, the major Cubists are George Braque, Juan Gris, and Fernand Leger.

➤ **Ashcan School**—The 1920s brought the Ashcan School, a realistic slice of city life. Much of this is good art, but the supply is quite limited.

➤ **Surrealism**—This movement's goal is to liberate our unconsciousness from the chains of reason. Like abstract art, surrealism uses shapes, forms, and colors that have no natural counterpart. The Big Man on Campus was Salvador Dali.

➤ **Expressionism**—Headquartered in Germany from 1905 to the 1920s, these paintings are marked by a revelation of the artist's personal emotions. Look for feeling conveyed on canvas through the use of brush and paint. The major players were George Grosz, Otto Dix, Max Beckmann, Vassily Kandinsky, and Paul Klee.

Know Thyself

Fortunately, there's no right or wrong art. There's no right or wrong reason for buying art. There's not even any right or wrong way to buy art. But you can learn to buy the paintings you like at prices you can afford. Here's how.

Connoisseur
Countless portraits of nameless English and European worthies painted by equally nameless English and European artists populate the walls of antique shops. If you are looking for a painted ancestor to match your 18th-century furniture, consider buying one of these anonymous—and affordable—portraits. Just make sure that you like the person's looks, because few things are more annoying than eating daily meals as someone you detest stares down at you.

When you feel the urge to collect paintings, start by identifying the kinds of art you like. You first have to describe your taste in art to figure out which styles touch your soul. Remember, you have to live with the painting, and it can be easier to get rid of a recalcitrant spouse than a mediocre painting. With the first, you're usually willing to take a loss; with the second, you'll likely want to recoup your initial investment.

Say you're looking for a painting with a little green and some peach to fit over the mantel, something light or floral like the one you saw in the model house down the street. Or perhaps you want a hunting scene to go in the den or a portrait of some ritzy-looking old guy for the dining room. Ritzy portraits always give a dining room some class.

If these scenarios fit your interest in art, then your goal is to locate decorative art. In that case, there's no need to blather on about the artist's qualifications. You like the picture, the picture likes you, and everyone is happy. And don't let anyone tell you differently. Remember—you have to live with the painting, not your arrogant neighbor, contemptuous in-laws, or conceited boss.

Do Squeeze the Charmin!

Next, locate and select the specific paintings that you might want to buy. In order to do this, you need a working knowledge of the art world. You have to become familiar with art personalities, art dealers, art galleries, and the art community. There are several price guides you will want to consult as well. I recommend *The Official Price Guide to Fine Art* by Susan Theran (House of Collectibles, Florida).

➤ **Love at first sight? Not.** You comparison shop for food and clothes; why not art? In order to select the best art for your taste and budget, stifle the impulse to buy immediately and instead make a point to shop around. Don't fall prey to the "one-of-a-kind" myth—that no two paintings are exactly alike. You can always find another painting that looks virtually identical to the first one. I promise.

➤ **Those in the know.** Stick to well-known galleries and dealers. This offers you protection that you can't get with fly-by-night fellas.

➤ **Dealing with dealers.** The same advice I gave you in earlier chapters holds true here, too: Get to know the dealers who sell the paintings you like. A reputable art dealer will scour the market and help you get the paintings you want at a fair price. Buying from a dealer can also help you avoid damaged art, which you may find in secondhand shops, frame shops, and resale outlets. But dealers aren't gurus offering you inner peace, so shop smart.

Hit the Books: Research

In order to make informed decisions about whether or not you really want to buy a particular painting, you need to learn more about the art and artist. Use the Hitting the Books Worksheet in this chapter.

Caveat Emptor
Even art experts have a difficult time determining the value of a painting that is under glass. If you cannot examine the work fully, pay no more than the frame is worth to you.

Hitting the Books Worksheet

Find out as much as you can about a painting before you consider buying it. Copy and use this worksheet to direct your research.

1. Who is the artist? _____

_____

2. What is the medium?

   ❏ acrylic   ❏ mixed media   ❏ pencil

   ❏ charcoal   ❏ oil   ❏ tempera

   ❏ gouache   ❏ pastel   ❏ watercolor

   ❏ ink

3. What is the subject?

   ❏ figure study   ❏ landscape   ❏ seascape

   ❏ folk art   ❏ marine   ❏ sporting scene

   ❏ genre (French courtiers,   ❏ portrait   ❏ still life
      Dutch farmers, etc.)

   ❏ hunting scene   ❏ primitive   ❏ wildlife

   ❏ illustration

4. What is the size? _____

_____

5. What is the framing? _____

_____

6. What is the condition? _____

_____

7. What is the style? _____

_____

8. What is the quality? _____

_____

9. What is the painting's historical importance? _____

_____

10. What is the provenance (prior ownership, shows or exhibitions, awards)?

_____

To get the answers, go to an art museum library. Try a private or state museum, college, or university that has a strong art history department. Kiss up to the research librarian; they can be of invaluable assistance.

An art treasure can appear at any time and in almost any place. If you think you have unearthed a true masterpiece, start by visiting an art museum. Study photographs of the paintings by the artist whose work you have. If you find your painting there, you know you have a copy. If not, there is a chance that you're onto something. In that case, take the picture to an art appraiser. Have the appraiser take a look at the picture to determine whether it merits appraising. If so, determine the fee in advance and get it in writing.

Big Deals

Provenance is profit. Provenance almost always makes a piece of art more valuable. Here are some things to look for concerning provenance:

➤ A signed statement of authenticity from a reputable art gallery

➤ An appraisal

➤ Names of previous owners

➤ Newspaper or magazine articles mentioning the painting

➤ Mention of the painting in a sales catalog

Paying the Piper

Paintings and drawings do not start out as just something else to buy and sell, but once they leave the artist's studio, they become a commodity like guns and butter. This brings us to the realities of the art economy: value and pricing.

Value

The art world is not a democracy: some art is worth more than other art. Collectors pay more for paintings that are judged to be of greater depth, significance, and quality. Table 17.3 lists the top ten artists whose work has commanded the most seven-figure price tags.

Connoisseur

A great pencil drawing is usually more valuable than a lousy oil painting, but as a general rule of thumb an oil painting will be more valuable than other media (such as watercolors or drawings) by the same artist.

Table 17.3 Artists with the Most Paintings Sold for More Than $1,000,000

Artist	Number of Paintings Sold
Pablo Picasso	148
Auguste Renoir	142
Claude Monet	126
Edgar Degas	64
Marc Chagall	53
Camille Pissarro	49
Henri Matisse	45
Paul Cezanne	42
Vincent Van Gogh	32
Jean Dubuffet	31
Amedeo Modigliani	31

Art prices can change over time. Changes in value can be the result of general outside forces such as shifts in public taste or fashion. With art, there is no obvious relationship between price and product. There are no formal laws for pricing art and art is not subject to quality control in any way. A fluctuation in the overall economic climate is also a factor in what a painting will cost. Take the case of the Impressionists.

After having their art derided during their lifetimes, several of the pioneer Impressionists got their revenge: they lived long enough to see their work accepted and even embraced. Nonetheless, even the most far-seeing of these painters could not have anticipated the outrageous prices their works fetch today. Around 1900, it was still possible to buy a painting by Vincent Van Gogh for about $190, a Cezanne for $1,000, a Manet for $2,000, a Monet for less than $5,000, and a Renoir for $10,000.

Caveat Emptor

The quality of the frame can be significant; in some cases, the frame can be worth more than the painting itself. This is a serious tip-off that the painting isn't a rare masterpiece.

Prices rose slowly but inexorably as the century marched on. In 1958, for instance, Van Gogh's *Public Gardens in Arles* set a record for a painting when it sold for $370,000; less than 12 years later, paintings by the Impressionists Van Gogh, Monet, and Renoir were selling for nearly $1,500,000 each. The upward trend continued: in 1980, Van Gogh's *Le Jardin de Poete, Arles* was sold for $5,200,000; five years later, his *Paysage au Soleil Levant* fetched $9,000,000. With this kind of investment potential, who needs to follow the Dow Jones?

An extraordinary price increase followed in the late 1980s, with Van Gogh's paintings leading the pack. In 1987, Van Gogh's *Sunflowers* sold for three times the price of any of his previous paintings; even this outrageous price was passed later that same year with the sale of *Irises* and three years later with the sale of *Portrait du Dr. Gachet*.

Big Deals

Seven of the ten most expensive paintings by women are by the American Impressionist Mary Cassatt (1845–1926). In first place is *The Conversation*, sold in 1988 for $4,100,000. *Black Hollyhocks with Blue Larkspur* by the American painter Georgia O'Keeffe (1887–1986) fetched $1,800,000 in 1987. Finnish artist Helene Schjerfbeck (1862–1946) is the other woman on this list; her *Balskorna—Dancing Shoes* sold in 1990 for $1,600,000.

You've learned how to buy paintings. Now find out how *not* to buy paintings. Here's the top ten list:

1. **Don't buy any painting when you are under the influence.** No "morning after" art, please.

2. **Don't buy paintings at night.** You tend to be more impulsive at night. Not a good time to spend big bucks.

3. **Don't buy serious paintings on vacation.** Buy fun art as a souvenir of your trip—but not serious art. You might forget how the couple next to you danced with the lampshades on their head, but you'll never forget the dreadful, overpriced painting you bought—because you're still paying off the charge card.

4. **Don't buy a painting because you are enchanted by the seller.** Good salespeople are charmers; that's why they're in sales and not dentistry or the post office. To help you resist the glib sales pitch, bring a cranky friend along.

5. **Don't buy paintings from trucks, street vendors, one-shot auctions, and other quickies.** Hot dogs, ice cream, and Danishes are all fine from trucks. No art or shellfish, please.

6. **Don't buy paintings over the phone.** Even though paintings are a visual medium, unscrupulous people sell them over the phone—and innocent people buy them. Caveat emptor.

7. **Don't buy any painting because it's "hot."** A hot painting can cool off faster than a hot pretzel.

8. **Don't buy any painting because the gallery is posh.** The appearance of the gallery is not a reliable indicator of its quality. Some of the best dealers operate out of modest quarters.

9. **Don't buy any painting under pressure.** What works for fire drills works for art sales: Stop, drop, and roll. Stop and think. If your credit is good, the picture will be there tomorrow or a week from tomorrow.

10. **Don't buy art based on predictions.** Past performance is no indication of future earnings. If it was, my stock portfolio would be worth a whole lot more than it is.

Connoisseur
Romantic and sentimental art from the 1850s has fallen out of favor in the past few decades. But the mid-1980s saw a revival of interest in the paintings of that period. The 1984 sale of the syrupy oil painting *Arrival of St. Nicholas* for $52,250 was a clear sign that cloyingly sweet art had come back into favor.

Connoisseur
Family portraits are rarely valuable, almost never as much as the owner anticipates. Unless painted by a recognized master, portraits usually have only sentimental or family value. Don't count on selling a family portrait to finance a world cruise.

Paintings as Investments

Don't. Art is not liquid. You cannot simply cash in a painting as you would stocks or bonds. Selling art takes time—and there are no guarantees that you will be able to make a profit, recoup your investment, or even sell the painting at all. Even if you do sell your Renoir at an upscale auction, you may have to wait at least six months from the time you place the art for sale until you cash the check. I would never recommend that anyone buy a painting or drawing as an investment.

Damaged Goods

Experienced art dealers and collectors generally avoid paintings that are damaged beyond a certain point. The most serious investors and collectors will not touch a painting that is damaged in any way. But depending on the type of art, some collectors will accept certain amounts and types of damage. The precise amount varies according to the usual suspects: age of the art, rarity, importance of the artist, and so on. For example, people who collect Gothic panel paintings from the 1600s will accept more damage on their paintings than those people who collect contemporary acrylic landscapes.

Here are three general guidelines to follow when assessing the relationship of damage to value:

1. **The greater the damage, the less the value.** Under five percent, damage is considered minor. Over that, things get a little dicey. Ten percent is generally the upper limit of "acceptable" damage.

2. **The location of the damage is as important as the extent.** Even the smallest amount of damage in the wrong place can destroy the value of a painting.

3. **Restorers will downplay the affect of the damage.** Restorers like to restore and are often justly proud of their work. There are many reputable, honest restorers, but some just want to get their brushes and rags on your painting. These restorers are apt to tell you that the damage isn't a problem. It usually is.

Caveat Emptor
Art fraud is one of the IRS's favorite targets.

Liar, Liar, Pants on Fire: Fakes and Frauds

Take this quick quiz. How many of the following statements are true?

1. Every kind of art is faked.

2. Forged art sells in every price range.

3. Forgeries are everywhere.

Unfortunately, they are all true. Great painters of every period have been imitated and faked. Many artists were even copied while they were still active because their work was so popular. While those paintings may have been sold as copies during the artist's lifetime, once the artist's work fades from the public eye, the line between real and reproduced is blurred. If the original artist is resurrected from obscurity, even art experts may be hard-pressed to distinguish the original from the copy.

And what happens if no one knows that an artist's works have been copied? Even greater confusion results. It's likely in this case that many pictures with the artist's signature—all fakes, of course—will be sold as authentic.

See Chapter 4, "Hey, Big Spender... Buying Like an Expert," for a detailed description of faked and fraudulent paintings.

The Least You Need to Know

➤ Know your taste, shop around, and research before you buy any painting that costs more than a box of cereal.

➤ Paintings are seriously devalued if damaged.

➤ Collect paintings for pleasure, not investment.

➤ Life is short, but art is long.

Chapter 18

Say Cheese, Please: Photographs

In This Chapter

➤ Learn all about "daguerreotypes"

➤ Find out how to build a collection of photographs that suits your taste—and pocketbook

➤ Discover what's hot and what's not in this field

Is photography art? Yes, and a highly collectible one at that. Most of the art photographers of the 19th century were ignored in their day but are highly prized in ours. Right now, American photographs from the 1920s and 1930s are sizzling collectibles. The images of contemporary shutterbugs are also widely sought after.

For some photography collectors, the appeal of this art lies in the fact that the camera captures a moment that can never be repeated again. For others, the allure lies in photography's realistic base. But whatever their reasons for seeking out fine photographs, these collectors are passionate about their interest.

In this chapter, you will first learn about the earliest photographic images, called *daguerreotypes*. Then you'll discover which 19th-century photographers are prized. Next I'll take you on a survey of contemporary American and British photography, so you can see what people are collecting and why. Finally, you'll get ballpark figures for each of the most collectible photographs, so you can price your own portfolio.

Look at the Birdie

Collectors of photographs cut across all class lines, but inquiring minds don't care that Mr. and Ms. John Q. Average collect snapshots. We care about the glitterati. So I'll just drop some names of famous collectors of photographs: actress Jodie Foster, musician Elton John, actress Diane Keaton, designer Ralph Lauren, and in a class by herself, the pop-culture icon Madonna.

Photographs greatly increase in value if they are autographed, like this one.

What photographs do they collect? Some favor the classics, prints by Edward Streichen, Alfred Stieglitz, Edward S. Curtis, Man Ray, Walker Evans, Edouard Baldus, Edward Weston, Tina Moditti, Dorothea Lange, William Henry Fox Talbot, Alexander Rodchenko, Lewis Carroll, Irving Penn, Hiro, and Henri Cartier-Bresson. Others crest the new wave: Francesco Scavullo, Steven Meisel, Patrick Demarchelier, Neil Winokur, William Klein, Karel Hajek, Adam Fuss, Mario Giacomelli, Mary Ellen Marx, Max Yavno, and Alfred Cheney Johnston. More on this later, shutterbugs.

What do they spend? Table 18.1 offers a list of the most expensive photographs ever sold at auction:

Table 18.1 The Most Expensive Photographs Ever Sold at Auction

Photographer/Sale	Price
1. Edward S. Curtis (American, 1868–1952) *The North American Indian 1907–30* Sotheby's, New York, 1993	$662,500
2. Alfred Stieglitz (American, 1864–1946) Georgia O'Keeffe: A Portrait— *Hands with Thimble* 1930 Christie's, New York, 1989	$398,500
3. Alfred Stieglitz (American, 1864–1946) *Equivalents (21)*, 1920s Christie's, New York, 1989	$396,000
4. Edward S. Curtis (American, 1868–1952) *The North American Indian 1907–30* Christie's, New York, 1992	$396,000
5. Man Ray (American, 1890–1976) *Noir et Blanch*, 1926 Christie's, New York, 1994	$354,5000
6. Man Ray (American, 1890–1976) *Hier, Demain, Aujourd'hui*, 1930–32 Christie's, New York, 1993	$222,500
7. Man Ray (American, 1890–1976) *Glass Tears*, c. 1930 Sotheby's, London, 1993	$195,000
8. Tina Moditti (Mexican, 1896–1942) *Two Callas*, 1925 Christie's, New York, 1993	$189,500
9. Alexander Rodchenko (Russian, 1891–1956) *Girl with Leica,* 1934 Christie's, London, 1992	$181,450
10. Tina Moditti (Mexican, 1896–1942) *Roses, Mexico,* 1925 Sotheby's, New York, 1991	$165,000

These are the three most expensive photographic collections ever sold at auction:

1. Edward S. Curtis: *The North American Indian 1907–30*

2. Alfred Stieglitz: *Equivalents (21)*

3. Man Ray: *Noir et Blanch*

But people who collect photographs are too diverse to categorize. If you can describe yourself as a philosopher, investor, aesthete, detective, and explorer, then this may be the collectible for you. Let's start with the birth of photography, daguerreotypes.

America in Amber: Daguerreotypes

Jacques Louis Mande Daguerre announced his picture-taking process in 1839. He had stolen the basic idea from a naive provincial, Nicephore Niepce, who had been playing around with the notion for nearly 20 years.

Although Daguerre's announcement marked the official birth of photography, it was actually a photographic dead end because of the process he used. A daguerreotype is produced by light striking a silvered copper plate. As a result, there is no negative. The image on the plate cannot be reproduced or enlarged. Bad for customers; great for collectors. How can you recognize this collectible? One way is appearance: Daguerreotypes have a characteristic amber color.

Connoisseur
Ever wonder why people in daguerreotypes never seem to be smiling? It's probably because of the way their pictures were taken. Sitters had to remain absolutely still for anywhere from 30 seconds to several minutes; cast-iron head clasps were often used to lock their noggins in place.

Tricks of the Trade
You can distinguish daguerreotypes from other cased images by their mirror-like reflection and precise detail.

Smile!

Nonetheless, daguerreotypes were enormously popular through the late 1850s. They were beautifully accurate images, and while not cheap by the standards of the time, still cost less than the alternative, painted portraits. Thousands of "daguerreian artists" and itinerant photographers combed the countryside seeking people who wanted their mugs immortalized. Around 30 million daguerreotypes were taken in America between 1840 and 1860. That's not counting the millions and millions taken throughout the rest of the world.

But as with any collectible, over the years the vast majority of these daguerreotypes were lost or damaged. Daguerreotypes are especially collectible because each one is unique—unlike photographs today that are made from negatives—and each captures people, places, and events from the first period in history ever to be recorded by photographic images. By 1860, daguerreotypes were supplanted by the *ambrotype*, tintype and paper images. Both of these images are also highly collectible.

Size Does Matter

Daguerreotypes vary in size. A "full plate" measures six-and-a-half inches by eight-and-a-half inches. Other sizes are divisions of a full plate. When you are collecting daguerreotypes, bigger *is* better. Most daguerreotypes were small, so anything large is out of the ordinary and thus potentially very valuable to collectors.

Big Deals

Likely the best daguerreotype collection in America has been amassed by Matthew Isenburg of Connecticut. It includes more than 2,000 daguerreotypes and 3,000 pieces of related gear such as cases, equipment, books, documents, and cameras. The collection cost Isenburg $4 million and almost 30 years to assemble. It's now worth an estimated $20 million.

In the mid-1960s, collectors could find daguerreotypes in flea markets and antiques shops for $2 to $5. A fine daguerreotype purchased in 1967 for $10 would be worth about $5,000 today.

No Red Eye

When determining what to buy, it's time to round up the usual suspects:

➤ **Size.** With daguerreotypes, bigger is better.

➤ **Condition.** As with most other collectibles, buy daguerreotypes in the best condition you can afford.

➤ **Subject matter.** Collectors of daguerreotypes seek out photos of animals, outdoor scenes, men at work. They also lust after portraits of people who became famous after their death and so were not widely photographed. Fan favorites include the writer Edgar Allan Poe and the philosopher Henry David Thoreau. Images of these men start at $10,000 each.

➤ **Maker.** The more famous the "daguerreian artist," the more the daguerreotype will be worth. All things being equal, a signed daguerreotype is worth more than an unsigned one.

➤ **Aesthetic beauty.** As with any artistic creation, form matters to collectors of daguerreotypes. Look for the interplay of composition, line, shape, and shadow.

Market Forecast

The market for daguerreotypes is stronger now than ever. A standard small "ancestor" daguerreotype sells for under $100, but for anything special, prices rise more quickly than

Connoisseur
Calotypes were the first process for producing more than one print from a single image.

a successful soufflé. For example, an early panorama of Paris and a portrait of Daguerre were sold privately for more than $100,000. In a 1992 auction, a half-plate Cincinnati scene by African-American James Presley Ball sold for $63,800. The previous auction record has been set in 1985, when the National Portrait Gallery paid $59,400 for a portrait of photographer Matthew Brady. Consult *Prints, Posters, and Photographs: Identification and Price Guide* for specific prices. The price guide, by Susan Theran, is published by Avon Books.

Better Safe than Sorry

Thanks to my sage advice, you rushed out and assembled a fine collection of daguerreotypes. Like a new puppy, they require special care.

All early photographic processes are susceptible to oxidization because of the metal used in their processing. The effect is intensified if they were exposed to high levels of relative humidity—such as that found on a flea market field. Follow these guidelines for safe storage:

➤ Store your daguerreotypes upright in photo envelopes or archival plastic sleeves.

➤ If you do display a photograph, have a professional framer use a non-acid matte and UV-filtering glass.

➤ Keep them away from undue levels of ultraviolet light.

➤ Keep daguerreotypes as clean as possible. Never attempt to clean them yourself.

So You Want To Put Together a Collection of Photos

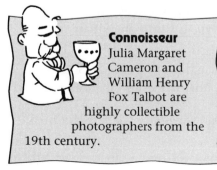

Connoisseur
Julia Margaret Cameron and William Henry Fox Talbot are highly collectible photographers from the 19th century.

Almost every serious collector of photography has a story of a lucky find that turned out to be a treasure. In most cases, it happened to his brother's-cousin's-sister's-third-cousin. This section will show you how to make your dream come true without waiting for lightning to strike. You *can* put together a quality collection of photographs at a reasonable price without a bolt from the blue.

Please keep in mind that the following ideas are just that—ideas, not guaranteed investments. Trust your own tastes and instincts. And always remember the cardinal rule of collecting: Buy only what you love and can live with. With art, it will usually be pieces that make a strong emotional connection, that touch your soul in some private way.

A Few Grand

So you have a few thousand to spend, discretionary money that you don't need to tithe to the dentist, plumber, or auto mechanic. If that's the case, consider adding prints from some of the following photographers to your collection.

➤ **Retro Chic**—One field ripe for the collecting is documentary photography, especially the realistic social photos of the 1960s or the conceptual photographs of the 1970s. Danny Lyon's photographs, fine examples of this genre, sell in the $3,000-$5,000 range.

➤ **California dreaming**—Some of the West Coast photographers are being hyped as up-and-coming collectibles. These include John Divola, Joann Callis, Eileen Cowin, and Richard Misrach. The Los Angeles Center for Photographic Studies offered a David Levinthal print for $250, what one dealer termed a "real steal." Levinthal's Polaroids (20 × 24 inches) usually fetch $4,000 apiece.

➤ **Hey, Abbott**—Berenice Abbott comes with impeccable credentials: she began her photographic career as an apprentice in Man Ray's studio. Born in 1898, Abbott is famous for her documentation of New York City life. Financed by the Works Progress Administration, she sought, in her own words, "to catch in the sensitive photographic emulsion the spirit of the metropolis, while remaining true to its essential fact, its hurrying tempo, its congested streets, the past jostling the present." The LitCrit crowd is no doubt familiar with her famous portrait of Irish novelist James Joyce.

➤ **A big Fuss**—Photographer Adam Fuss is making a big hoopla in collector circles. A lucky find is one of his prints in the $3,000 range; an average picture goes for about $8,000.

➤ **Trail blazers**—Cindy Sherman and Sherrie Levine put photography on the art map in the early 1980s. This makes them a solid investment.

➤ **Songs of self**—Nan Goldin, born in 1953, has been the art world's photographer of the hour for several years now. Her "warts and all" style is steeped in passion, immediacy, and rich color. Her photographs have been exhibited at all the first-class spots, including the Whitney Museum of American Art in New York City.

➤ **Batter up**—Take a look at Robert Riger's sports photos. Riger, who was an artist for *Sports Illustrated* magazine, started by using his photos as reference materials for his illustrations.

➤ **A Rose by any other name**—Among the most promising photographers is Aaron Rose. Although not well-known, he is working in the tradition of such masters as Alfred Stieglitz—but with a modern twist. Rose is in his 70s and just had his first exhibition, so we're talking virgin collector territory here. Each of Rose's photographs goes for about $5,000. They are created with a special camera that Rose made himself.

➤ **Surf's up**—Hiroshi Sugimoto has attracted attention for his soothing photos of the ocean. They start around $2,500.

➤ **Movers and shakers**—Lee Friedlander, Helen Levitt, Robert Adams, Eadweard Muybridge, Nicholas Nixon, Neil Winokur, J. John Priola, Andres Serrano, McDermott and McGough, Germaine Krull, and Joel-Peter Witkin are all fabulous photographers; some offer prints that start around $1,000.

➤ **See the world**—In general, American masters of photography are hot right now. You can capitalize on this by collecting the photographs of European whiz kids. The images created by Patrick Faigenbaum, a French photographer, go for around $3,500. Another hot prospect is Roger Parry, a yet-to-be-discovered French photographer. His photos are in the same range as Faigenbaum's.

See Susan Theran's *Prints, Posters, and Photographs: Identification and Price Guide* (Avon) for a list of other "best-bet" collectible photographs.

A Fist Full of Bucks

Feeling a little more flush? You can buy photographs by Henri Cartier-Bresson, Walker Evans, Robert Frank, or Edouard Baldus. These are considerably more pricey; a Baldus photograph, for example, can run as much as $45,000—or more.

Connoisseur
When he wasn't sailing down the Thames with little Alice or writing storybooks for her, the 19th-century author/photographer/mathematician Lewis Carroll took some highly collectible photographs.

Here's a brief price survey to give you an idea of the current market for collectible photographs:

➤ $5,000 buys

Maurice Tabard (surreal images from the 1920s)

Eugene Atget (surreal images from the 1920s)

Michael Rovner (contemporary, Israel-born)

Ann Hamilton (conceptual-based, documenting her performance pieces)

➤ $10,000 buys

Edward Weston (portraits)

➤ $20,000 buys

Raoul Ubac (surreal images from the 1920s)

William Henry Fox Talbot (classic chic)

Safekeeping

Who are we kidding? You paid a bundle for a gorgeous photograph, so of course you're going to frame it and enjoy it. And so you should, says our hedonistic side. Let the neighbors drool and the picture fade. But our obsessive side says: No, no, no! Don't store your collectible photos that way! Here's what you should do... and why.

Be Good

The American National Standards Institute recommends that you store black-and-white prints and negatives in special materials. They really want you to store *all* your photos in the dark and under cover in the driest possible environment. What works for prudes works for photos.

Here's Why

Color photographs are less stable than black-and-white photographs because their dyes fade erratically. For example, blues may fade out before yellows. It's because color transparencies use organic dyes that are not durable. Color photos are especially sensitive to UV light. They can be kept more stable if they are stored at cool temperatures.

The Least You Need to Know

➤ Those old daguerreotypes in your attic could be worth a lot of money.

➤ Photographs by American masters are hot right now. Capitalize on this by collecting the photographs of European whiz kids.

➤ Display and store your photographs properly. Frame them under UV glass or store them in a dark, dry place in special storage containers.

Pretty as a Picture: Drawings

Since oil painting gets all the press, novice art collectors are apt to think that drawings take a back seat in the art collecting world. Not so. To the right crowd, drawings are every bit as important as their more assertive cousins, paintings.

In this chapter, I'll convince you that drawings are a noble collectible, featured in any museum worth its endowment and entrance fee. You'll also learn how drawings are created so you can distinguish among the different types. Then comes a detailed survey of the different kinds of drawings, with special attention paid to those that you may not realize are trendy collectibles, such as *fractura*, silhouettes, paper cutting, and caricatures. I'll help you see what types of pictures to collect to fit your taste and budget.

Pain on Paper?

Draw•ing (dro'ing) *n.* 1. a representation by lines; a delineation of form without reference to color; 2. a sketch, plan, or design, especially one made with pen, pencil, or crayon [ME].

Since the word "drawing" goes back to the Middle Ages (although people have been drawing since caveman Og first put charcoal to a wall), you'd figure by now that we'd all have a clear idea of what a drawing is. No one has a problem recognizing a drawing when little Janey scrawls something on paper with a crayon, but from then on, the definition and purpose are up for grabs. Take the Drawing Quiz to see how you envision collectible drawings.

Drawing Quiz

Complete this quiz to see how you define the purpose of a drawing.

Drawings should...

(Check as many as apply)

- ❑ Express psychological penetration.

- ❑ Be intense and expressive.

- ❑ Capture fragmented images.

- ❑ Exhibit a tortured sensibility.

- ❑ Create order out of chaos.

- ❑ Depict pleasant, bland families.

- ❑ Have interesting shapes and designs.

- ❑ Poke fun at people or institutions.

- ❑ Satirize social foibles.

- ❑ Look nice on the wall.

Fortunately, there's no wrong answer; every choice is correct. It all depends on your taste. You can collect pen-and-paper anguish or sweet paper cuttings. Squirrel away an arduous and authentic hand-drawn legacy or seek out ebullient theater caricatures. Ain't art grand?

Quick Draw McGraw: A Brief Survey of Drawings

Usually an artist draws to convey information or work out ideas, rather than impress. This does not mean that all drawings are purely sketches and rough drafts, but it does explain why it was not until the 16th century that it became fashionable to buy and keep drawings. Ever since, connoisseurs of this art form have attempted to form collections of drawings that are both decorative and valuable.

Collectors are not restricted to people like you and me, who have "collector" written across their foreheads; artists also feel the desire to amass things of beauty. For example, the famous German artist Albrecht Dürer (1471–1528) traded drawings with his buddy and fellow famous artist Raphael; Rembrandt and Rubens also formed massive collections of drawings.

Culture Vulture

Let's take a brief armchair museum tour to get to know a little more about drawings. Sometimes the famous drawings collections stayed together and remained so to our day; if you're ever at dinner in Windsor Castle, be sure to take a peek at the Royal Collection. It features a stack of nifty drawings by Domenichino. There are also impressive collections of drawings at the usual spots:

➤ The Louvre in Paris boasts Louis XIV's collection

➤ The Uffizi in Florence has drawings collected by the light-hearted Medici clan (when they weren't busy poisoning each other)

➤ The Albertina in Vienna

➤ The Hermitage in Leningrad

➤ The British Museum

➤ The Victoria and Albert in London

The Material Is the Message

Unless the artist is the newfangled sort who executes drawings on subways and sidewalks, a drawing will be made on paper of some kind using ink of some kind. (That's why you have to be 18 to buy markers and spray paint, especially around Halloween.) But to buy drawings with confidence, you have to know a little bit about how they are made. Let's start with paper.

Paper Trail

Paper was first produced in China nearly 2,000 years ago, but the process remained within the country. The Egyptians went their own way, stripping the thin membranes from papyrus reeds to write on it. In the days before animal rights, some people even made parchment from the skins of sheep and goats and the finer-grained vellum from the skins of calves and kids. Soon, paper-making techniques spread across the world, and animals breathed a sigh of relief.

During the Renaissance, all the paper used for drawings in Western Europe was made from cotton or linen rags. The rags were washed, shredded, and pulped until a thick white mash filled the vat. The "paper soup" was poured out on tightly stretched cloth (later, mesh) to let the extra water drain away. The residue was then pressed and dried, forming a tight sheet of paper. Often, the mesh marks remained. The paper would be sized to make it less absorbent.

In the early 1800s, economical paper makers realized that wood pulp would make an equally nice—and far cheaper—paper. Paper used for watercolors was still made with cloth, however. After 1860, esparto grass was also used to make paper.

Connoisseur
While paper is the most common drawing medium, there are also drawings on cloth, wood, bone, ivory, and other materials.

What does all this paper stuff mean to you as a collector of drawings? It means that experts examining a drawing under a microscope can tell by the paper when it was made. We give them a few years in either direction, but they are still remarkably accurate.

Of course, this doesn't stop forgers from trying to artificially age paper to trick the unwary collector. Some efforts are as blatant as dipping drawings in tea to make the paper look aged. Sophisticated forgers, on the other hand, use chemicals to produce convincing age marks and even acid to simulate the appearance of a watermark.

Inky Dinky Bottle of Inky

The earliest inks were likely made from charred bones, ground to a powder and mixed with a binder liquid. In the Middle Ages, ink was made from fluids produced by the cuttle fish. There were also inks made from different kinds of salts. In the second half of the nineteenth century, aniline inks were introduced. These inks are made from coal tar. An expert can sometimes date a drawing and determine if it is authentic by examining the ink.

Get the Point: Pens and Pencils

The style of a drawing will be influenced by the type of drawing implement the artist uses, the range of choices limited by what was available at the time the drawing was made. Dürer, Da Vinci, and Michelangelo didn't have easy access to an OfficeMax or Staples, so they most often used chalks to make their rough drawings. Here are some other common drawing implements:

➤ **Pens.** Medieval scribes and illustrators often used pens cut from the quills of large birds such as swans and geese. These large fowl were probably pleased when reeds were used instead. Metal pens did not appear to have been produced until late in the 1700s. The introduction of the steel pen nib at the end of the 18th century led to a new interest in pen-and-ink drawings. Today, artists have fountain pens, ballpoint pens, and felt-tipped markers available.

Big Deals

Drawing in charcoal was especially popular during the Victorian period. Most of the pictures were done on regulation paper, but some were executed on sandpaper, called "marble," giving strange results. On the low end of the scale, these sell for $150–$350; upper-end pieces can go for as much as $2,000. Most of these pictures are landscapes, often copied from earlier European oil paintings. They are attracting a wide following, so now is the time to snap them up.

➤ **Pencils.** The pencils available in the early 18th century were rough affairs, made from lead and tin. Graphite (called "plumbago" or "black lead") was discovered in the English Lake District quite early in the century, but it was not until the very end of the 1700s that it was refined and made into drawing implements. In 1795, N.J. Conte devised a way to make graphite leads into sticks. These were fired in a kiln and voilà! Pencils were born. The process whereby pencils are made is still based on this method.

➤ **Pastels.** Pastel drawings are admired for the purity of their color, a result of the process whereby pastels are made. The pigments are unusually pure, making the color vibrant. Unfortunately, pastel drawings are fragile and especially prone to damage.

Caveat Emptor
If you add pastel drawings to your collection, be sure that they are correctly framed under glass to prevent smudging. Also, hang pastel drawings in a place where they will not be disturbed. Vibrations can cause smudging.

Just Plain Folk

Many attempts have been made to formulate a precise definition of American folk art, with mixed success. So let's just say it's like the judge's famous definition of pornography: You can't put it into words, but you know it when you see it.

The pioneer collectors of folk art, in the early decades of the twentieth century, swooped down first on oil paintings, followed by watercolors. However, under the twin pressures of decreasing supply and increasing demand, interest has swelled in drawings, silhouettes, and cut paper.

Drawings

Folk artists didn't start making pencil drawings until oil painting was a well-established art form. There are a few pencil portraits, mainly from the 1870s and 1880s, but much of the work consists of sketches done as studies for oil paintings or watercolors. Ink drawings, however, are a different matter.

Connoisseur
Larger calligraphic pieces are very desirable at present and so are quite pricey. Calligraphy is fancy, decorative penmanship distinguished by many flourishes. Smaller works, such as those found in autograph books, can be purchased for prices that won't break the bank.

Tricks of the Trade
Never pass up an old autograph book without looking through it. Good calligraphy is often discovered this way.

Fancy Schmancy Fractura

When they weren't busy milking the cow or birthing the lambs, Pennsylvania calligraphers of the 18th and 19th centuries wrote certificates: birth, baptismal, wedding—whatever needed to be attested. The "drawing" part of fractura is the decorative illustration on the certificate. Calligraphy (decorative writing) is used for the certificate text. Many of the American examples, done in the 1800s, clearly show the influence of the Mother Country in style and subject.

At the beginning of the 20th century, one Dr. Henry Mercer made a pioneer study of these certificates and named them "fractura," reviving a term from the 16th century. Fractura combined lettering and pictorial embellishment. The work of Pennsylvania German calligraphers is especially prized by American collectors of this art form. Good fractura costs thousands of dollars, but there are small examples and figures without the lettering that can go for less than $100. European versions, still not a major collectible, are very affordable. Consult *Currier's Price Guide to American and European Prints at Auction* by William P. Carl (Currier Publications, 1994) for specific pricing information.

The Shadow Knows: Silhouettes

A *silhouette* is a profile portrait cut out of black paper, a shadow outline. The contrast between the black and white and the precision of the cutting combine to produce a very dramatic effect. Since they were cut quickly by an expert, silhouettes were inexpensive. Until the camera preempted the field, silhouettes served as the most accessible form of a family portrait.

The word *silhouette* came directly from the name of Etienne de Silhouette, an author and public servant initially respected as a financier. In 1759 he became controller-general of France and took immediate steps to meet the country's financial crisis. At first he was lavished with praise for his ingenuous belt-tightening measures. But when he proposed reforms to restrict the royal household's wastefulness, the bloom was off the rose. "Pick their pocket—not mine!" the royals bellowed.

Poor Monsieur Silhouette was suddenly an object of scorn. At the same time, outline drawings had become a fashionable art form. People quickly linked the drawings to Silhouette's fiscal reforms; before you could say "downsize," outline drawings came to be called "silhouettes" and regarded as a bargain-basement cut-rate art form. The brevity of his career matched the brief time it took to make a silhouette.

Connoisseur
In America, silhouettes were called **shades**. Portraits are the most popular collectibles, but landscapes and pictures of people in action are also eagerly sought.

Silhouettes provided an inexpensive, fast type of portraiture.

Silhouettes were at the height of their popularity from 1800 to 1850. Galleries making them flourished on both sides of the Atlantic. A substantial number of silhouette cutters earned a living in the first half of the 19th century by cutting likenesses of their customers, often adding embellishments such as tinted facial color and hair. Many silhouettes are signed by their makers.

A silhouette from the mid-19th century sells on the average for about $250. An unusual family record illustrated with silhouettes, made in 1830, went for $1,250. Since silhouettes are easily faked, I recommend that you buy them from a reputable dealer.

Cut and Paste

Another collectible offshoot of drawing is paper cutting, a folk art form practiced mainly by women. In addition to cut paper, watercolor was also used in many instances. Cut-paper pictures from Pennsylvania, made in the late 1880s, sell for anywhere from $275 to $450. An elaborate cut-paper picture from the same time and place recently fetched more than $1,000 at an auction.

You can also find cut-paper tinsel pictures. The tinsel creates a beautiful shimmering effect. Tinsel work is found mainly in the latter half of the 19th century. A neglected art form, they are still underpriced. A tinsel painting from the mid-19th century sells for $250-$550.

The Line Kings

Caricatures are another type of highly collectible drawing. For our purposes, a *caricature* is a drawing that exaggerates a particular physical or facial feature, clothing, dress, or manners of a person to produce a ludicrous effect. *"Caricatures"* comes from an Italian word that means to "exaggerate" or "overload," and so these drawings do. They may also poke fun at political, social, or religious situations.

Back in Time

In the modern sense, caricature originated at the end of the 1500s. To relieve stress, the students at a Bologna art school often drew pictures of visitors in the likeness of the animals whose traits they embodied. The engraver Pier Leone Ghezzi (1674–1755) took it to the trade, drawing caricatures for tourists. Political caricatures that poked fun at major figures took off in England around the middle of the 18th century. George Townshend, William Hogarth, Thomas Rowlandson, James Gillray, and George Cruikshank were the prime practitioners.

In 1841, the satirical magazine *Punch* burst into the English scene and soon became one of the most famous magazines in the world for its humor and caricatures. George du Maurier, John Leech, and Sir John Tenniel were well-known for their *Punch*-es. You might be familiar with Tenniel's distinctive illustrations in Lewis Carroll's *Alice in Wonderland*.

Big Men on Campus

In the late 19th and early 20th century, Sir Max Beerbohm, Sir Leslie Ward, and David Low were the best known caricaturists. In France, we had Charles Philipon, Honore Daumier, Gustave Dore, and Henri Toulouse-Lautrec holding the standards high. Toulouse-Lautrec caricatured theater and music hall habitués; Daumier landed in prison for using his pencil to take on King Louis Philippe. In Germany, George Grosz was another vehement social critic, known for his fierce attacks on the growing militarism in his homeland after World War I.

Takin' Care of Business

Perhaps the most important 19th-century American caricaturist was Thomas Nast, whose drawings helped to overthrow the corrupt political Tweed Ring. We also have Nast to thank for creating the symbols for the Republican and Democratic parties, the elephant and the donkey.

In the 20th century, standout caricaturists include Bill Mauldin, Herbert Lawrence Block ("Herblock"), Pat Oliphant, Jules Fieffer, Walt Kelly, and Al Hirschfeld. Hirschfeld's caricatures of theatre and movie stars are especially popular now; he has been dubbed the "line king" for his expressive use of line. His caricatures, especially those that contain "Ninas" (the name of his daughter) hidden in the folds, command top collector dollars. Original cartoons, editorial or otherwise, are considered fine art. There's a flourishing collectible market for this work.

Connoisseur
Drawings—pen or pencil work in a single color on paper—are almost identical to watercolors from the collector's standpoint.

The Least You Need to Know

➤ Don't treat drawings as wannabes; they are happenin' collectibles.

➤ In addition to pen/pencil drawings, other popular collectibles in this genre include *fractura*, silhouettes, paper cutting, and caricatures.

➤ Don't throw out your kid's scribbles. Hey, you never know.

SOMEDAY MY PRINTS WILL COME...

Chapter 20

Someday My Prints Will Come: Prints and Lithographs

In This Chapter

➤ Learn how prints are made

➤ Distinguish between different types of prints

➤ Find out which prints send collectors into a frenzy of acquisition

Any original work of art worth its paint, clay, or ink will tend to be pricey because it is unique. On the other hand, prints are likely to fall within the budgets of a much larger group of collectors since there are more of them (prints, not collectors). The price of a print tends to become inflated only when it is very rare or autographed. By collecting prints you can get superb examples of many first-class artists into your home, with a surprisingly affordable outlay of cash.

Prints are made in deliberately limited numbers, usually under the guiding hand of the artist who created the original picture. Such prints are often numbered and signed.

If you buy a quality print from an etched plate, you will most likely find it both signed and numbered. Normally, the figure in some margin indicates the number of prints produced in that edition, separated by a stroke from the number of that impression in order of printing.

In this chapter, you'll learn how prints are made. Exploring the different printing methods will help you understand the value, rarity, and pricing of this collectible. Along the way, you'll do some shopping to find the hidden values in the print market. Then I'll explain how you can avoid being ripped off in the print biz. So let the presses roll!

Psst! Wanna Come to My Room and See My Etchings?

Before you start shelling out any serious bucks for prints, you'd better learn a little about the different types of prints that are available. Some printing techniques are relatively modern, while others have a long and noble history. Let's take a look at each one in turn. Some methods are subcategories of others, but I've listed every term in alphabetic order to make it easier for you.

Engraving

With this method, an engraver uses a small tool to etch a metal (often copper or steel) plate. Furrows are plowed, ink is applied, the plate is wiped clean, paper is pressed on top, and pressure is applied. The quality of the engraving is determined by the variety of the lines. The finest and rarest engravings (such as Hogarth's) are very expensive, but fortunately for collectors, modern and affordable examples abound.

Hand-colored engravings were intensely collected in the 1920s. Because they are largely ignored today, they're a rich field for modern print collectors. Great bargains include a framed print in the low $100s.

Intaglio Printing

With this method, recesses are made by etching or engraving the flat surface of a plate. The recessed portions are then filled with ink, and the rest of the plate is wiped clean.

The print is made by transferring the ink to damp paper or other material. Again, the process requires considerable pressure. This is not a process for sissies.

American intaglio prints tend to be less detailed than European examples. Simple prints by lesser artists can be had for the low $100s.

Etching

This is a subcategory of intaglio. Included are etchings on hard plates, soft grounds, drypoint, aquatint, and mezzotint. Each achieves a different effect. Drypoint, for example, is an etching technique in which a pointed needle is used to make soft furrows.

This produces a print characterized by soft, velvety black lines. Aquatint includes tones (degrees of lightness and darkness) as well as lines. Hence the name: "tinted water." Mezzotint, created by engraving on copper or steel by brushing or scraping away a uniformly roughened surface, creates a stronger line. The first dated etching is marked 1513.

Rembrandt's etchings, dated a century later, are most often associated with this technique. It doesn't take a rocket scientist to know that Rembrandt's etchings are going to cost a pretty penny, but if you yearn uncontrollably for an original Rembrandt, there are later prints from the same plates that are affordable for the reasonably well-heeled.

Mezzotints were a very popular collectible in the 1930s, but interest later faded. As a result, these prints can often be picked up today for sensible prices.

Tricks of the Trade
Prints by Impressionists are generally very expensive (as is anything by the Impressionists), but etchings by the landscape artists of the Barbizon school can sometimes be found for decent prices.

Lino Cutting

This is the printing technique you probably learned in school, when you attacked an innocent piece of linoleum with a sharp tool. We usually created cheesy prints of the Starship Enterprise and gouged all our fingers in the process, but in the hands of a skilled artist, lino cutting results in striking posters.

Lithography

Fortunately, oil and water don't mix. Otherwise, we wouldn't have salad dressing or lithography. *Lithography* is a process in which a greasy crayon is used to trace a design on a very porous stone. The stone is then soaked in water, and it absorbs the moisture in its clear areas. Ink is rolled onto the surface and it clings to the crayon areas and is repelled by the wet parts. A sheet of paper is then rolled on the stone, picking up the design from the remaining ink.

Want to collect lithography? Then read on!

➤ **Color my world.** Around the turn of the century, color lithographs were hot stuff, but collector interest faded fast. To the modern eye, many of these colored lithographs seem fussy and stodgy, so there hasn't been terrific collector interest. But if you're the fussy and stodgy type, you're in luck. You can pick up original lithographs to your liking for reasonable prices.

➤ **Pulling no punches.** In contrast to the out-of-favor picturesque views of the early nineteenth century, political lithographs from the same era are keenly collected today. Satirical lithos, especially those of Daumier and Gavarni, are especially hot now.

➤ **I'm dreaming of a white Christmas.** Currier and Ives was the most famous 19th-century American lithography firm. Active from 1834 to 1906 under several names, this New York company recorded important social scenes, big ships, and senti-mental glimpses of American life. The prints have a simple, folksy quality that endeared them to millions of buyers. Although the prints were originally priced from a few cents to a few dollars, they have been collected fervently for many years. As a result, rare examples go for more than $1,000 each.

Caveat Emptor

Since Currier and Ives prints are so popular they have been repro-duced widely, especially on overpriced Christmas cards. If you plan to buy an original Currier and Ives print, check the paper stock carefully to make sure that you are getting a genuine original print, not a recycled Christmas card.

Tricks of the Trade

If you like the Currier and Ives look but not their prices, check out the prints made by Sarony & Major and Kellogg, two contemporaries of Currier and Ives. They are very similar in style but much less costly.

➤ **Poster child.** Lithography was also important to the world's poster makers. There are striking examples from England, France, and America. Color lithography techniques improved after the 1860s, so there was a marked increase in the poster output after that. Posters were made to announce just about any type of occasion and to advertise any product. Some have elements of folk art, while others are more sophisticated. Art Nouveau styles and theater themes are especially popular with collectors. Check *Prints, Posters, and Photographs: Identification and Price Guide* (Susan Theran, Avon Books) to price litho prints and posters.

➤ **Modern times.** There is a revival in lithography today and some fine artists are quickly being recognized and their work collected. Check major city newspapers for announcements of important exhibits and sales. You may favor modern masters such as LeRoy Neiman and Andy Warhol, or go with more traditional works.

Relief Printing

In relief printing, a block of wood or metal is cut into so that parts of the original flat surface remain. These raised parts are coated with ink, leaving the cut-away parts clean.

The print is made by transferring the image from the inked surface to the paper. Pressure is applied to make a clear print.

Surface Printing

This modern printing process, kissing cousins to *planographic printing* and *screen printing*, involves ink being forced through a fine mesh of silk or some silk-like synthetic material.

Woodcut Printing

This is probably the most ancient form of relief printing, used by the Chinese early as the 9th century A.D.. To create a woodcut print, an artist draws a design in reverse on a block of wood. The outlines are defined and the extra wood is cut away. You can usually tell a woodcut print because of its bold, heavy, and plain lines, although some prints are characterized by more complex shadings.

Tricks of the Trade
Shopping for woodcut prints? Most 18th-century broadsides (advertisements, announcements, and poems) include woodcuts. Many 19th-century folk prints are also woodcuts.

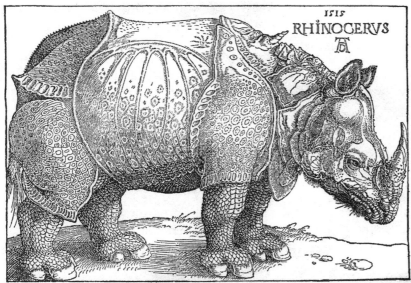

18. A rhinoceros: from a woodcut by Albrecht Dürer, 1515

This Albrecht Dürer woodcut print, made in 1515, is an outstanding example of the art form.

Masters of woodcutting include Albrecht Dürer (1471–1528), Hans Holbein (1497–1543), and Hans Burgkmair (c. 1473–c. 1531). Among the most famous wood-block prints made during this time include the *Dance of Death* series and the *Triumphal Arch and Car*. Of course these prints are seriously collectible, but they very rarely come onto the market and command out-of-this-world prices when they do.

There are also colored woodcut prints. Here are two of the most common techniques:

➤ **In living color.** These color woodcuts were created with more than one block, each color requiring a separate printing.

➤ **Hand-colored.** Even more rarely, you may see woodcuts in which the colors have been applied by hand. These are most often found in Japanese wood-block prints.

It's not difficult to find simple 18th-century and 19th-century woodcuts for less than $100.

Wood Engraving

This technique is similar to woodcuts except that differences in materials result in finer drawing and more detail. The most famous old masters of this art are the romantic visionary Edward Calvert (1799–1883) and the romantic visionary madman William Blake (1757–1827). Some more modern masters include Robert Gibbings, Eric Ravilious, and Joan Hassall.

False Profits

Now that you know how prints are made, it's time to study as many prints as you can and decide which ones appeal to you. Whatever types you collect and whatever organizing principles you use, a few basic guidelines are in order.

First off, neither age nor quantity is a factor in the price of a old prints: Dürer etchings are costly (one such print recently sold for $14,000 at auction), but so are some 19th-century prints. A collector may pay top dollar for the work of a specific artist, subject matter, or technique. With newer series (such as each new release by Bev Doolittle), the quantity can be a factor.

➤ **Playing the Numbers.** What does the numbering on a print mean? For example, a print numbered "5/500" is the fifth impression in a series of 500. The higher the second number, the more prints there are—and the less valuable each one potentially is when you're talking about a newly released series of prints as opposed to an older collector's item like a Dürer.

➤ **Condition, condition, condition.** A torn, cropped, or sheared print is not going to be as valuable as one that is in mint condition. Also be on the lookout for prints that have been "backed" (stuck down on backing) or blurred by rubbing and handling. These are not good collectibles because their value is already diminished.

➤ **Buying on margins.** Some collectors are willing to pay more for old prints that have clean, wide margins. This has resulted in some fakery—I bet you're shocked. In the hands of a skilled forger, a print can be trimmed back to the edge of the printed surface and carefully inlaid into a new (and obviously not original) mounting. Pretty—and worth much less than an untouched original.

➤ **Plate mark.** The "plate mark" is the indentation in the paper made by the edge of the sheet of metal from which the print has been taken. A print expert can use the plate guide to help date the print. Prints made before 1800 are always unbevelled; more modern prints are finished off with a bevel.

➤ **First impressions count.** Try to avoid later prints made from early engravings. Many of the early blocks or plates were saved and then reused. How can you tell if you're getting a later print from an early engraving? First, the color of the new paper may make the print look odd; second, the background may look overly fuzzy from wear; and third, the background may look overly sharp from a tool-time touch up.

> **Connoisseur**
> Ideally, every print that you buy should look as if it had just come straight from the presses.

> **Connoisseur**
> Prints without plate marks are not necessarily forged. The prints may have been commissioned for use as book illustrations and so were engraved on plates larger than the plates on which they were to appear. As a result, the margins were trimmed and the plate marks cut away.

Stop the Presses!

So how can you avoid being ripped off in the print biz? Here are some tips:

1. **See the light.** Hold every print you want to buy up to the light. This will help you see repairs such as patches and redrawings.

2. **Check the paper.** Forgers often try to pass off modern prints as older ones but the paper is a real tip-off that something isn't kosher. Old paper will feel silky; new paper has a harder, stiffer feel.

3. **Offsetting and upsetting.** Offset printing has made it possible to create faithful reproductions of old prints. If you're into old prints, be sure to carefully examine each one to see if it really is old.

4. **Who is number one?** Beware that some contemporary print makers number their works in a short series and then sell complete sets in different parts of the country.

Buyers are tricked into thinking they are buying limited edition originals. The best defense is a good offense; buy investment-grade prints only from a reputable dealer.

5. **I've been framed!** Sometimes modern prints are tarted up in fancy frames to make them look like more than they are. Although the prints may cost only a few cents to make, the frames make them look like a million bucks.

6. **Set the *Limits!*** Remember earlier in the book I warned you to avoid collectors' plates and figurines? The marketing of some prints is identical to the collector plates and figurines. These are the prints you see advertised in the Sunday newspapers. Signed and numbered limited-edition prints now being produced are poor investments. They should be considered only as decoration. There are some exceptions to this, but they are reserved for the advanced collectors with prior knowledge.

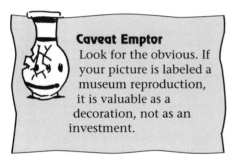

Caveat Emptor
Look for the obvious. If your picture is labeled a museum reproduction, it is valuable as a decoration, not as an investment.

Overall, always check the price of any print you are considering buying—before you buy. Use a reputable price guide. Here are two that I recommend: *Currier's Price Guide to American and European Prints at Auction* by William P. Carl (Currier Publications, 1994). You can also consult *Prints, Posters, and Photographs: Identification and Price Guide* by Susan Theran (Avon Books, 1993). Prices can fluctuate a great deal in the art world. To protect yourself, get the most up-to-date guide being published. This will help ensure that you're getting the most reliable prices.

Go West, Young Collector

Trigger may be dead and stuffed, but Roy Rogers and Dale Evans are still going strong. That's because the Old West is once again rip roarin'. Partly as a result of the renewed interest in anything Old West, the art of Frederick Remington is enjoying a comeback.

Remington was born in New York in 1861, moved West, and captured the excitement of the wide open spaces in his paintings, sketches, and bronzes. Remington is to the West as blondes are to Hollywood. In 1990, one of Remington's paintings sold for almost $4.5 million.

Tricks of the Trade
Look in boxes of papers at auctions, flea markets, old house sales, and country sales to see if you can find any of Remington's woodblock prints.

It's not likely that either of us can afford one of his paintings, but there *is* still a niche for you and me— Remington's woodblocks. Early in his career, Remington created a series of woodblock prints for *Harper's Weekly*. This is the only place such work appears and the original woodblocks seem to have vanished. These prints date from 1886; in 1980, 119 of his prints appeared in the magazine. Some are signed, some are not.

Go East, Too

Japanese woodblock prints are as collectible as Remington's prints. There are a far wider range of Japanese woodblock prints available, however, which makes this a much easier collection to amass. Some of the prints show beautiful scenery; others, portraits of citizens. There are woodblock prints that document important events in Japanese life, too.

The golden age of Japanese woodblock printing is generally accepted as the 1700s and 1800s. These prints were quite popular; in some cases, more than 100,000 impressions were made from the same scene. Some collectors seek woodcut prints from the Meiji Period (1868–1912), for their lush color. If you like Asian art, this might be an area to examine in greater depth.

The Least You Need to Know

➤ When you collect prints, look for condition, rarity, artist, and subject matter.

➤ Hot areas include Currier and Ives lithographs, art nouveau posters, Japanese woodcuts, and Frederick Remington prints.

➤ The entertainer formerly known as "Prints" doesn't collect woodblocks.

Chapter 21

Feathering the Nest: Furniture and Rugs

In This Chapter

➤ Find out which types and styles of furniture are most collectible

➤ Discover how to judge the age and authenticity of a piece of furniture

➤ Learn how to buy Oriental rugs with confidence

For the typical collector, buying furniture is more nerve-wracking than buying any other collectible. Perhaps this is because furniture tends to be so big that mistakes are hard to hide—where *can* you put that hideous armoire? Also, furniture costs a lot more than everyday tchotckes like Howdy Doody glasses. Finally, the average collector buys far less furniture when compared to other objets d'art, making each furniture purchase monumental.

This chapter is designed to allay your fear of furniture. No more panic over patina, dread over desks, or hysteria over Hepplewhite. Since entire series of books have been written on furniture, there's no way I can cover all facets of style, construction, and value in one chapter. Instead, I'll give you the most useful information to help you assess and collect furniture—the furniture that's right for you. You'll learn about the major periods of furniture, the key manufacturers, and the characteristics of each. You'll see which pieces are the most popular collectibles and why.

Strike a Pose: Identifying Furniture Style Periods

Let's play a quick game of matching. I say beehive hairdos and sequined glasses; you say Aunt Ethel in the '50s. I say bell-bottoms and bandannas; you say first cousin Moonbeam Sunflower in the '70s. Before you buy furniture, you have to be able to match style and era. It's easier than matching odd relatives to their strange clothing. I promise.

Start with Table 21.1, which is a simple chart of design periods in English and American furniture.

Table 21.1 Furniture Design Periods

Ruler	Date of Reign	Name of Furniture Period or Type of Furniture
James I	1603–1625	Jacobean
Charles I	1625–1649	Carolean
Commonwealth	1649–1660	Commonwealth or Cromwelian
Charles II	1660–1685	Restoration
James II	1685–1689	Restoration
William and Mary	1689–1694	William and Mary
William III	1694–1702	William III
Anne	1702–1714	Queen Anne
George I	1714–1727	George I (early Georgian)
George II	1727–1760	Early Georgian
George III	1760–1811	Later Georgian Chippendale Hepplewhite Sheraton
George III	1811–1820	Regency Empire
George IV	1820–1830	Regency Empire
William IV	1830–1837	Late Regency Empire
Victoria	1837–1901	Early Victorian (to 1860) Late Victorian (1860–1901) Empire Victorian Cottage
Edward VII	1901–1910 1905–1920 1925–1945	Edwardian Mission (Arts and Crafts) Art Deco

I've made this a nice, neat chart so you don't have undue furniture-collecting anxiety, but every period of furniture has transitions where one style may show the influence of another style. For example, Empire furniture may have some Victorian influence as the beginning of the Victorian period started and furniture became more ornate. We call these pieces "transitional pieces." They fall in both periods and confuse a lot of people. Furniture from the 1700s is the most popular and expensive collectible in this field. Louis XV and Chippendale are the head weenies at the roast. Earlier fine furniture—Louis XIV and William and Mary—are as heavy as dumplings and so attract less attention. Later examples—Hepplewhite and Sheraton—are more austere. Nonetheless, each has its cheering section. Let's look at some of the most popular styles so you can discover where your taste lies.

> **Connoisseur**
> The benchmark date for "manufactured" furniture is 1830. If a piece of furniture has tool marks and screws, it was made after 1830.

We Americans had some furniture styles of our own, like Pilgrim and Mission, but we also cribbed a lot of our styles from the Mother Country.

Grim and Guilt-Ridden Pilgrim Furniture

This big, cumbersome, squarish, heavy furniture has the added allure of being uncomfortable. Since there were fewer people in the seventeenth century, there's not a whole lot of Pilgrim furniture, which is not a bad thing to my way of thinking.

> **Learn the Lingo**
> A **trestle table** is a long picnic-like table with a crossed base. Benches, rather than individual chairs, were typically used with trestle tables.

But if you're still inclined to collect this style of furniture, be on the lookout for trestle tables, joint or joined stools, butterfly and gateleg tables, and chests. You'll be able to spot Pilgrim furniture by its large panels and turned parts. Nearly all the pieces are made of oak or pine. The lack of authentic furniture from the Pilgrim era is balanced by the abundance of reproductions. The quality of these repos runs the gamut from custom-made to bargain basement, so beware.

> **Connoisseur**
> Recognizing furniture forms that did not exist in the original period is an effective way of identifying "adaptations" and outright fakes.

A Well-Turned Leg: Queen Anne

With its graceful lines and lovely curves, the Queen Anne style of furniture has achieved and maintained great popularity. To identify this style, start at the bottom and work your way up. The foot may be slippered, ball-and-claw, or padded. The cabriole leg tapers to the ankle and then curves outward at the knee. The top is equally graceful and may be embellished with a shell motif. While authentic Queen Anne furniture is hard to find and thus pricey, it is not rare.

The Best Seat in the House: Chippendale

Chippendale furniture, produced from 1750 to 1790 during the Georgian period, is like Queen Anne's mother: straighter and heavier. Mahogany was the favored wood. Many collectors consider Chippendale the height of elegance for its balance between strong, bold lines and inherent grace. Even good reproductions are costly.

Queen Anne and Chippendale side chairs made in America should feature removable slip seats. If the seat is upholstered around the framing so that it cannot be removed, it is either European or a reproduction.

This Chippendale armchair demostrates the style's blend of grace and strength.

Hepplewhite

The Hepplewhite period dominated American taste from the 1780s until the end of the century. Look for inlaid shields and urns and a lighter, more delicate feeling. Pieces are often beautifully inlaid. You'll also see a simple square tapered leg, which many feel is the purest in design.

You can tell American from English Hepplewhite because the former is often embellished with symbols of our nation: eagles, arrows, and stars. Not so with English Hepplewhite.

Recently, Hepplewhite has enjoyed a boost in the ratings. Its delicate frame and light wood make it more suitable for many small homes and co-ops.

Sheraton

Often lumped with Hepplewhite because they developed around the same time, Sheraton nonetheless has a style all its own. Sheraton has a rounded, fluted leg; the Hepplewhite leg is square and tapering. Sheraton fronts are plain; tops are solid or veneer. One style of Sheraton chair, often called "Duncan Phyfe," has a wide horizontal back rail. Since Sheraton is not as popular as Chippendale and Hepplewhite, it is less expensive. That doesn't mean it hasn't been copied extensively, however, so beware of imitations.

Learn the Lingo
Duncan Phyfe made furniture in several styles, so "Duncan Phyfe" isn't a particularly useful term for describing specific furniture. Of course, that hasn't stopped most people from using it.

The Empire Strikes Back

Empire furniture, made from about 1810 to 1850, comes in both skim milk and heavy cream. The low-fat version is heavy, bold, and starkly plain. The rich end is carved, gilded, and ornamented with everything from dolphins to serpents.

If you like the Empire style, you can often pick up pieces for a song—even if you can't sing particularly well. Why? Since these pieces were often heavily varnished, the surfaces have crackled, making them less appealing. As a result, the furniture's *patina* (rich surface quality) is poor. Also, many people shun Empire-style furniture because it is monster-sized. But the wood is solid and the craftsmanship good, making it an exceptional value.

Learn the Lingo
Patina is the surface quality of a piece of furniture, the finish that develops after years.

Victorian

Queen Victoria reigned from 1837 to 1901, bringing peace and contentment to England. But what's good for national stability can be bad for dating furniture. Why? Because over sixty-four years, designers had a chance to come up with several different styles—all called "Victorian." Here are the three main divisions in "Victorian" furniture:

➤ **Early Victorian.** Also called "Victorian Gothic," this furniture is as massive as the cathedral style it mimics, replete with arches and rosettes. Understandably, it's not the Prom Queen of furniture.

➤ **Late Victorian.** Victorian rococo is elaborately embellished with carved flowers, shells, grapes—and just about anything else you can imagine. It's the most popular of the Victorian styles, beloved for its flowing lines, burl woods, and rich veneers.

➤ **Jenny Lind.** At the same time, the simple "cottage" style caught on. You'll know it by the spool (or Jenny Lind) turnings.

Mission Impossible?

A reaction to the intricacy of Victorian furniture, the Mission style is linear and nearly devoid of decoration. In America, the prime craftsmen of this style were Elbert Hubbard and Gustav Stickley. Collectors eagerly seek this furniture. Here are some basic guidelines to help you identify original Mission pieces:

➤ First look for manufacturers' labels or other identifying marks.

➤ If there are no labels or marks, look for exposed pegs that join one piece of wood to the next. Copies often use screws.

➤ The hardware will often be hand-hammered and copper, but Stickley's pieces often have round wooden knobs rather than hand-hammered metal pulls.

➤ Mission sofas and chairs upholstered in the original green, brown, or red leather are extremely hot collectibles.

The legs of this Mission-style Stickley table show obvious wood joinery.

Art Deco

This sleek furniture, characterized by bleached wood and a chrome body, is as highly collectible as the art deco accessories described in Chapter 16 "As Clear as Crystal" and Chapter 22, "Are Diamonds a Collector's Best Friend?"

Two key designers are Louis Majorelle and Josef Hoffmann.

Rock 'Round the Clock: Furniture from the 1940s and 1950s

Levittown. Conformity. Happy homemakers. The cookie-cutter sameness of the 1950s is belied by the innovative furniture produced by high-end designers of the time. With this type of furniture, designer matters, so go for a big name. Check out the highly collectible pieces created by these five big-name designers:

➤ **Charles Eames (1907–1979).** Remember those molded polyester chairs shaped like shells? We have Eames to thank for those. He also made some nifty laminated wood and bentwood pieces, often combined with steel bases. When you inspect furniture that you suspect may be original Eames, look for the logo of the "Herman Miller Company" of Michigan, his home base. It's well worth the search. An original "Eames chair" in mint condition sells for more than $1,000 today.

➤ **Eero Saarinen (1910–1961).** He is best known for his famous "womb chair," a molded plastic shell upholstered and mounted on a steel frame. His furniture came out under the name "Kroll International."

➤ **Harry Bertoia (1915–1978).** Also associated with Kroll, Bertoia used iron to create whimsical chairs, tables, and sofas.

➤ **Gilbert Rohde (1894–1944).** During his years with the Herman Miller Company, Rohde created new styles of furniture by mixing traditional mahogany and maple with innovative chrome and glass. An original Rohde dresser sells for $500 to $800 today. A steel-and-vinyl settee in good condition will fetch $250.

➤ **Wharton Esherick (1887–1970).** Famous for his unique hand-crafted furniture.

Caveat Emptor
Upholstery repair is very expensive, so try to buy upholstered furniture in good condition.

Connoisseur
European furniture made between 1940 and 1950 is often more expensive than its American counterparts. European designer desks, for example, can sell for as much as $3,000.

Buy pieces with manufacturers' marks or unmarked items that are clearly the work of important designers. Avoid furniture by lesser-known designers unless it's love at first sight. Although these pieces cost less now, they will not appreciate in value as rapidly as pieces by famous designers. Avoid pieces that have been extensively refinished because restoration reduces their value.

Shake and Bake

The Shaker sect in New England designed their beautiful, simple furniture so that it could be hung on pegs around the walls. Every evening the Shakers hung the furniture on the walls in case they were disturbed during the night by the Second Coming of the Lord. Only the larger pieces of furniture, such as chests and tables, were left on the floor.

The Shakers were the biggest and most successful Utopian venture in America. Founded in 1774 on the principles of equality and divine order, the celibate sect passed their time praying, being self-reliant, and making some extremely collectible furniture. Above all, the Shakers believed that the outward appearance revealed the inner spirit, and that the greatest value an object could have was usefulness. Their superbly made furniture and objects are simple, beautiful, and useful.

Among the most eagerly sought Shaker furniture are storage cupboards, chests of drawers, work counters, desks, tables, ladderback side chairs, rocking chairs, washstands, large trestle tables, and benches. Some pieces were painted as well as stained. Because of their outstanding craftsmanship, Shaker furniture has survived in relatively large quantities in good condition. Here's what to look for when you collect Shaker furniture:

➤ Normal wear-and-tear is acceptable.

➤ Pieces with their original paints and stains intact are the most desirable.

➤ Signed pieces command the highest prices.

The elegant simplicity of Shaker furniture attracts avid collectors.

Moving in for the Kill

Although there are plenty of furniture fakes around, this is one area of collecting where you can relax—somewhat. For a furniture faker to earn enough to make his efforts worthwhile, he's got to sell the piece to a first-class dealer. If the faker can fool the dealer, the chances are the fake will go undetected until the piece is old enough to really become a genuine antique. Besides, if the fake is of such high quality, it's likely not a bad deal.

Follow the Rules

So what should you obsess over? Here are the four basic rules to follow when you're buying antique furniture:

1. Learn not only how to identify styles and periods, but also what pieces of furniture were made in what time periods. There were not a whole lot of computer desks made during the 17th century, for instance.

2. Learn how much each piece is worth. You can do this by consulting price guidebooks. Here are two handy ones: *The Wallace Homestead Price Guide to American Country Antiques* by Don Raycraft (Wallace Homestead, 1991) and *Current Antique Furniture—Style and Price Guide with Decorative Accessories* (Doubleday, 1993).

> **Tricks of the Trade**
> Subscribe to auction catalogs to get the price ranges for specific pieces of antique furniture you want. You can find names and addresses in your local telephone book and from antiques and collectible magazines.

3. Use all your senses. The furniture should *smell* old as well as look and feel it.

4. Watch for refinished and repainted pieces. Refinishing and repainting affect the value of a collectible piece of furniture to varying degrees. Check the price guides mentioned above for more detail on this.

Check and Double-Check

OK—so you think you've stumbled on the furniture find of a lifetime, or at least of this year. What's next? Use the Furniture Buyer's Checklist to see if you've got a chip off the old block—or just chipwood.

Furniture Buyer's Checklist

Follow these steps in order to make sure you're on the money.

- ❏ The furniture should show the expected amount of wear and tear for its age, especially the feet and drawers.

- ❏ Original handles and screws are unlikely. Instead, look for post holes. If handles and screws were replaced, the old holes should be there.

- ❏ Old locks were large and held in place by handmade screws or hand-forged nails.

- ❏ Check that all inside wood matches. If not, the furniture may have been assembled from many different old pieces.

- ❏ The outside patina is not an accurate guide to age; check the inside carefully for color changes. Air causes unfinished wood to darken.

- ❏ Early dovetails in drawer corners were irregular.

- ❏ Circular saw marks indicate the piece was made *after* 1830 or 1840.

- ❏ Plane marks are a good sign that the piece was made *before* 1860.

- ❏ Authenticate your "finds" in print sources.

- ❏ If you think you've stumbled on real goodies, don't hesitate to contact an expert. That's why they're the experts.

Magic Carpet Ride

You might be walking on a treasure—so take your shoes off! Even though some collectors and rug aficionados speak in hushed tones of the warp and weft of the weave, don't get distracted by the hyperbole. Buy a fine rug for the same reasons that you buy any collectible—you like its color, design, feel, and value.

Flying Carpets: Oriental Rugs

Oriental carpets are an especially good value now because countries that export these rugs have stepped up production. Oriental carpets now cost about half of what they did in the 1980s. Unfortunately, the law of supply and demand does not guarantee you a good deal. Some Oriental carpets are originals, others are clever copies—and it's hard to tell the difference between the two. Sears, Ikea, and Home Depot all sell "one of a kind" Oriental rugs, for about a third less than a dealer would charge.

There are three keys to the value of an Oriental rug: age, origin, and caliber of wool. As a rule, the older the rug, the higher a price it will fetch—but only if it's first class. For example, an antique Persian usually runs about $200 a square foot, as compared to about $50 a square foot for a new one.

Here are my suggestions for getting the most for your money when you collect Oriental rugs:

1. **There are no bargains.** With Oriental rugs, you get what you pay for. As a general rule, any hand-woven rug is more expensive than the best machine-made rug.

2. **Persians are still the standard for Oriental rugs.** As a result, they cost more than other similar rugs. It has been illegal to import Persian carpets since 1987, but they are smuggled into America nonetheless.

3. **Costs are fairly standard for new Oriental rugs.** On the average, you'll pay about $1,500 to $2,500 for a new 6 × 9 rug or $3,000 to $5,000 for a 9 × 12 Oriental rug made in Afghanistan, China, India, Pakistan, Romania, and Russia. A Persian of the same size can cost double.

> **Connoisseur**
> By the 5th century B.C., carpet weaving was already a fine art. In structural terms, there is no difference between a carpet found in the fifth century and any symmetrically knotted rug made during the last 500 years.

> **Learn the Lingo**
> **Kilims** are flat-weave carpets. **Dhurries** are such carpets made in India from cotton or cotton and wool.

4. **Looks count.** It's sad, but true: pretty rugs are worth more than ugly ones. Color and design are important.

5. **Knots to you.** Traditionally, collectors were told to look at the knots in the back of the rug. There should be between 64 to 400 knots per square inch. The more knots, they were told, the better the rug. Forget about knots, they are not a reliable indicator of quality.

6. **Don't pile it on.** Thick pile is not necessarily better than a tighter weave. In fact, heavy-pile, sculptured rugs from China are some of the least desirable collectible rugs being sold today.

7. **Look around.** A dealer's mark-up ranges from 30% to 100%, so it pays to comparison shop. I suggest that you examine the merchandise in at least three shops before you buy.

8. **"Is that the best you can do?"** Most dealers expect you to haggle. But beware of excessive discounts. That may mean that the rug is greatly overpriced.

9. **Read the fine print.** Check the label to be sure that the rug is properly marked with the place of manufacture and its materials.

10. **Stick with it.** It can takes years of study to make sure you are getting what you paid for with Oriental rugs.

Connoisseur
Almost all Oriental carpets are made of silk and wool.

While fine Oriental rugs often appreciate in value, don't let anyone sell you one as an investment. The world's oldest, rarest, and most beautiful rugs *do* hold their value—like the world's oldest, rarest, and most beautiful jewels, furniture, and artwork. But this is true for only the best of the big-buck best.

Hooked Rugs

The hooked rug, a type of floor covering widely used since the 1850s, is one of the most popular and collectible of all American folk arts. Hooked rugs were made by using a hook to pull narrow strips of fabric over and over through a coarse backing, such as burlap. A series of loops is left on the surface. The closer the loops, the more durable the rug. Hooked rugs have been collected avidly since the 1920s.

Hooked rugs often depict everyday scenes like these.

THEY HAD TO LEAVE

What should you look for when you buy an antique hooked rug? Here are some basics:

➤ **Condition.** Although of all collectibles, rugs surely get used the most heavily, condition matters. First, the rug should not be heavily worn. Next, the colors shouldn't be overly faded. Examine the underside of the rug where the colors should be the brightest. Also, the backing should be in good condition, without rips or tears.

Tricks of the Trade
You can sometimes date a hooked rug by the colors. The earliest hooked rugs were made with fabrics colored with vegetable dyes that faded.

279

➤ **Pictorial rugs.** These rugs show animals or figures. Those most similar to folk paintings are the most desirable. Scenes of activities, such as celebrations, are also hot.

➤ **Design.** Original designs are generally most valuable, although some collectors do favor rugs worked from commercial patterns.

➤ **Modern Pieces.** Don't reject twentieth century examples; they are also highly collectible.

The Least You Need to Know

➤ Furniture from the 1700s is the most popular and expensive collectible in this field.

➤ Louis XV and Chippendale are the most hotly sought types.

➤ Then comes Shaker furniture and selected pieces from the 1940s and 1950s.

➤ When you buy an Oriental rug, look for age, origin, and caliber of wool.

Part 5

All that Glitters Isn't Gold—but It's Probably Collectible

In 1903, a Canadian blacksmith, Fred La Rose, threw his hammer at a marauding fox, missed—and struck silver. The hammer landed on what turned out to be the world's richest vein of silver. La Rose sold his claim for $30,000. By 1913, the vein had yielded silver worth more than $300 million.

Today, throwing a hammer is more likely to land you a stay in the county jail than a fortune. But there is another way that you might amass a fortune, or at least have a whole lot of fun. How? By collecting precious metals, jewelry, and gems.

For thousands of years, people have collected and worn precious stones and metals for decoration and talismans to protect them from ill health and misfortune. The stones are treasured for their color, translucence, durability, and monetary value. Gold has been prized by human beings since the Stone Age; the Egyptians were probably the first to cut and polish gems to increase their beauty.

There's a wealth of precious metals, jewelry, and gemstones for every collector's taste and budget. In the following chapters, you will discover riches from the earth that have been crafted into wondrous possessions.

Chapter 22

Are Diamonds a Collector's Best Friend? Collecting Jewelry

In This Chapter

➤ Find out about collecting antique jewelry

➤ Learn about precious gemstones

➤ See why all that glitters isn't necessarily gold

➤ Get the scoop on Native American jewelry, netsuke, and other collectible personal ornaments

In 1987, the Duchess of Windsor's jewels were auctioned off amid great publicity. The sale marked a frantic revival of interest in collecting jewelry. In fact, the market was so stable that sales didn't even tremble when the stock market tumbled later that year. It's no surprise that gems hold such allure, for jewelry has always been a symbol of wealth and status.

If you want to collect jewelry, you must first learn to identify the metals and gems (and in the case of the 1950s, the plastics and woods!) that comprise it. This isn't as tricky as it sounds, which you'll discover in this chapter. You'll also learn that you don't need a million bucks to put together a beautiful—and valuable—jewelry collection.

Oldies but Goodies: Antique Jewelry

> Rare gold, blue, green and white enamel, pearl and diamond cornucopia brooch, circa 1840... $8,500.

> Gold, silver, blue enamel and diamond bracelet, circa 1820... $15,000.

> Gold, platinum cabochon sapphire and diamond ring, circa 1885... $12,500.

Ever drool over ads like these? People who collect antique jewelry like to explain their extravagance by claiming they are buying a piece of history, but I think they are glossing over the truth: a lot of antique jewelry is just plain gorgeous.

According to law, antique jewelry isn't antique until it can make a birthday appearance with Willard Scott because it's a hundred years old. However, this definition has been broadened to include any jewelry that looks old and wasn't made yesterday. Table 22.1 can help you place "antique" jewelry into manageable periods. History is rarely as tidy as we'd like, so you'll find some overlap in time spans.

Table 22.1 Jewelry Periods

Name	Dates
Georgian	1790–1837
Early Victorian	1837–1860
Mid-Victorian	1860–1880
Late Victorian	1880–1901
Art Nouveau	1880–1914
Arts and Crafts	1890–1914
Edwardian	1901–1910
Art Deco	1920–1940

Plunging In!

First stop: a store that sells antique jewelry. Study as many pieces of antique jewelry as you can. Discover what periods, styles, artists, and materials appeal to you. Buy a jeweler's loupe so you can examine each piece carefully.

Then consult a reliable and up-to-date price guide. I recommend *The Official Identification and Price Guide to Antique Jewelry,* edited by Arthur Kaplan (House of Collectibles, Florida).

Dating

How can you figure out when a piece of antique jewelry was made? Here's a run down of the characteristics of the jewelry produced in each era:

➤ **Georgian.** Brooches tend to be square or rectangular, and chunky. Pearls are often used as borders and black and white enamel are common. Most pieces are 18K gold. The Georgians were a mournful lot, so expect a lot of memorial jewelry.

This Georgian ring has a characteristic rectangular stone.

➤ **Early Victorian.** Pieces are lighter in feeling and construction. Rings have flat sides and often incorporate enamel in the design. Some mourning pins include snippets of hair from the deceased. Necklaces often sport garnets, pearls, and swirls of gold. An early Victorian gold locket brooch, with pearl and blue enamel motif, costs about $1,000.

The gold swirls clearly mark this as an early Victorian necklace.

➤ **Mid-Victorian.** Elaborate lockets and chains suit mid-Victorian taste; silver makes a bold stand. You'll find the influence of ancient Greece and Rome. Pieces once again get as large as Queen Victoria's considerable brood. A mid-Victorian gold and opal cluster brooch with a butterfly and a sword sells for about $900.

This large brooch is from the mid-Victorian period.

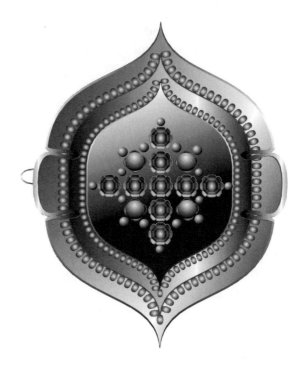

➤ **Late Victorian.** Engraved patterns combine an interest in naturalism and a fascination with the crescent motif. There's already a whiff of Art Nouveau. Lots of simple and delicate pendants, called *lavalieres*.

➤ **Art Nouveau.** Look for lush enamels and exotic forms. The iris and the idealized female form were especially popular. This style of jewelry is currently a very hot collectible. Fancy an airy Art Nouveau diamond pendant with a pearl drop? Figure it will set you back about $900. An Art Nouveau pendant with two birds on a twig, decorated with beads and turquoise, costs about the same.

➤ **Arts and Crafts.** Soft colored enamels, mother-of-pearl, silver, twisted braid trim, ornate clasps. An Arts and Crafts enamelled and moonstone brooch, with openwork mounts and a large central moonstone, runs about $1,500.

➤ **Edwardian.** These pieces are light and delicate. Look for diamonds and white metals such as platinum. Settings are airy and pierced. An Edwardian half-pearl swag necklace, for example, should cost about $800; a half-pearl and tourmaline open-work pendant, about $500.

➤ **Art Deco.** Art Deco jewelry captures the flashiness of the 1920s. Onyx, carnelian, and marcasite are popular stones. These pieces are eagerly sought by collectors, perhaps because they mirror the excesses of our own day.

Big Deals

Carol McFadden of Oil City, Pennsylvania, had collected 18,750 different pairs of earrings as of January 1995. Her collection earned her a place in the *1996 Guinness Book of World Records.*

Material Girl

Don't overlook the costume jewelry of the 1800s. Much of it is beautiful—and quite valuable today. Its value derives from the odd materials from which it was made as much as from its age and appearance. Here are some of the materials you may encounter in antique costume jewelry:

➤ **Aluminum**, a rare and costly metal in the 1850s, was very popular for jewelry until the 1880s.

➤ **Bog oak**, from the Irish bogs or swamps, was carved with various designs and made into jewelry.

➤ **Cut steel** was often faceted to mimic more expensive metals.

➤ **German silver**, also called *nickel silver*, is an alloy made from copper, zinc, and nickel.

➤ **Gutta-percha**, a brown-to-black mixture of resin, sawdust, and latex, was molded into beads and brooches.

➤ **Hair jewelry** is just what it sounds like, locks cut from the head of the beloved, who was usually deceased. Ornaments made from hair were very popular in the Victorian era.

Gemstones: Gravel with an Attitude

Gemstones are uptown versions of the gravel on your driveway. A *gemstone* can be cut and polished into a *gem*. When it's set, it becomes a *jewel*. The market is flooded with inferior versions of every possible gemstone—nothing more than gravel with an attitude.

Truth or Dare

How can you tell a noble gemstone from a common chunk of glass? Here are some tests:

1. First, take its temperature. Touch it with your tongue. Gemstones (with the exception of an opal) will remain cool; glass warms up fast. This is not to say that you don't want glass; you just want to make sure you're paying the right price for it.

2. Try a little water torture. A drop of water will hold its shape on a real gemstone; on glass, it spreads out like a couch potato's rear end.

3. Look at the setting. Glued stones are likely worth a lot less than those held in place with prongs.

4. As a very last resort, try the scratch test. If you can etch glass with the stone, it's likely genuine. Unfortunately, you've probably damaged any gem but a diamond in the process, which is why this is your last resort.

Amethyst to Zirconium

Let's survey the most collectible gemstones, so you can better recognize what's being collected—and why.

1. **Amethyst.** According to myth, these stones protect the wearer against intoxication. A variety of quartz, the rich purple is the most desired color.

2. **Aquamarine.** This gem shades from a light bluish green to deep blue, which is the rarest. The deeper the blue, the more collectible the gem.

3. **Amber.** Amber is petrified pitch. It often contains bits of insects and bark, which most collectors feel enhances its value. They look for rich amber brown pieces filled with relics from ages long gone. Some collectors seek out rosaries made of amber, which date back to the 1400s.

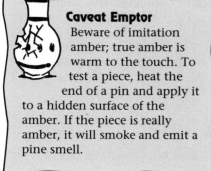

Caveat Emptor

Beware of imitation amber; true amber is warm to the touch. To test a piece, heat the end of a pin and apply it to a hidden surface of the amber. If the piece is really amber, it will smoke and emit a pine smell.

4. **Coral.** No one knows if this gem is a plant or an animal, but we do know that the most prized coral is the dark red variety found off the coast of Tunisia and Algeria. Black coral is next in value; pink coral trails behind. Coral is now a protected part of the underwater landscape, at least in the U.S. In places like the Caribbean, coral reefs are being decimated to make cheapo coral trinkets. You'll want to steer clear of newer coral pieces for environmental reasons.

5. **Diamonds.** Diamonds are the hardest and brightest of the gems. When collecting diamonds, look for the four C's: cut, color, clarity, and carat. The clearest, largest, best-cut stones are the most valuable. It is rare for any diamond less than a carat to be purchased for investment. Further, investment-grade diamonds are rarely mounted and worn, Liz Taylor's habits notwithstanding.

6. **Emeralds.** These are the most highly prized of all gems—even more valuable than diamonds! Fortunately, an emerald is one of the easiest gemstones to identify because of its *occlusions* or flaws; a totally flawless genuine emerald is almost impossible to acquire. A true emerald will not change color under the light.

7. **Garnets.** Garnets are found in several colors, including pink, brown, and black, although the ruby-red shade is the most common. A violet garnet is called a "rhodolite." The stones will change color under the light. Most garnets are considered costume jewelry.

8. **Ivory.** Ivory from Asian elephants cannot be legally imported into the U.S. because the Asian elephant is protected as an endangered species. The African elephant, however, is just "threatened," so its tusks *can* be imported. Nonetheless, I could make a good case that we're splitting (elephant) hairs here so you shouldn't collect *any* ivory. If you do decide to buy ivory, make sure that you are buying from a first-class dealer who gives you clear documentation of the ivory's source.

> **Connoisseur**
> Early diamonds were cut in as few as 24 facets, which accounts for their lack of brilliance when compared with modern diamonds cut to 58 facets.

9. **Jade.** The jade you're likely most familiar with comes in greens that range from emerald to spinach, but it also occurs in brown, yellow, black, blue, and an off-white. Jade has long been revered by the Chinese; it is still used in China as a symbol of high rank and authority.

10. **Jet.** A variety of coal that's dense and glossy, jet is making a strong comeback on the collector trail. It's hard to tell jet from black plastic, so beware. The real thing is heavy, feels warm when touched, and like amber, will take an electrical charge when rubbed.

11. **Lapis Lazuli.** The most valuable varieties of this soft, deep blue gemstone are uniform in color, although lapis often has flecks of iron pyrite (fool's gold) and occasionally real gold. If it is streaked with white, it is considered of lesser quality.

12. **Opals.** Look for a fiery stone. Some are milky white and tinted with flashes of color. So-called "black opals" have a dark color.

13. **Pearls.** *Natural pearls* form in oysters all by their lonesome. *Cultured pearls* are seeded and returned to their ocean homes to grow. *Mikimoto pearls* are a brand name for a company that started culturing pearls in 1908. *Biwa pearls* are cultured freshwater pearls. The majority of modern pearls are cultured.

14. **Ruby.** Rubies were said to preserve the body and health of the wearer and to remove evil thoughts. The rubies with an orange-yellow color are the most desired. Star rubies reveal a star when they are cut.

Caveat Emptor

Most colored stones on the market today have had more dye-jobs than even *my* hair. Heat, chemicals, and radiation are used to improve the color and smooth out imperfections. Because some color enhancements are not permanent, ask what's been done to the stone before you buy it.

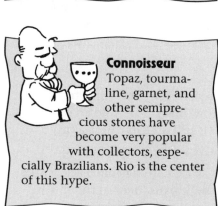

Connoisseur

Topaz, tourmaline, garnet, and other semiprecious stones have become very popular with collectors, especially Brazilians. Rio is the center of this hype.

15. **Sapphire.** Although the word *sapphire* comes from a Greek word that means "blue," these stones come in yellow and green as well as blue and violet.

16. **Topaz.** According to an ancient superstition, topaz can cure insomnia and avert sudden death. Commonly, these stones range in color from gold to deep brown, but blue topaz are not uncommon. Citrine is a less-expensive variation.

17. **Zircon.** Zircon is a real gemstone but considerably more common and thus less valuable than its first cousin, diamonds. Do not confuse a zircon with a *cubic zirconia*, which is an artificial diamond.

Many types of stones, emeralds and rubies in particular, now can be manufactured. Mother Nature has the edge in the collectible market: Manufactured gemstones aren't as valuable as the natural versions. Unfortunately, it is very difficult to tell natural gemstones from manufactured ones. This isn't something you can eyeball with a jeweler's loup. Even trained gemologists often have to remove the stone from its setting to see what's what. Sometimes, they have to weigh it to see if it's real or not. The moral of the story? If the deal seems too good to be true, it probably is. Take gems to a trained, licensed gemologist for identification before you plunk down your hard-earned bucks.

Truth in Advertising

Beware of how a gemstone is labeled. Here are some examples of deceptive labeling:

➤ **Cape May diamonds**, **Bohemian diamonds**, and **Herkimer diamonds** are *quartz*— the stuff on your sidewalk.

➤ **Gilson opal** and **Slocum opal** are *plastic*—the stuff used to make your food storage containers.

➤ **Girasol pearls**, **Laguna pearls**, and **Majoica pearls**—fake, fake, fake. Even confirmed landlubbers have been closer to oysters than a simulated pearl has ever been.

To avoid problems later, ask these five questions when you buy a colored gemstone:

1. Is this a genuine stone or a synthetic stone?

2. Is the color natural?

3. Is the color permanent?

4. What is the gem called and what does its name mean?

5. Is the clarity acceptable, or are there too many flaws?

All That Glitters Isn't 14K

What's the allure of gold? First of all, it doesn't tarnish, rust, corrode, or fade. It can withstand thousands of years in a pharaoh's tomb; it is impervious to salt and water. It is malleable (able to be molded) and ductile (flexible). One ounce of gold can be formed into a wire 50 miles long. It also looks really neat around your neck, wrist, or dangling from any port.

Somewhere Over the Rainbow

To make gold sturdier, it is usually mixed with another metal, such as copper, silver, nickel, or platinum. How many of these golds do you collect?

➤ **Yellow gold** is an alloy of gold, copper, and silver.

➤ **White gold** is an alloy of gold, copper, and nickel or platinum.

➤ **Pink gold** has gold, copper, and silver. The pink color comes from greater amounts of copper.

➤ **Red gold** has even more copper.

➤ **Green gold** has silver as its main component, along with gold, zinc, and copper.

➤ **Purple gold** is an alloy of gold and aluminum.

What's Up, Doc?

The purity, or fineness, of gold is measured in *karats*. ("Carat" is used for gemstones). The word probably comes from ancient times, when the seeds of the carob plant were used to measure the weight of gemstones.

The scale goes from 1 to 24, with 24 karats (abbreviated as 24K) as the purest form of the metal. One standard alloy sold in America is 18K gold (18 parts out of 24 are gold), which would be 75 percent pure gold. You will also find 14K, 12K, and 10K. Antique rings are sometimes 22K, which explains why they are often very thin and worn.

Connoisseur

How can you tell real gold from fake? Phony gold will dissolve in nitric acid whereas real gold won't.

Caveat Emptor

The Federal Trade Commission requires that all gold jewelry sold in America be labeled with karats. Therefore, a 14K piece of gold jewelry cannot be advertised solely as "gold"; it must also be stamped "14K."

Imported gold jewelry will often have the amount of gold expressed in a fraction or decimal rather than the K format. For example, 750/1000 or .750 are the same as 18K. To make your life more complex, there is no international gold scale. Japan, for instance, recognizes nine grades of gold between 24K and 9K, while Italy has five (from 18K to 8K).

Anything less than 14K gold is generally considered costume jewelry; anything less than 10K is definitely the jewelry equivalent of a fun fur. There are a number of ways to cover base metal with gold; all are considered costume jewelry. Here they are:

➤ **Vermeil** is gold-coated silver or other metals.

➤ **Gold-filled** pieces have a gold coating $1/20$ or *more* of the total weight of the piece.

➤ **Gold-plated** pieces have a gold coating $1/20$ or *less* of the total weight of the piece.

➤ **Gold electroplate** is a coating no less than 7 millionths of an inch.

➤ **Gold wash** is anything thinner than electroplate.

Big Deals

In contrast to gold, which has been the stuff of jewelry forever, platinum didn't become the stuff of jewelry until the early years of the twentieth century. "Platinum" refers both to a specific metal and to a group of six related metals whose names suggest they would be equally at home on the periodic table: *platinum*, *palladium*, *rhodium*, *ruthenium*, *iridium*, and *osmium*.

One of my favorite gold guides is Tomart's *Price Guide to Garage Sale Gold* (Tomart Publishers; Dayton, Ohio; 1992). I always carry it with me when I cruise the garage-sale circuit.

Native-American Jewelry

The days when a tourist could buy an exquisite squash-blossom necklace in a teepee are as long past as the buffalo. During the past few decades, every Native-American art form has zoomed up faster than a harried executive's blood pressure. The finest examples of American Indian art are already in museums or noted private collections.

A few years ago, there was a real rush of interest in Native-American jewelry, but the interest has slacked off somewhat. Buyers have become disillusioned because of imitations and lack of knowledge about what they were buying. "Turquoise" may be plastic. Unwary collectors have bought pieces from gift shops in Arizona and New Mexico, returned home, and discovered their prizes were stamped "Taiwan" on the back. If you are planning to buy Native-American jewelry, make sure you receive a valid bill of sale guaranteeing what you got.

Connoisseur
Some collectors of American Indian art have turned to Eskimo items in an attempt to get in on the bottom floor. Soapstone figures, bone masks, jewelry, and scrimshaw pieces are affordable.

Netsuke

Some of the smallest items valued by collectors are netsuke (pronounced net-ski). These button-size toggles were used by the Japanese to hold the drawstrings on their purses that they hung from their belts as part of their traditional dress.

Netsuke were made for hundreds of years and reached their peak as an art form between the 1600s and 1800s. Usually made of wood or ivory, they were carved in a great many shapes, the one proviso being that they should not have any sharp points to catch on clothing.

More than 2,000 artists made signed netsuke, and there are many more unsigned ones. Since the 1850s, fake netsuke have been made. The price of the genuine article reached a peak in 1980–1981, when one collector reputedly paid $250,000 for a single netsuke. Since then, prices have come down.

Happy Days Are Here Again: Jewelry of the 1940s and 1950s

The 1940s and 1950s boasted big cars, big families, and some big jewelry. *Costume jewelry*—inexpensive funky pieces—from this era are in great demand among collectors. With costume jewelry, the design is often more important than the material content.

Jewelry from half a century ago varies greatly in materials and look. Some rings and bracelets were made from wood, glass, inexpensive metal, and plastic—which makes them very reasonable collectibles. Here are some of the most highly collected pieces, arranged by materials:

➤ **Enamel.** Enameled silver jewelry is very much in demand by collectors. Even small pieces can cost $50 to $200 each.

➤ **Metal and Glass.** These materials were often combined to simulate the look of diamonds and silver. Many of the pieces have a Victorian look, but there are some hideously gaudy pieces that Liberace would have loved. Actually, I collect them, too. Rhinestone expansion bracelets run between $50 and $100; plastic and rhinestone specimens cost less than $50 on average.

➤ **Plastic.** Collectors seek out Bakelite bracelets, rings, brooches, pins, and hair clips in bright orange, green, red, yellow, and blue. These usually sell for under $10 each. Character pins featuring Mickey Mouse, Donald Duck, Goofy, and other Disney characters are also highly collectible but still reasonably priced.

➤ **Sterling silver.** Geometric necklaces, pendants, and earrings are sought-after by sophisticated collectors. George Jensen pieces command prices starting around $100. Big, clunky charm bracelets have enjoyed a rebirth in popularity, and the trend shows no signs of abating.

➤ **Wood.** Wooden pins and earrings, often boasting large jungle plants and animals, are very popular. They go for about $5 to $10 each.

Big Deals

The outbreak of World War II was marked by a new fashion for women: brooches with the insignia of various army regiments, the Royal Air Force, and the Royal Navy. To cater to all pocketbooks, these were made in diamonds and gold as well as rhinestones and base metals. Both varieties are hot collectibles today.

Fortunately for collectors of this type of jewelry, it's relatively easy to find great pieces. I've hit up all my aged aunts as well as the aged relatives of friends and co-workers. My nifty ice-blue sequined clip-on earrings came from Betsy's 90-year old aunt.

Yard sales, charity bazaars, and estate auctions are also great sources. Better-quality examples such as those by Jensen are offered at auctions specializing in 1940s and 1950s memorabilia. Make sure that all sets are complete—they are worth much more that way. Earrings and necklaces, for example, often came with bangles. Compare all pieces in a set to make sure that they match.

Caveat Emptor
Broken costume jewelry is very difficult to get repaired. Only the rarest pieces are worth the trouble and expense of repair. In nearly all instances, you're better off waiting for a piece in good or excellent condition to come to market.

The Least You Need to Know

➤ Technically, antique jewelry must be 100 years old, but now anything two or three generations old is considered an antique.

➤ Gold must be labeled in karats to indicate its purity.

➤ It is very tricky to find authentic Native American jewelry.

➤ Be wary of how gemstones are labeled and colored.

➤ If you want as many rings as a frat house coffee table, consider collecting 20th-century costume jewelry.

Chapter 23

Heavy Metal

In This Chapter

➤ Slide into silver, the siren of metals

➤ Learn about pewter, copper, brass, bronze, iron, and steel collectibles

➤ See what makes bottle tickets, brass beds, and lithographed tins hot metal-based collectibles

History remembers Paul Revere for his midnight ride in 1775 from Boston to Lexington to warn the armed American patriots, the Minutemen, that the British troops were on the march. But Revere had already assured himself of a lasting reputation among discerning collectors for his skill as a silversmith. Today, Revere's finely engraved silver pieces still generate high bids in the world's auction rooms. FYI: Revere was the son of a French Huguenot refugee, Apollos Rivoire, who changed his name to Revere "so that the bumpkins could pronounce it easier."

Today, the "bumpkins" are creating great collections in silver, copper, brass, bronze, and pewter. But silversmiths and metalworkers have always had a place in history, from the Egyptians of more than 3,000 years ago to the armorers of the Middle Ages, from Paul Revere to the present. In this chapter, you will learn about how to evaluate the different types of silver, from sterling to plate. Then you'll find out all about the base metals used to make collectible items: pewter, copper, brass, bronze, iron, and steel. Finally, I'll clue you in on some other important metal collectibles: bottle tickets, brass beds, and lithographed tin cans.

The Silver Standard

Collecting silver poses both problems and opportunities. The main problem is that pieces from the 1700s that are clearly marked with their maker are out of the reach of the average collector—that's you and me, kiddo. But in the plus column, there is still a lot of beautiful, collectible silver available. Most of it was made between 1840 and 1930, and there's enough to go around.

In its pure state, silver is too soft to be made into anything but mush. Add a dash of copper, however, and you get a shiny, strong alloy known as "sterling silver." Let's look at some of the different types of silver that collectors seek.

American Sterling

"Sterling silver" is .925 pure silver. "Sterling" is the most frequently found mark on American sterling silver, but you may also find the notations "925," "925/1000," and "Sterling. Weighted" on pure silver pieces. "Sterling. Weighted" means that the piece is sterling silver but a dark, powdery lead-like substance has been added to the base to provide additional balance and weight to the piece. Almost any piece that is marked "Sterling" will be more valuable than one marked "Sterling. Weighted."

Caveat Emptor
American silver marked "Sterling" was usually made after 1860.

Looking for some interesting and affordable sterling silver to collect? Art Nouveau may fit your bill. For example:

➤ A small sterling silver dish from the late 1800s goes for less than $100.

➤ You can find a sterling silver magnifying glass or a letter knife for about $100 each.

➤ A sterling silver dressing table set from the turn of the century runs more than $300. Add some cut crystal to the set and you add about $100.

Dresser sets featuring ornate silver-backed hairbrushes like this one are an affordable and graceful addition to a silver collection.

298

American Coin Silver

Before 1850, "solid" silver pieces contained only 900/1000 parts of pure silver (or less), with 100/1000 parts other metals. Known as "coin silver," it was often marked *coin, pure coin, standards, premium,* or *dollar.* Sometimes the letters "C" or "D" were used; other times, coin silver was marked with the maker's name. Just to make your collecting life a little more difficult, sometimes it was not marked at all.

Or it could be marked with "pseudo-hallmarks." American silversmiths slapped these faux silver hallmarks on their products to suggest that their silver was as fine as British silver, which had clear hallmarks. The American hallmarks included profiles, animals, and stars. Since American coin silver can be marked in so many ways, it is often overlooked and even shunned as (horrors!) plated silver.

Here are some prices to give you an idea of the market for coin silver collectibles:

➤ Small coin silver spoons from the early 1800s sell for between $10 to $25 each. Large spoons go for $250 for a set of six.

➤ A coin silver serving dish from the late 1700s might fetch as much as $300.

Caveat Emptor
Old silver pieces not marked are often worth more than those that are marked.

Coin silver or sterling? Regardless, never put your silver flatware in the dishwasher!

English Sterling Silver

Early Americans may have cornered the market on freedom, wide-open spaces, and bears, but the Brits had it all over us in silver. Collectors of antique silver drool at the very hint of English sterling silver because to many people, it epitomizes the silversmith's art.

Antique English sterling silver can be marked in several key ways:

1. A full lion, facing left.

2. A letter. These changed over the years, so consult an English silver book for the full alphabet.

3. The silversmith's hallmark, usually his initials. The most valuable antique English silver was produced by Hester Bateman, Paul Storr, Paul de Lamerie, and Matthew Boulton. Beware: their marks have been remade as many times as Michael Jackson's face.

4. "Guild" marks that tell where the silver was made. The most frequently seen ones are the anchor (Birmingham), crown (Sheffield), castle (Edinburgh), and harp (Dublin).

5. The head of a monarch may or may not appear.

The fine work on this piece distinguishes it from many other silver coffepots.

Continental Silver

The Yanks and Brits didn't have the silver market cornered; the silver centers in Europe also produced high-quality sterling. Unfortunately, it is very difficult to identify continental silver—even experts sometimes err. Here is some general information so you can tell if you might have stumbled upon a genuine Continental silver "find":

➤ Antique French silver sometimes carried an ornate capital letter with a crown or a fleur-de-lis.

➤ Antique German silver often sports a half-moon or crescent and a crown, along with the number "800."

➤ Eastern European countries marked their silver with a castle or shaped center design encircled with numbers.

➤ Old Italian silver can have a Roman or classical portrait with other hallmarks.

Sterling Silver from the Former Soviets

Russian artisans are noted for their artistry with silver. In the main, fine Russian silver is quite valuable and certainly an important part of a silver collection. In addition, Polish and Hungarian silversmiths created (and continue to create) magnificent pieces. Many religious artifacts were made by these countries in silver and are highly prized by collectors.

This sterling silver piece is a fine example of Hungarian silver.

Danish Silver

In addition to some great butter cookies and the Little Mermaid, the Danish people produced some highly collectible silver. George Jensen (1866–1935) heads the list for his beautiful Art Nouveau and Art Deco styles. Other top-notch Danish silver designers include Johan Rohde, Harold Nielsen, Sigvard Bernadotte, Kay Bojesen, Evald Nielson, Frantz Hingelberg, Holger Kyster, Hans Hansen, Mogins Ballin, Peter Hertz, and Henning Koppel.

Fortunately for collectors, Danish silver is easy to authenticate because the maker's mark appears on all the silver the Danes produced between 1490 and 1893. Since then, retailers have added their names to the makers' marks as well.

Victorian and Modern Silverplate

Once shunned by serious collectors of silver, many silver-plated pieces from those stuffy Victorians are now hot. The rising prices of sterling silver, the dearth of fine examples, and the general lust for collectibles has fueled this fire. How can you tell which silverplate pieces to collect? Try these guidelines:

1. Look for pieces with copper bases; they are often the best quality silverplate.

2. Examine the piece for smoothly finished surfaces, crisp designs, and the depth of the raised work.

3. Among the hottest silverplate collectibles are pieces that are no longer made, such as Victorian pickle castors, epergnes, baskets, and lemonade pitchers.

Not to make your life any more difficult than it already is, but silverplate can have nearly as many marks as a Dalmatian. Well, at least silverplate doesn't shed or drool. Look for these marks to identify silverplate:

A1	Triple plate
Quadruple	Silver plate
Plate	Sheffield Reproduction
NS (nickel silver)	EPC (electroplate on copper)
Silver on copper	EPNS (electroplate silver on a nickel base)
EPWM (Electroplate on nickel, white metal mounts)	EPBM (electroplate on Britannia metal)
German silver	Nevada silver
Alaska silver	Argentine silver
Craig silver	Inlaid silver

This Victorian silver caster stand is eagerly sought after by collectors.

Price check:

➤ A silverplate creamer, sugar bowl, and tray made by B.F. Rogers in the early 20th century runs about $100.

➤ Commemorative spoons your bag? One from the 1893 Columbia Exposition can join your collection for a mere $50.

➤ A silverplate brush and mirror set from the turn of the century runs less than $250 and is a good investment.

Caveat Emptor
Collector alert: Avoid silverplate produced in the East, especially India. It is not high quality.

How can you tell if unmarked silver is really silver and not silverplate? Look at the place of greatest wear, such as the back of a spoon. If you see a different color showing through, usually brass-looking, you will know that you've got silverplate, not solid sterling or coin silver.

In addition, always consult a reliable price guide, such *as The Official Identification and Price Guide to Silver and Silverplate* by Jeri Schwartz (House of Collectibles, Florida).

Check a price guide to determine the value of this silver spoon holder.

The Baser Metals: Pewter, Copper, Brass, Bronze, Iron, Steel

Silver gets a lot of good press because it's shiny and sexy. But that's not to say that other collectible metals don't have their day in the sun. For every collector who covets silver, there's one who lusts after pewter, copper, brass, bronze, iron, or steel.

Collectors don't seek out these metals because they can't afford silver, either. True collectors like these "base" metals because of their unique qualities. Like children in a large family, each one of these metals is special in its own way and valued for its unique qualities. Let me introduce you to the pleasures of pewter, copper, brass, bronze, iron, and steel.

"The Poor Man's Silver": Pewter

As you learned in Chapter 6, pewter is an alloy of tin. For nearly 500 years it was one of the most important metals found in any home; even a pauper owned a pewter plate. Since it is a soft alloy, pewter had a relatively short working life. As a result, there are few survivors from the zillions of pewter items that were in daily use. The earliest pieces found date from the 1600s. The most commonly found antique pewter objects are plates and dishes from the 1700s and mugs from the 1800s. American pewter from the 1700s is harder to find than a parking spot in Manhattan during rush hour.

It was not until the 20th century that pewter became a collectible. Almost at once, fakes were created. Unfortunately, old pewter is easy to fake. In France, clever scam artists place modern reproductions of valuable old pewter in grass cuttings to give the new pewter a convincingly old patina. Acid is also used to make new pewter look old. Some of these methods are so convincing that even sophisticated auctioneers have had the pewter pulled over their eyes, so to speak.

So how can you tell a valuable old pewter piece from a fake? Fakers are savvy enough to stamp "genuine" marks on their work, so cross out this method. But even if they leave the marks off, genuine old pewter was not always marked, so it's a wash. Instead of searching for marks, examine the surface of the piece carefully. Ask yourself these questions:

➤ How did the piece get its bruises?

➤ Do the bruises match real wear? Fakers tend to bang away at a piece in a pattern to make it look old.

➤ Is the piece oxidized where you would expect it to be? It takes at least 50 years for a real oxide to develop. Look for bubbles—these are very hard to fake.

Big Deals

Victorian factory-made pewter is a good investment. In general, it is much cheaper than earlier pewter and it comes in a wide variety of forms. Best of all, most metal collectors haven't cornered the market yet.

Interested in prices? Here are some benchmarks:

➤ A porringer with openwork handles from the 1700s recently sold for $400.

➤ A teapot made in Connecticut in the early 1800s fetched $350.

➤ A pewter coffeepot made before 1850 sells for $150–$300, depending on condition and style.

➤ A pewter bowl made in New York around 1850 should set you back less than $200. A very large plate (16 inches), about $350.

The Alloy Kids: Copper, Bronze, Brass

Since copper is too soft to be used on its own, it became an alloy. The most common alloys of copper are *bronze* and *brass*. Bronze is made by adding tin to copper; brass is an alloy of zinc and copper.

Big Deals

It was not until 1945 that brass and bronze pieces were widely collected; as a result, there were few fakes produced until later. Today, the market is flooded with excellent reproductions of wall sconces, alms dishes, ladles, candle molds, and other popular and valuable forms.

Tricks of the Trade

Hand-cut screws are a tip-off that an object was made before or during the Industrial Revolution. Machine-made modern screws date from after 1850.

Copper alloys present special difficulties to connoisseurs because these pieces are difficult to date and authenticate. But, hey, that doesn't stop determined collectors like you and me. As a result, prices for brass and copper are high and have been so for many years. Pieces in great demand—marked andirons, kettles, and early buttons—command princely sums. Are you of more modest means? Consider focusing on smaller utensils and later spun-brass kettles.

Check out these prices before you go shopping:

➤ Copper saucepans with brass handles from the mid-1800s sell for $100 and up.

➤ Copper cooking pots with wrought-iron handles, dating from the 1800s, cost about $100.

➤ Turn-of-the-century copper funnels? About $25–$75. Mugs or oilcans? Around $50 each.

➤ Brass Pennsylvania-Dutch punch-decorated bed warmers from the 1800s go from $150–$400.

➤ A brass cattle bell fetches cattle if rung and about $50 if sold. A brass spoon goes for about $60.

Bronze figures are an extremely popular collectible. The signed statues, most of which were made in France and Russia, are among the most eagerly sought. Bronze statues produced today command astronomical prices—if the artist is famous. Some collectors are happier buying the work of known contemporary artists than investing in older pieces that have no history.

Man of Steel (and Iron)

Until the 1800s, steel was difficult to make, so it was used chiefly for tools, weapons, and some jewelry. Improved manufacturing techniques led to better combinations of carbon and iron, and so steel became a major player from the early Victorian period on.

Iron, in contrast, has been used since earliest times. Until the Industrial Revolution, wrought iron was by far the most common use of this metal. Iron tends to oxidize fast, so it is easy to make reproductions look old. But wear isn't so easy to fake, which makes this a good way to separate the real from the fake. Look for wear at the points where an object would have been put to the hardest use.

Here are some sample prices:

➤ A cast-iron tea kettle from 1860 sells for about $250.

➤ Large wrought-iron serving tools from 1830 cost about $200 each; a hanging griddle from 1850, about $150.

Connoisseur
Brass bells are a popular collectible—and still affordable.

➤ Wrought-iron New England trivets dating from the 1800s should cost you less than $100 each, while a wrought-iron candy mold from the turn of the century should go for about $150.

Collectors' Darlings

Here are a few metal items that hold a special place in collectors' hearts and wallets.

Ring Around the Bottle: Bottle Tickets

Bottle tickets are silver beverage labels used in 18th-and 19th-century England and America before modern packaging techniques. They are labeled with the names of the liquor, such as *whiskey, port,* and *brandy.* Important manufacturers include Tiffany and Gorham.

A Good Night's Sleep: Brass Beds

In the 1950s, most brass beds were tossed on the trash heap. No doubt the tossers kicked themselves soon after when brass beds became a highly popular collectible. Contrary to public opinion, most brass beds are not made entirely of brass since the posts would be too soft to support the weight of the mattress. On good quality brass beds, the ornaments will be solid brass.

Tricks of the Trade
How brassy is your bed? Check it with a magnet. The magnet will cling to the steel, but not to solid brass.

With brass beds, more is better. The fancier the bed, the better. The more decorations, the more collectible. Condition is also crucial. Worn brass beds are a bad deal, because replating is expensive.

Lithographed Tins

In the 1870s, new machinery made it possible to print in color. In the resulting avalanche of printed items, one stands out to collectors of metal items: tin containers. These containers held everything from coffee to cookies, grease to gunpowder. What matters to collectors of these tins?

➤ Age, color, and condition are the touchstones.

➤ Avoid repainted tins.

➤ Rust harms value.

➤ Oddly shaped tins and those holding unusual products command high prices.

The Least You Need to Know

➤ Silver comes in different grades. From most to least silver content, these are *sterling silver*, *coin silver*, and *silverplate*.

➤ Many objects made of pewter, copper, brass, bronze, iron, and steel are also hot collectibles.

➤ Bottle tickets, brass beds, and color lithographed tins are popular metal-based collectibles.

Future Collectibles

The forecast is good—collecting will continue be a pleasurable and lucrative hobby into the next century. Certainly collectors in the year 2096 will be willing to pay a fortune for today's ephemera. It's not too late to get in on the fun and profits. Here's how.

How do items become hot collectibles? Which pop-culture icons are going to rise in value—and which ones should be heaved into the trash compactor now?

> Rule #1: When the demand for an item is greater than the supply, the market price will rise.

> Rule #2: When enough people begin to collect an item that was previously only functional, the item will increase in price.

OK, so how do you do it? To determine which things will become the sizzlin' collectibles of the future, figure out what people are *not* collecting today. I know, that's easier said than done. The collectors' explosion has called attention to the fact that virtually anything can become collectible. Items that people sneered at a decade ago—beer cans, magazines, bottle caps, toothpick holders, modern toys—have all become valuable today. As a result, people are saving everything—or so it seems. But there are still a few untouched areas to explore.

Below is my forecast. If you decide to squirrel away any of these items, make personal pleasure rather than profit your prime motive.

Ephemera

I think ephemera of all sorts is going to continue to be a much-desired collectible. I see all throw-away items growing in popularity. Today's hottest items are discussed in Chapter 7, "Pulp (Non)fiction," so here's my prediction for future collectibles:

➤ **It's All in the Packaging: Advertising.** While tin, glass, and wood advertising pieces from the nineteenth century and early twentieth century are already very collectible, their counterparts from the present are often ignored. Consider looking more carefully at contemporary promotional items for cigarettes, drinks, and automobiles.

➤ **Trick or Treat.** As the world becomes increasingly politically correct, we'll see fewer Halloween masks and costumes. Right now, witch masks are on the wane because they discriminate against those who practice the ancient religion called "Wicca"; hobo masks are a no-no because they mock the homeless. So stash those costumes in a safe place. And don't forget to keep the boxes!

➤ **A Day at the Races.** Anything associated with gambling has captured the public's imagination. Think about assembling a collection of ephemeral items associated the racetracks (both horses and dogs), the different state lotteries, and casinos.

➤ **A Night at the Opera.** Culture is a biggie, too. Go for contemporary theater posters, programs, and autographs. Menus are especially promising.

➤ **I'm All Business.** Save personal business cards from famous people—especially if you can get the cards with autographs.

➤ **Hope on the Horizon.** AIDS ephemera—posters, leaflets, and the like—are already being collected in anticipation of a cure.

➤ **Blast Off.** Space-age toy models from the '50s and '60s, inspired by Sputnik and the Apollo missions, are usually tin and sell for $50 to $250 now. The '70s bought less desirable, but still collectible, plastic toys. These should cost you $5 to $25 at local flea markets. Space-related items, such as postcards and pamphlets, can still be obtained for very little. Now is the time to look carefully at space-related items, especially ephemera such as stamps, photographs, autographs of astronauts. Get on the shuttle before the race for spaceiana blasts off!

Tricks of the Trade
Consider coffins as collectibles. People will still die in the future, but we may not have six feet in which to plant 'em. A choice coffin from today may command a hefty price in the next century.

➤ **Hit the Road.** If every car is going to be equipped with a computerized guidance system, there will be no more Wrong Way Corrigans in the future. And there won't be any maps, either. As a result, gas station maps may be next century's antiquities.

Pundits predict that the most valuable maps will be those of today's wide open spaces that will become tomorrow's suburbs. Think Colorado, Idaho, and the Dakotas.

The Future Is Plastic

Plastic is currently not popular among collectors. Because of this, I think that plastic items such as cereal bowls, banks, figurines, and novelty toys will become hot when people see how rare they are. Buy plastic items that are special in some way. Look for a clever design, bright color, unusual action, and interesting purpose.

Here are some specific ideas:

Snowglobes

These globes are little plastic paperweights filled with water and "snow" that depict a scene. When the globe is shaken, it looks like it is snowing. It's pretty… and no one has to shovel real snow. What could be better?

What's Up, Doc?

You know that Disneyana is already an important collectible. I predict that in the future, many items that bear a famous cartoon character will be hot. Peanuts, Garfield, Star Trek, comic book superheroes—look for characters that made a great impact on the public's consciousness now.

Bits and Bytes

Remember that most collectibles are items that are still being produced, albeit in a different form. We still collect china, which has been made for centuries; glassware, comics, books, and paintings are all popular collectibles.

Computer memorabilia seems a likely bet for the future collectibles markets because it is changing very quickly yet will be around in the future. Pamphlets, books, advertising, hardware, software, postcards, computer watches, and hand-held calculators are all things to consider saving.

Caveat Emptor
Collecting plastic is not without its perils. The Tupperware collection at the Museum of Modern Art is discoloring and smells terrible. A set of 1946 plastic nesting bowls in the same collection is a molten mess—toxic as well as unsightly. Some plastics are so unstable and subject to uncharted chemical reactions that no one quite knows how to protect them. Let the collector beware.

Tricks of the Trade
When putting aside an item that you think will become a future collectible, remember to save the entire package: the box, instructions, and the item.

The Medium Is the Message

The T-shirt craze took off about thirty years ago, when simple shirts became the canvas for advertising and personal expression. By the 1970s, young and old alike were sporting T-shirts hyping their favorite drink, band, state, political affiliation, drug, leisure-time activity, sport, movie, food, or belief. Hand-lettered, silk-screened T-shirts might just be the clothing collectibles of the future.

Royal Nonsense

If the naughty behavior of Chuck and Di (not to mention Fergie's toe-sucking escapades) are any indication, we may be seeing the end of the royal line in England. Devout Anglophiles have always cherished the likeness of their favorite royal on a beaker (mug), but if the royals go the way of the Edsel, royal family souvenirs may be worth more than the pound.

Get the Scent

For years, people have been collecting lovely perfume bottles. What about the contents? The scents of today are the memories of tomorrow. Ever since the late pop artist and cultural trend-setter Andy Warhol began collecting designer perfumes, those in the know got on the scent. So think about stashing away today's best perfumes.

VidKids

Video madness is upon us, as people line up outside their local movie store clamoring for the latest release. In just a few short years, video has become a way of life for most Americans. Consider saving material related to videos. Here are some ideas:

➤ Original releases, especially of movies that were released in two or more versions

➤ Posters

➤ Novelties

➤ Toys and games

➤ Stickers

➤ Video games and game systems

A few final suggestions. First, look for items linked to big stories, such as national scandals, historical events, and national movements. Possibilities include Watergate, the first test-tube baby, and feminism. There is already a hot market for items linked to the Kennedy assassination; a market is developing for Watergate memorabilia.

Second, take a look at what children are playing with now. These toys and novelties are apt to be popular in 30 years—when those same children have grown up. They will create the demand for the items of their youth.

Today's toy may be tomorrow's collectible.

Vice

What are the three hot symbols of vice? Cigarettes, condoms, and playing cards. In the future, they may be the hot collectibles as well.

➤ **Cigarettes.** In the 1600s, the Puritans believed that tobacco was good for whatever ailed you. They even gave their horses a puff from the old cheroot to whisk away evil spirits. Today we know enough to keep the stogies away from Mr. Ed. See how much progress we've made in 300 years? Any century now, tobacco will be outlawed. When that happens, the smart cookies who have unopened packages of cigarettes, cigars, and chewing tobacco will command more than smoke. Remember how the invention of lighters made matches a collectible?

➤ **Sex.** Like chastity belts, the day will come when condoms will be a curiosity and collectible. In the future, people will have developed less cumbersome methods of birth control than condoms... or they will have figured out another way to pass the time when there's nothing on cable.

➤ **Gambling.** Remember Atari's Pong? It was the first of the video games. That little ball went boing, boing, boing across the screen until you were ready to scream. How prehistoric that video game seems now. But in the future, even today's glitzy video poker will seem as old-fashioned as virginity. So stash away unopened packages of playing cards against the day when all games beep and buzz.

313

Further Reading

Below are some additional resources you may wish to consult. Their inclusion here in no way constitutes an endorsement. Caveat emptor; judge each source carefully by weighing it against its competitors' books, expert advice, and your own common sense.

General Guides

Know Your Antiques [videorecording]. Washington, DC: PBS Video, 1988.

Atterbury, Paul and Lars Tharp. *The Bullfinch Illustrated Encyclopedia of Antiques.* Boston: Little Brown and Company, 1994.

Collector's Information Bureau Collectibles Price Guide, 5th edition, 1995. Collector's Information Bureau, 5065 Shoreline Road, Suite 200, Barrington, IL 60010. *This book includes information on plates, figurines, cottages, bells, graphics, Christmas ornaments, dolls, steins. There are more than 40,000 collectibles listed.*

Kovel, Ralph and Terry. *Kovels' Guide to Selling, Buying, and Fixing Your Antiques and Collectibles.* New York: Crown Publishers.

Kovel, Ralph and Terry. *Kovels' Know Your Antiques.* New York: Crown Publishers, 1990.

Kovel, Ralph and Terry. *Kovels' Quick Tips—799 Helpful Hints on How to Care for Your Collectibles.* New York: Crown Publishers, 1995.

Kovels' Antiques and Collectibles Price List for the 1996 Market. New York: Crown Trade Paperbacks, 1996. 28th edition.
This is a book for the average collector.

Kovel, Ralph and Terry. *Kovels' Antiques and Collectibles Fix-It Source Book.* New York: Crown Publishers, 1990.

Kovel, Ralph and Terry. *Kovels' Collector's Source Book.* New York: Crown Publishers, 1983.

Kovel, Ralph and Terry. *Kovels' Antiques and Collectibles Price List.* New York: Crown Publishers.

Maloney, David J. *Collector's Information Clearinghouse Antiques and Collectibles Resource Directory.* Homestead Price Guide. Radnor: PA, 1992.
This book includes auction services, matching services, repair and restoration services, and suppliers.

Miller, Martin and Judith Miller. *The Antiques Directory.* London: G.K. Hall, 1985.

Miller, Martin and Judith Miller. *Miller's Collectibles Price Guide.* 1995–96. London: Reed Consumer Books, Ltd. 1995.
All prices are quoted in British pounds.

Forgery and Fakes

The Chase, The Capture: Collecting at the Metropolitan. New York: The Metropolitan Museum, 1975.

Goodrich, D.L. *Art Fakes in America.* New York: Viking, 1973.

Grafton, Anthony. *Forgers and Critics: Creativity and Duplicity in Western Scholarship.* London: Collins & Brown, 1990.

Hebborn, Eric. *Drawn to Trouble: Confessions of a Master Forger.* New York: Random House, 1991.

Hoving, Thomas. *False Impressions: The Hunt for Big-Time Art Fakes.* New York: Simon and Schuster, 1996.

Jeppson, Lawrence. *The Fabulous Frauds: A Study of Great Art Forgeries.* London: Arlington Books, 1971.

Jones, Mark, ed. *Fake? The Art of Deception.* Berkeley and Los Angeles: University of California Press, 1990.

Jones, Mark, ed. *Why Fakes Matter: Essays on Problems of Authenticity*. London: British Museum, 1992.

Kurz, Otto. *Fakes: A Handbook for Collectors and Students*. New Haven: Yale University Press, 1948.

Mendax, Fritz. *Art Fakes and Forgeries*. London: W. Laurie, 1955.

Savage, George. *Forgeries, Fakes and Reproductions*. London: Barrie and Rockcliff, 1963.

Chapter 7: Pulp (Non)fiction

Advertising Items

Kovel, Ralph and Terry. *Kovels' Advertising Collectibles Price List*. New York: Crown Publishers, 1986.

Baseball Cards

Beckett, James and Dennis Eckes. *The Sport Americana Baseball Card Price Guide*. Laurel, MD: Den's Collectors Den, 1982.

Erbe, Ron. *The American Premium Guide to Baseball Cards*. Florence, AL: Books Americana, 1982.

Movie Memorabilia

Dietz, James S. Jr. *Price Guide and Introduction to Movie Posters and Movie Memorabilia*. San Diego, CA: Baja Press.

Gallo, Max. *The Poster in History*. New York: American Heritage Publishing Company, 1974.

Hake, Theodore and Robert D. Cauler. *Six-Gun Heroes: A Price Guide to Movie Cowboy Collectibles*. Des Moines: Wallace Homestead Books, 1976.

Chapter 8: Comic Books

Overstreet, Robert. *The Overstreet Comic Book Price Guide*. New York: Avon Books, 1996.

Chapter 9: Stamps

Dunair, Gary. *Stamps: The Beginning Collector*. New York: Mallard Press, 1992.

Schwarz, Ted. *Beginner's Guide to Stamp Collecting*. New York: ARCO Publishers, 1983.

Chapter 10: Coins

Alexander, Davit T. et. al. *Coin World Comprehensive Catalog & Encyclopedia of United States Coins*. New York: World Almanac, 1990.

Bowers, Q. David. *A Buyer's Guide to the Rare Coin Market*. Wolfeboro, NH: Bowers and Merena Galleries, 1990.

Bowers, Q. David. *Adventures with Rare Coins*. Los Angeles: Bowers and Ruddy Galleries, 1980.

Bowers, Q. David. *Coins and Collectors*. Wolfeboro, NH: Bowers and Merena Galleries, 1988.

Bowers, Q. David. *Commemorative Coins of the United States: A Complete Encyclopedia*. Wolfeboro, NH: Bowers and Merena Galleries, 1991.

Bowers, Q. David. *United States Coins by Design Types*. Wolfeboro, NH: Bowers and Merena Galleries, 1989.

Brown, Martin R. and John W. Dunn. *A Guide to the Grading of United States Coins*. Racine, WI: Western Publishing Co., 1969 (5th edition).

Ganz, David L. *The World of Coins and Coin Collecting*. New York: Charles Scribner's Sons, 1985.

Handcock, Virgil and Larry Spanbauer. *Standard Catalog of Counterfeit and Altered United States Coins*. New York: Sandford J. Durst, 1979.

Hudgeons, Mark. *The Official Guide to Detecting Altered & Counterfeit U.S. Coins & Currency*. Orlando: The House of Collectibles, 1985.

Porteous, John. *Coins*. New York: G.P. Putnam's Sons, 1964.

Shafer, Neil. *A Guide to Modern United States Currency*. Racine, WI: Whitman Coin Products, Western Publishing Co., 1975.

Chapter 11: Paper Money

Beresiner, Yasha. *A Collector's Guide to Paper Money*. New York: Stein and Day, 1977.

Beresiner, Yasha and Colin Narbeth. *The Story of Paper Money*. New York: ARCO Publishing, 1973.

Criswell, Grover C., Jr. *Colonel Grover Criswell's Compendium, a Guide to Confederate Money*. Brannon Publishing Company, 1991.

Friedberg, Robert. *Paper Money of the United States*. Clifton, NJ: The Coin and Currency Institute, 1989. (12th edition)

Nussbaum, Arthur. *A History of the Dollar*. New York: Columbia University Press, 1957.

Pick, Albert. *Standard Catalog of World Paper Money*. Iola, WI: Krause Publications, 1990.

Rochette, Edward. *Making Money*. Frederick, CO: Renaissance House Publishers, 1986.

U.S. Secret Service (Department of the Treasury). *Know Your Money*. Washington, DC: U.S. Government Printing Office, 1991.

Chapter 12: Books

Bradley, Van Allen. *The Book Collector's Handbook of Values*. New York: G.P. Putnam.

Bookman's Price Index: A Guide to the Value of Rare and Out-of-Print Books. Detroit, MI: Gale Research Company.

Mandeville, Mildred S. *The Used Book Price Guide*. Kenmore, WA: Price Guide Publishers.

Chapter 13: China

Kovel, Ralph and Terry. *Kovels' Illustrated Price Guide to Royal Doulton*. New York: Crown Publishers.

Kovel, Ralph and Terry. *Kovels' Dictionary of Marks—Pottery and Porcelain*. New York: Crown Publishers, 1986.

Kovel, Ralph and Terry. *Kovels' American Art Pottery: The Collector's Guide to Makers, Marks, and Factory Histories*. New York: Crown Publishers, 1974.

Kovel, Ralph and Terry. *Kovels' Guide to American Art Pottery*. New York: Crown Publishers, 1994.

MacDonald-Taylor, Margaret. *A Dictionary of Marks*. London: Barrie & Jenkins, 1989.

Chapter 14: Toys and Games

Disneyana

Tumbusch, Tom. *Tomart's Disneyana Catalog and Price Guide*. Dayton, Ohio: Tomart Publications, 1989.

Mechanical Banks

Rogers, Carole G. *Penny Banks: A History and Handbook*. New York: E.P. Dutton, 1977.

Toys and Games

Marsh, Hugo. *Toys and Games*. London: Miller's Antiques, 1995.

Mackay, James. *Childhood Antiques*. New York: Taplinger Publishing Company, 1976.

Chapter 15: Household Items

Kovel, Ralph and Terry. *Kovels' Book of Antiques Labels*. New York: Crown Publishers.

Kovel, Ralph and Terry. *Kovels' Bottles Price List*. New York: Crown Publishers, 1992.

McDaniel, Patricia. *Drugstore Collectibles*. A Wallace-Homestead Price Guide. Radnor, PA, 1994.
This book includes a price guide.

Petretti, Alan. *Petretti's Coca-Cola Collectibles Price Guide,* 9th edition. Nostalgia Publications, 21 South Lake Drive, Hackensack, NJ 07601. Wallace-Homestead Book Company. Radnor, PA: 1994.

Raycraft, Don and Carol. *American Country Antiques*. Wallace-Homestead Book Company. Radnor, PA: 1995.

Chapter 16: Crystal

Cottle, Simon and David Battie, General Editors. *Sotheby's Concise Encyclopedia of Glass*. London: Conran Octopus Ltd., 1995.
This is a beautiful survey volume.

DiBartolomeo, Robert E. *American Glass. Vol. II: Pressed and Cut*. New York: Weathervane Books, 1972.
An excellent group of articles for the aspiring glass collector.

Kovel, Ralph and Terry. *Kovels' Depression Glass & American Dinnerware Price List*. New York: Crown Publishers.

Phillips, Phoebe. *The Encyclopedia of Glass*. New York: Crown Publishers, 1981. *Beginning with the worldwide history of glass, this volume continues into the modern age of Art Glass and Art Nouveau glass.*

Schwartz, Marvin D. *American Glass. Vol. I: Blown and Molded*. New York: Weathervane Books, 1972

Chapters 17–20: Fine Art

Jacobsen, Anita. Jacobsen's Third Painting and Bronze Price Guide: Auction Records.

Miller's Picture Price Guide. Kent, England: Miller's Publications, 1992.

Naifeh, Steven. *The Bargain Hunter's Guide to Art Collecting*. New York: Morrow, 1982.

Serullaz, Maurice. *The Concise Encyclopedia of Impressionism*. New Jersey: Chartwell Books, Inc. 1974.

Chapter 21: Furniture and Rugs

Kovel, Ralph and Terry. *American Country Furniture 1780–1875*. New York: Crown Trade Paperbacks, 1965.

Hammond, Dorothy. *Pictorial Price Guide to American Antiques and Objects Made for the American Market*. New York: EP Dutton, 1988.

Miller, Edgar G. *American Antique Furniture*. New York: Dover Publications, 1966.

Owens, Mitchell. "Carpets that Fly... and Some that Crash: Smart Rug Buying in Eight Easy Lessons." *The New York Times*, February 8, 1996.

Payne, Christopher, General Editor. *Sotheby's Concise Encyclopedia of Furniture*. London: Conran Octopus, 1989.

Rinker, Harry L. *Warman's Furniture*. Wallace-Homestead Book Company. Radnor: PA, 1993.

Silver, Marc. "The Oriental Rug Revolution." *US News and World Report,* August 8, 1994, p. 76.

Chapter 22: Jewelry

Darling, Ada W. *Antique Jewelry Identification with Price Guide*. 1973.

Edwardian, Art Nouveau, and Art Deco Jewelry, Circa 1887–1930s [videorecording]. 1994.

Kaplan, Arthur Guy. *The Official Identification and Price Guide to Antique Jewelry*. Orlando: House of Collectibles, 1985.

The Official Identification and Price Guide to Antique Jewelry. Orlando: House of Collectibles, 1990.

Victorian Jewelry, Circa 1837–1901 [videorecording]. Pittsburgh, PA (PO Box 4290, Pittsburgh 15203) Antique Images, Inc. 1994.

Chapter 23: Precious Metals

Kovel, Ralph and Terry. *A Directory of American Silver, Pewter, and Silver Plate*. New York: Crown Trade Paperbacks.

Kovel, Ralph and Terry. *Kovels' American Silver Marks: 1650 to the Present*. New York: Crown Publishers.

Index

A

Abbott, Berenice, 243
accumulator, defined, 118
acquiring, *see* collecting
acquisition guidelines, 26-29
Action Comics #1, 106, 110
advantages of collecting, 9-10
advertising
    in classified ads, 56-57
    in newspapers, 56
    yard sales, 57
African elephant ivory (legal), 289
albums, 75, 127, 207-208
alcohol (isopropyl), 80
Alexis de Tocqueville, 144
All-American Comics, 110
amber, 288
ambrotypes, 240
American art pottery, 170
American coin silver, 299
American sterling silver, 298
American Tobacco Company, 92
amethyst, 288
antiques
    appraising, 53-55
    buying, 26-30, 55
        checklists, 48

for profit, 42-44
    provenance, 43
    risks of, 45-48
damaged, 46
defining, 20-21, 38
    government, 44-45
fraudulent, 47-48
pricing, 38, 52-55
repairing, 38-39
selling, 52-55
    in private, 56-57
    yard sales, 57-58
shops, 33
shows, selling at, 58-60
speculating, 46
trading, 41-42
see also collectibles
Antiques publication, 29
Antiques Trader (St. Louis), 29
appraising, 52
    antiques, 53-55
    charts, 54
aquamarine, 288
Arctophily (teddy bears), 194
art
    collectible, defining, 20
    comic books, 115
    see also paintings;
        drawings

Art Deco furniture, 273
Art Deco jewelry, 287
art glass, 215-217
Art Nouveau jewelry, 286
Arts and Crafts jewelry, 286
Arts Weekly (CT) magazine, 29
Ashcan School, 228
Asian elephant ivory (legal), 289
atlases, 165
attracting customers, 59-60
auctions
    bidding, 33
    catalogs, 31
    categories, 60
    fees, 61-62
    price estimates, 32
    pricing items, 32, 61
    reading reference
        literature, 32
    reserves, 32
    selling at, 60-62
    shopping, 30-33
    stamps, 124-125
    timing, 61
    viewing items, 32
authors' first editions, 163-164
    signed, 165
autographs, 99
Avon bottles, 200

B

Ball, James Presley, 242
Baltimore quilts, 206
banks
     mechanical, 190-192
     penny-banks, 191-192
barbed wire collections, 4
Barbie dolls, 187
Barbizon, 227
bargaining, 39-41, 56-57
baseball cards
     collectibles, 92-96
     golden era, 92
     history, 92-94
     second golden era, 93
     World War II, 93
     see also paper collectibles
Batman (comic books), 110
beauty (collectible
     qualities), 7-8
beds (brass), 307
beer cans, 16, 198-199
Beerbohm, Sir Max, 255
Belleek (porcelain), 175
benefits of collecting, 9-10
Bertoia, Harry, 273
Bibles, 160-161
bidding
     auctions, 33
     jumping, 62
Bill Gaines, 107
Bing & Grondahl
     porcelain, 175
bisque dolls, 185
bitters bottles, 201
Black Arrow, 166
black light, 53
Block, Herbert Lawrence,
     255
board game collections, 21
bone china (ceramics), 173
booklets, 120
bookplates, 97-98

books
     19th-century, 168
     atlases, *see* atlases
     Bibles, 160-161
     buying, 167-168
     children's, 159-160
     collecting, 159-161
          dust jackets, 164
          expensive manuscripts,
               165-166
          genres, 167
     comics, *see* comic books
     first editions, 161-165
          popular authors,
               163-164
     investing, 166-167
     printing, 159
booths, attracting custom-
     ers, 59-60
bottle tickets, 307
bottles, 200-203
     cleaning, 202-203
     finding, 202
     most collectible types,
          200-202
          Avon bottles, 200
          inkwells, 201-202
          medicine bottles, 201
          soda bottles, 201
          whiskey bottles,
               200-201
bourse, 125
Brady, Matthew, 242
brass, 305-306
     beds, 307
breweriana collections,
     198-199
bronze, 305-306
brooches (military insignia),
     294
buying
     antiques, 26-30, 55
          checklists, 48
          fraudulent, 47-48
          for profit, 42-44

     provenance, 43
     risks of, 45-48
     by trading, 41-42
     books, 167-168
     porcelain, 179, 181
     stamps, 131-132
     see also shopping
buzzwords (comic books),
     113-114

C

cabinets, 75
call-ups, 62
Callis, Joann, 243
candy containers, 221
cans (beer), 198-199
Capodimonte porcelain,
     175
Captain America Comics,
     110
cards
     baseball, *see* baseball
          cards
     playing, 98
     sports, 96-97
Carl, William P., 252
carnival glass, 217
carpets, *see* rugs
caricatures, 254-255
Cassatt, Mary, 233
cataloging, 66-74
catalogs
     auctions, 31
     stamps, 128
categories
     auctions, 60
     ephemera, 90
celluloid, 100
cels (movie memorabilia),
     100
ceramics
     bone china, 173
     cleaning, 79

defining, 170-178
earthenware, 170-172
history, 170
ironstones, 173-174
limited-edition col-
lectibles, 179-180
porcelain, 174-178
types of, 175-177
reproductions, 180
stoneware, 172-173
see also porcelain
Cezanne, 232
character dolls, *see* movie
dolls
characteristics of
collectibles, 7-9
charcoal drawings, 251
charging fees (auctions),
61-62
charts, appraisal, 54
checklists
Antiques, Buying, 48
Furniture Buyer's, 276
children's books, 159-160
china, *see* porcelain
Chippendale furniture, 270
circulating coins, 138
Citizens' Stamp Advisory
Committee, 121
classified ads (advertising),
56
cleaning, 78-82
bottles, 202-203
ceramics, 79
copper collectibles, 80
glass collectibles, 80
iron collectibles, 80
paper collectibles, 81
paper money, 152
pewter collectibles, 81
silver, 81
stuffed toys, 82
wooden collectibles, 82
clocks, 203-204
coil format, 119
coin silver, 299
coins

circulating, 138
collecting, 136-138
guidelines, 139
methods, 138-139
tools, 137
WWW (World Wide
Web), 139
colonial, 135
dealers, 138-139
grading, 137-138
Greek, 134
history, 134-135
investing, 140-141
Medieval, 134
parts of, 136-137
Roman, 134
United States Mint, 135
collectibles
collectibles craze, 6
defining, 20
future collectibles,
310-313
list of hottest collectibles,
22-24
collecting
guidelines
acquisition, 26-29
coin collecting, 139
penny-bank collecting,
191-192
yard sales, 58
history of, 4-6
methods (paper money),
152-153
tools, 208
coins, 137
Disneyana, 188-189
stamps, 126-128
Collection Inventory
Worksheet, 11-12, 73-74
collections, defining, 24
Collector Quiz, 17-18
Colonial
coins, 135
currency, 144
colored lithographs, 259

colored woodcut prints, 262
comic books, 109-111
art, 115
collecting, 109-111
grades, 111-112
history, 106-109
investing, 109-111
most valuable, 110
overview, 109
restoring, 112-113
selecting, 111
stages, 108
superheros, 108-109
vocabularies, 113-114
commemorative stamps,
121
comparing collectors to
investors, 18-19
Confederate currency, 145
consignments, 62
Continental silver, 301
copper alloys, 305-306
copper collectibles,
cleaning, 80
coral, 288
costume jewelry, 287
1940s and 1950s era,
294-295
costumes, 99
covers, 120
Cowin, Eileen, 243
crystal, 210-213
cut crystal, 210-212
distinguishing from
pressed glass, 212
manufacturer mark-
ings, 212
Steuben, 213
Waterford, 213
see also glass collectibles
Crystal (Degenhart) Glass,
219
Cubism, 228
currency, *see* paper money
Currier and Ives lithography

firm, 260
Curtis, Edward S., 238-239
customers, attracting to
    booths, 59-60
cut glass, 210-212
    distinguishing from
        pressed glass, 212
    manufacturer markings,
        212

D

Daguerre, Jacques Louis
    Mande, 240
daguerreotypes, 238-242
    size, 241
    storage, 242
damages
    antiques, 46
    paintings, 234-235
    repairing, 38-39
Danish silver, 301-302
dating
    dolls, 186
    porcelain, 178
Daumier, Honore, 255
dealers
    coins, 138-139
    selling to, 58
    stamps, 123
deceptive labeling (gem-
    stones), 290-291
Declaration of Independence,
    30
decorative art, 229
defining
    antiques, 20-21
        legal definition, 44-45
    ceramics, 170-178
    collectibles, 20
    collections, 24
    collectors, 18-19
    investors, 18-19
    mechanical banks, 191
    papers, 91
Delft earthenware, 171

Depression glass, 217-218
    selection guidelines, 218
Detective Comics, 110
diamonds, 289
die-cast toys, 190
Dinkie toys, 190
Disneyana
    pricing, 189
    tools, 188-189
displaying, 75-78
    albums/scrapbooks, 75
    cabinets, 75
    glass collectibles, 75-76
    paper collectibles, 76-77
    pewter collectibles, 77
    stuffed toys, 77
    wooden collectibles,
        77-78
Divola, John, 243
dollar bills, 146-151
    foreign, 149-150
    formats, 147-148
    trashing, 147
dolls
    Barbie, 187
    bisque, 185
    collecting, 184-187
    dating, 186
    houses, 187-188
    movie, 187
    paper, dating, 186
    papier-mâché, 185-186
    wooden, 185
Domenichino, 249
Dore, Gustave, 255
Dr. Who Annual, 166
drawings, 248-255
    caricatures, 254-255
    charcoal, 251
    collections, 249
    folk art, 252
    fractura, 252
    history, 249
    ink, 250
    marble, 251
    paper, 250
    pastels, 251

pencils, 251
pens, 251
silhouettes, 253-254
sandpaper, 251
Dresden porcelain, 175
drypoint (etching tech-
    nique), 258-259
Dunbar Glass, 219
Durer, Albrecht, 249
dust jackets (books), 164

E

Eames, Charles, 273
early Victorian jewelry, 285
earthenware (ceramics),
    170-172
editions, defined, 161
Edwardian jewelry, 286-287
emeralds, 289
Empire furniture, 271
English sterling silver, 300
engraving, 258
ephemera, 90-103, 310-311
    categories, 90
Esherick, Wharton, 273
estimates, price (auctions),
    32
etchings, 258-259
everlasting ephemera
    (commemoratives), 90
Expressionism, 228

F

faience earthenware, 172
Faigenbaum, Patrick, 244
fakes
    antiques, 47-48
    furniture, 275
    paintings, 235
    porcelain, 180-181
Favrile (Tiffany glass), 215
Federal Reserve, 150
fees (auctions), 61-62

Fieffer, Jules, 255
finding bottles, 202
fine rugs, 277-280
    hooked rugs, 278-280
    Oriental rugs, 277-278
first editions (books),
    161-165
    popular authors, 163-164
first-day covers, 120
flea markets
    selling at, 58-60
    shopping, 33-34
fleeting ephemera (lottery
    tickets), 90
folk art, 252-254
    drawings, 252
    paper cutting, 254
foreign currency, 149-150
forgeries, *see* fakes
formats
    dollar bills, 147-148
    stamps, 119-121
fractura, 252
Frank Horwath, 45
Friholm, Helge, 82
furniture
    fakes, 275
    price guides, 275
    selection guidelines,
        275-276
        buyer's checklist, 276
    style periods, 268-273
        1940s and 1950s,
            273-274
        Art Deco, 273
        Chippendale, 270
        Empire, 271
        Hepplewhite, 270-271
        Mission, 272
        Pilgrim, 269
        Queen Anne, 269-270
        Shaker, 274
        Sheraton, 271
        transitional pieces, 269
        Victorian, 271-272
Fuss, Adam, 243
future collectibles, 310-313

G

Gaines, Bill, 107
garnets, 289
gemstones, 287-291
    deceptive labeling,
        290-291
    identifying, 288
    list of most collectible,
        288-290
    manufactured, 290
genres (books), collecting,
    167
Georgian jewelry, 285
Ghezzi, Pier Leone, 254
glass
    1940s and 1950s era,
        218-220
    art glass, 215-217
    candy containers, 221
    carnival glass, 217
    collectibles
        cleaning, 80
        displaying, 75-76
    crystal, 210-213
        cut crystal, 210-212
        Steuben, 213
        Waterford, 213
    Depression glass, 217-218
        selection guidelines,
            218
    fakes, 222
    Lalique glass, 218
    paperweights, 220-221
    pressed, 213-214
        distinguishing from
            cut glass, 212
    selection guidelines,
        221-222
gold, 291-293
    covering base metals, 292
    karats, 292
    mixtures, 291
    pennies, 136
    price guides, 293

golden era of baseball cards,
    92
Goldin, Nan, 243
Goodwin and Company, 92
government definition of
    antiques, 44-45
grades
    coins, 137-138
    comic books, 111-112
    paper money, 151
Greek coins, 134
green gold, 291
Grosz, George, 255
guidelines
    acquisition, 26-29
    coin collecting, 139
    penny-bank collecting,
        191-192
    yard sales, 58
guides, *see* price guides

H

hard-paste porcelain, 174
Haviland china, 175
Heisey glass, 219
Hepplewhite furniture,
    270-271
hinges (stamps), 126
Hirschfeld, Al, 255
historical links (collectible
    qualities), 9
history
    baseball cards, 92-96
    ceramic, 170
    coins, 134-135
    comic books, 106-109
    doll houses, 187-188
    drawings, 249
    paper money, 144-145
        Confederate currency,
            145

printing, 158-159
 books, 159
 toys, 184
Hitting the Books
 Worksheet, 230
homeowner's insurance, 83
Honus Wagner baseball
 card, 95
hooked rugs, 278-280
 selection guidelines,
 279-280
Horwath, Frank, 45
hot collectibles, 22-24
household collectibles,
 204-205
Household Inventory
 Worksheet, 67-72
houses, doll, 187-188
Hummel porcelain, 176
hygroscopic, 76

I

identifying furniture style
 periods, 268-273
Imari (porcelain), 177
Impressionism, 227, 232
incunabula, 159
ink, 250
inkwells, 201-202
insurance, 83-85
 homeowner's, 83
intaglio printing, 258
Inventory Worksheet, 67-72
investing
 books, 166-167
 coins, 140-141
 comic books, 109-111
 stamps, 130-131
investments
 paintings, 234
investors
 defining, 18-19
iron, 306-307

iron collectibles
 cleaning, 80
ironstone (ceramics),
 173-174
 see also ceramics
Isenburg, Matthew, 241
isopropyl alcohol, 80
ivory, 289

J

jade, 289
Japanese woodblock prints,
 265
jargon, comic books,
 113-114
jet, 289
jewelry, 284-287
 costume, 287
 1940s and 1950s era,
 294-295
 gemstones, 287-291
 deceptive labeling,
 290-291
 identifying, 288
 list of most collectible,
 288-290
 manufactured, 290
 gold, 291-293
 covering base metals,
 292
 karats, 292
 mixtures, 291
 price guides, 293
 history periods, 284
 identifying, 285-287
 Native-American, 293
 netsuke, 293
 platinum, 292
 price guides, 284
Jim Beam bottles, 201
Johann Bottger, 169
jumping bids, 62

K

kaolin (china clay), 174
karats (gold), 292
Kelly, Walt, 255
Kidnapped, 166
kitchen utensils, 204-205

L

Lalique, Rene (Lalique
 glass), 218
lapis lazuli, 289
late-Victorian jewelry, 286
law of supply and demand,
 21-22
Le Moulin Rouge, 101
Leech, John, 254
Levine, Sherrie, 243
Levinthal, David, 243
lignin-free boards, 77
limited-edition collectibles
 (ceramics), 179-180
Limoges (porcelain), 177
Lincoln Cents, 138
links to the present (collectible qualities), 8
lino cutting, 259
Lion King, 166
liquor bottle tickets, 307
literature, reference, 32
lithographed tins, 308
lithography, 259-260
Little Red Riding Hood, 166
Lladro (porcelain), 177
loose papers (movie memo-
 rabilia), 102
Low, David, 255
lusterware, 174
Lyon, Danny, 243

M

magazines, *see* publications
magnifying glasses
(stamps), 128
mail-order shopping, 34-35
stamps, 124
Maine Antiques Digest, 29
Majolica tinware, 172
makings of a collectible, 7-9
*Maloney's Antiques and
Collectibles Resource
Directory*, 29
Manet, 232
manufactured gemstones,
290
marble (drawings), 251
marbles, 194
markets (flea)
selling at, 58-60
shopping, 33-34
Marvel Comics, 110
matchbooks, 102
Mauldin, Bill, 255
Maurier, George du, 254
mechanical
banks, 190-192
toys, 189-190
medicine bottles, 201
Medieval coins, 134
Meissen china, 177
Meisterstuck Solitaire Royal
fountain pen, 204
memorabilia, 99-102
autographs, 99
movies, 100-102
programs, 100
stage set designs, 99
Mennonite auctions, 206
metals
brass, 305-307
beds, 307
copper alloys, 305-306
gold, 291-293

covering base metals,
292
karats, 292
mixtures, 291
price guides, 293
iron, 306-307
pewter, 304-305
identifying fake
pieces, 305
Victorian factory-
made, 305
platinum, 292
silver, 298-303
American sterling, 298
bottle tickets, 307
coin silver, 299
Continental, 301
Danish, 301-302
English sterling, 300
price guides, 303
Russian sterling, 301
silverplate, 302-304
steel, 306-307
tin containers (litho-
graphed), 308
mezzotint (etching tech-
nique), 259
mid-Victorian jewelry, 286
military insignia brooches,
294
millefiori weights, 220
Misrach, Richard, 243
Mission furniture, 272
mixtures (stamps), 123
modern toys, 195
Moditti, Tina, 238-239
Monet, 232
money, *see* paper money;
coins
motivations for collecting, 6
movie dolls, 187
movie memorabilia,
100-102
Mylar, 77

N

Nast, Thomas, 255
Native-American jewelry,
293
netsuke, 293
New Fun Comics, 110
New Martinsville Glass, 219
newpapers (advertising), 56
Nicholson, Wheeler, 106
Niepce, Nicephore, 240
numbering (on prints), 262

O

*Official Price Guide to
Fine Art*, 229
offset printing, 263
O'Keeffe, Georgia, 233
Oliphant, Pat, 255
opals, 289
Oriental rugs, 277-278
*Overstreet's Comic Book Price
Guide*, 113

P

packets, stamps, 123
paintings
Ashcan School, 228
Barbizon, 227
Cubism, 228
damaged, 234-235
decorative art, 229
Expressionism, 228
forgeries, 235
Impressionism, 227, 232
investments, 234
most expensive, 226
provenance, 231
purchasing, 229
restoration, 235
Surrealism, 228
value, 231-234

paper, 250
paper collectibles
  cleaning, 81
  displaying, 76-77
  hygroscopic, 76
paper cutting, 254
paper dolls, 186
paper money
  cleaning, 152
  collecting, 146, 150-151
    methods, 152-153
  dollar bills, 146-151
    collecting, 146-148
    foreign, 149-150
    formats, 147-148
    trashing, 147
  grading, 151
  history, 144-145
    Confederate currency,
    145
  preserving, 152-153
  storing, 153
papers
  collectibles, 91
  loose, 102
paperweights, 220-221
papier-mâché dolls, 185-186
Parry, Roger, 244
pastels, 251
pearls, 290
pencils, 251
pennies, gold, 136
penny-banks, 191-192
pens, 204, 251
perforation gauges
  (stamps), 128
permit imprints, 121
pewter, 304-305
  collectibles
    cleaning, 81
    displaying, 77
  identifying fake pieces,
    305
  Victorian factory-made,
    305
Philatelic Exhibitions
  (stamp shows), 125

Philco radios, 207
Philipon, Charles, 255
photography, 238-245
  ambrotypes, 240
  daguerreotypes, 238,
    240-242
    size, 241
    storage, 242
  storing, 245
Pilgrim furniture, 269
Pilgrim Glass, 219
pink gold, 291
plate blocks, 119
plate mark (prints), 263
plate-number coils, 119
platinum, 292
playing cards, 98
political lithographs, 260
polyethylene bags, 77
polypropylene bags, 77
porcelain (ceramics),
  174-178
  buying, 179, 181
  collecting, 178-179
  dating, 178
  fraudulent, 180
  reproductions, 180-181
  types of, 175-177
  see also ceramics
Portland Vase, 213
postage meters, 120
postal stationery, 120
postcards, 98-99
poster girls (movie memorabilia), 100-101
posters (lithography), 260
preserving paper money,
  152-153
pressed glass, 213-214
  distinguishing from cut
    glass, 212
price (collectible qualities),
  8
price guides, 315-322
  furniture, 275
  gold, 293

jewelry, 284
prints, 260, 264
silver, 303
pricing
  antiques, 38-39, 52-55
    damaged, 38-39
  auctions, 61
  bargaining, 39-41, 56-57
  Disneyana, 189
  guides, 315-322
  items at auctions, 32
  regional differences in, 55
  reserves, 32
printing
  history, 158-159
    books, 159
  stamps (methods),
    121-122
prints
  Frederick Remington, 264
  Japanese woodblock
    prints, 265
  price guides, 260, 264
  printing techniques,
    258-262
    engraving, 258
    etching, 258-259
    intaglio printing, 258
    lino cutting, 259
    lithography, 259-260
    relief printing, 260-261
    surface printing, 261
    wood engraving, 262
    woodcut printing,
      261-262
  selection guidelines,
    262-263
    avoiding ripoffs,
      263-264
  see also paper collectibles
programs, 100
provenance, 231
  buying antiques, 43
publications
  Antiques, 29
  Antiques Trader
    (St. Louis), 29

Arts Weekly (CT), 29
Maine Antiques Digest, 29
*Maloney's Antiques and
   Collectibles Resource
   Directory*, 29
Punch, 254
purchasing, *see* buying
purple gold, 291

Q

qualities of collectibles, 7-9
quantity (collectible qualities), 8
Queen Anne furniture,
   269-270
quilts, 205-206
Quimper tinware, 172
quiz (Collector), 17-18

R

radios, 207
Ray, Man, 238-239
records, 75, 127, 207-208
red gold, 291
reference literature (auctions), 32
relief printing, 260-261
Rembrandt etchings, 259
Remington, Frederick, 264
removing stamps, 122
Renoir, 232
reproductions
   ceramics, 180
   porcelain, 180-181
reserves (defined), 32
restoring
   antiques, 38-39
   comic books, 112-113
   paintings, 235
rewards of collecting, 9-10
Riger, Robert, 243
risks of buying antiques,
   45-48

Rodchenko, Alexander,
   238-239
Rohde, Gilbert, 273
Roman coins, 134
Rose, Aaron, 244
rubies, 290
rugs, 277-280
   hooked rugs, 278-280
   Oriental, 277-278
Russian sterling silver, 301

S

Saarinen, Eero, 273
sales, yard, 57-58
   advertising, 57
   guidelines, 58
   scheduling, 57
sandpaper drawings, 251
sapphires, 290
Schjerfbeck, Helene, 233
Scott all-wave receivers, 207
scrapbooks, 75
second golden era of baseball cards, 93
selecting comic books, 111
self-adhesive stamps, 120
selling
   antiques, 52-58
      prices, 56-57
      in private, 56-57
      showing, 56
      shows, 58-60
      yard sales, 57-58
   auctions, 60-62
   to dealers, 58
   flea markets, 58-60
semi-durable ephemera
   (postcards), 90
Sèvres (porcelain), 177
Shaker furniture, 274
sheet format, 119
Sheraton furniture, 271
Shergold, Craig, 97
Sherman, Cindy, 243

shopping
   antique shops, 33
   auctions, 30-33
   flea markets, 33-34
   house sales, 33-34
   mail-order, 34-35
   swap meets, 33-34
   while on vacation, 35
   see also buying
shows
   antiques, 58-60
   stamps, 125
silent films (poster girls),
   100-101
Silhouette, Etienne de,
   253-254
silhouettes, 253-254
silver, 298-303
   bottle tickets, 307
   cleaning, 81
   coin silver, 299
   Continental, 301
   Danish, 301-302
   price guides, 303
   silverplate, 302-304
      identifying, 302-303
      selection guidelines,
         302
   sterling
      American, 298
      English, 300
      Russian, 301
soda bottles, 201
soft-paste porcelain, 174
souvenir sheets, 120
speculating (antiques), 46
sports cards, 96-97
   see also baseball cards
SQ (Shopper's Quotient), 27
Staffordshire (ironware),
   174
stage set designs, 99
stamps
   auctions, 124-125
   buying, 131-132
   catalogs, 128

collecting, 118-130
    tools, 126-128
commemorating, 121
dealers, 123
format, 119-121
investing, 130-131
mail-order, 124
mixtures, 123
most valuable, 125
mounts, 126
packets, 123
printing methods,
    121-122
removing, 122
shows, 125
terms, 130
trading, 126
used, 122
steel, 306-307
sterling silver
    American, 298
    English, 300
    Russian, 301
Steuben (Corning) glass,
    213
Stieglitz, Alfred, 238-239
stock book (stamps), 128
stones, *see* gemstones
stoneware (ceramics),
    172-173
storing
    daguerreotypes, 242
    paper money, 153
    photographs, 245
    see also displaying
stuffed toys
    cleaning, 82
    displaying, 77
Sugimoto, Hiroshi, 244
superheros (comic books),
    108-109
Superman (comic books),
    106-107, 110
supply and demand, 21-22
surface printing, 261
Surrealism, 228

swap meets, 33-34
Sweet Caporal Tobacco
    Company, 95

T

teddy bears, 193-194
Tenniel, John, 254
terms (stamps), 130
Terren, George E., 78
The Black Arrow, 166
Theran, Susan, 229, 242
Tiffany art glass, 215
timing (auctions), 61
Tin-glazed earthenware,
    171-172
tins (lithographed), 308
tinsel paintings, 254
tips, *see* guidelines
toby jugs (ironware), 174
tongs (stamps), 126
tools, 208
    coins, 137
    Disneyana, 188-189
    stamps, 126-128
Tootsie toys, 190
topaz, 290
Topps Company, 94
Toulouse-Lautrec, Henri,
    255
toys
    die-cast, 190
    history, 184
    mechanical, 189-190
        banks, 190-192
    modern, 195
    teddy bears, 193-194
    stuffed
        cleaning, 82
        displaying, 77
trading
    antiques, 41-42
    stamps, 126

transitional pieces
    (furniture), 269
Treasure Island, 166

U

United States Mint (coins),
    135
used stamps, collecting, 122
utensils (kitchen), 204-205

V

vacations, shopping on, 35
Van Gogh, 232
vendor pricing (auctions),
    61
Victorian furniture, 271-272
Victorian silverplate,
    302-304
viewing auction items, 32
vocabularies, comic books,
    113-114

W

Ward, Sir Leslie, 255
Waterford crystal, 213
watermarks (stamps), 128
Wedgwood china, 180
Westmoreland Glass,
    219-220
Wheeler Nicholson, 106
whiskey bottles, 200-201
white gold, 291
Whiz Comics, 110
wood engravings, 262
woodblock prints, 264
woodcut printing, 261-262
wooden collectibles
    cleaning, 82
    dolls, 185
    displaying, 77-78

worksheets
    Collection Inventory,
      11-12, 73-74
    Hitting the Books, 230
    Household Inventory,
      67-72
World War II era baseball
  cards, 93
WWW (World Wide Web),
  coins, 139

X-Y-Z

yard sales, 57-58
    advertising, 57
    guidelines, 58
    scheduling, 57
yellow gold, 291
zircon, 290

Notes

Notes

Notes

When You're Smart Enough to Know
That You Don't Know It All

For all the ups and downs you're sure to encounter in life,
The Complete Idiot's Guides give you down-to-earth answers
and practical solutions.

The Complete Idiot's Guide to Buying Insurance and Annuities
ISBN: 0-02-861113-6 ▪ $16.95

The Complete Idiot's Guide to Managing Your Money
ISBN: 1-56761-530-9 ▪ $16.95

Complete Idiot's Guide to Buying and Selling a Home
ISBN: 1-56761-510-4 ▪ $16.95

The Complete Idiot's Guide to Doing Your Income Taxes 1996
ISBN: 1-56761-586-4 ▪ $14.99

The Complete Idiot's Guide to Making Money with Mutual Funds
ISBN: 1-56761-637-2 ▪ $16.95

The Complete Idiot's Guide to Getting Rich
ISBN: 1-56761-509-0 ▪ $16.95

You can handle it!

Look for The Complete Idiot's Guides at your favorite bookstore, or call 1-800-428-5331 for more information.

The Complete Idiot's Guide to Learning French on Your Own
ISBN: 0-02-861043-1 ▪ $16.95

The Complete Idiot's Guide to Dating
ISBN: 0-02-861052-0 ▪ $16.95

The Complete Idiot's Guide to Cooking Basics
ISBN: 1-56761-523-6 ▪ $18.95

The Complete Idiot's Guide to Hiking and Camping
ISBN: 0-02-861100-4 ▪ $16.95

The Complete Idiot's Guide to Learning Spanish on Your Own
ISBN: 0-02-861040-7 ▪ $16.95

The Complete Idiot's Guide to Gambling Like a Pro
ISBN: 0-02-861102-0 ▪ $16.95

The Complete Idiot's Guide to Choosing, Training, and Raising a Dog
ISBN: 0-02-861098-9 ▪ $16.95

The Complete Idiot's Guide to Trouble-Free Car Care
ISBN: 0-02-861041-5 ▪ $16.95

The Complete Idiot's Guide to the Perfect Wedding
ISBN: 1-56761-532-5 ▪ $16.99

The Complete Idiot's Guide to Eating Smart
ISBN: 0-02861-276-0 ▪ $16.95

The Complete Idiot's Guide to First Aid Basics
ISBN: 0-02-861099-7 ▪ $16.95

The Complete Idiot's Guide to the Perfect Vacation
ISBN: 1-56761-531-7 ▪ $14.99

The Complete Idiot's Guide to Trouble-Free Home Repair
ISBN: 0-02-861042-3 ▪ $16.95

The Complete Idiot's Guide to Getting into College
ISBN: 1-56761-508-2 ▪ $14.95

You can handle it!

continued

	Extremely Important					Not At All Important
____ Author's name and/or qualifications	6	5	4	3	2	1
____ Like the *Complete Idiot's Guide* series	6	5	4	3	2	1
____ Feel like an idiot when it comes to this subject and think that this book will offer helpful advice	6	5	4	3	2	1

We'd like to know your thoughts on this book. What did you like? What would you like to see changed?

_____

_____

_____

Please tell us something about yourself?

Age: ____

Gender: ____ Male ____ Female

Education Level: ____ high school ____ college ____ advanced degree

Would you like to be on our mailing list to receive the *Idiot's Newsletter*?
____ yes ____ no

Thank you for your reply. We will mail your free gift to the address you indicate below.

Name _____

Address _____

City, State, ZIP _____

Mail this completed form to:

Idiot's Guides
c/o Macmillan Reference
Marketing Department
1633 Broadway, 6th Floor
New York, NY 10019

Free gift offer expires December 31, 1997.

RAP WITH THE IDIOTS AND GET A FREE GIFT!

Okay...we're not smart enough to know what you're thinking, but we'd like to!
If you can take a few minutes to fill out the information below, we'll mail you a free gift in return.

Did you purchase this book for ___ yourself ___ friend ___ relative
Other _____

Had you heard of the *Complete Idiot's Guide* series prior to your purchase of this book?
___ yes ___ no

Have you purchased any other *Complete Idiot's Guide* titles? ___ yes ___ no

If yes, what other titles do you own?

_____
_____
_____

What other topics would you like to see as *Complete Idiot's Guides*?

_____
_____
_____

How did you become aware of *The Complete Idiot's Guide to Buying and Selling Collectibles?*

____ book was recommended by a friend or relative
____ saw it on the bookstore shelf
____ advertisement
____ review of book
Other _____

Did you go into the store looking for a book on this topic? ___ yes ___ no

On a scale where 6 is extremely important and 1 is not at all important, could you rate the following factors that influenced you to purchase this book?

	Extremely Important				Not At All Important	
____ Price	6	5	4	3	2	1
____ Attractiveness of cover	6	5	4	3	2	1
____ Thickness (or length) of book	6	5	4	3	2	1
____ Like the way that the information is presented in the book	6	5	4	3	2	1

continues

342